Kaplan Publishing are constantly finding new ways to make a difference to your studies and our exciting online resources really do offer something different to students looking for exam success.

This book comes with free MyKaplan online resources so that you can study anytime, anywhere. **This free online resource is not sold separately and is included in the price of the book.**

Having purchased this book, you have access to the following online study materials:

CONTENT	AAT	
	Text	Kit
iPaper version of the book	✓	✓
Progress tests with instant answers	✓	
Mock assessments online	✓	✓
Material updates	✓	✓

D0522902

How to access your online resources

Kaplan Financial students will already have a MyKaplan account and these extra resources will be available to you online. You do not need to register again, as this process was completed when you enrolled. If you are having problems accessing online materials, please ask your course administrator.

If you are already a registered MyKaplan user go to www.MyKaplan.co.uk and log in. Select the 'add a book' feature and enter the ISBN number of this book and the unique pass key at the bottom of this card. Then click 'finished' or 'add another book'. You may add as many books as you have purchased from this screen.

If you purchased through Kaplan Flexible Learning or via the Kaplan Publishing website you will automatically receive an e-mail invitation to MyKaplan. Please register your details using this email to gain access to your content. If you do not receive the e-mail or book content, please contact Kaplan Flexible Learning.

If you are a new user register at www.MyKaplan.co.uk and click on the link contained in the email we sent you to activate your account. Then select the 'add a book' feature, enter the ISBN number of this book and the unique pass key at the bottom of this card. Then click 'finished' or 'add another book'.

Your Code and Information

This code can only be used once for the registration of one book online. This registration and your online content will expire when the final sittings for the examinations covered by this book have taken place. Please allow one hour from the time you submit your book details for us to process your request.

Please scratch the film to access your MyKaplan code.

Please be aware that this code is case-sensitive and you will need to include the dashes within the passcode, but not when entering the ISBN. For further technical support, please visit www.MyKaplan.co.uk

KAPLAN PUBLISHING

COMPUTERISED ACCOUNTING

Qualifications and Credit Framework

AQ2013 Level 2 Certificate in Accounting

British Library Cataloguing-in-Publication Data

A catalogue record for this book is available from the British Library.

Published by
Kaplan Publishing UK
Unit 2, The Business Centre
Molly Millars Lane
Wokingham
Berkshire
RG41 2QZ

ISBN 978 1 78415 391 5

The text in this material and any others made available by any Kaplan Group company does not amount to advice on a particular matter and should not be taken as such. No reliance should be placed on the content as the basis for any investment or other decision or in connection with any advice given to third parties. Please consult your appropriate professional adviser as necessary. Kaplan Publishing Limited and all other Kaplan group companies expressly disclaim all liability to any person in respect of any losses or other claims, whether direct, indirect, incidental, consequential or otherwise arising in relation to the use of such materials.

Printed and bound in Great Britain

We are grateful to the Association of Accounting Technicians for permission to reproduce past assessment materials and example tasks based on the new syllabus. The solutions to past answers and similar activities in the style of the new syllabus have been prepared by Kaplan Publishing.

We are grateful to HM Revenue and Customs for the provision of tax forms, which are Crown Copyright and are reproduced here with kind permission from the Office of Public Sector Information.

We are grateful to Sage (UK) Limited for their support in the preparation of this Text.

CONTENTS

INTRODUCTION

HOW TO USE THESE MATERIALS

These Kaplan Publishing learning materials have been carefully designed to make your learning experience as easy as possible and to give you the best chance of success in your AAT assessments.

They contain a number of features to help you in the study process.

The sections on the Unit Guide, the Assessment and Study Skills should be read before you commence your studies.

They are designed to familiarise you with the nature and content of the assessment and to give you tips on how best to approach your studies.

STUDY TEXT

This study text has been specially prepared for the AQ2013 qualification introduced in September 2013.

It uses a case study approach to guide you through the syllabus and builds up your knowledge and skills chapter by chapter. The text is based upon Sage One Accounts.

Quality and accuracy are of the utmost importance to us so if you spot an error in any of our products, please send an email to mykaplanreporting@kaplan.com with full details, or follow the link to the feedback form in MyKaplan.

Our Quality Co-ordinator will work with our technical team to verify the error and take action to ensure it is corrected in future editions.

UNIT GUIDE

Purpose of the unit

The AAT has stated that the general purpose of this unit is about using a computerised accounting application to maintain records of business transactions including sales and purchases, receipts and payments, and to prepare reports. The unit requires skills needed to record accounting transactions with credit customers and credit suppliers as well as recording transactions involving the bank, petty cash and other nominal ledger accounts.

Learning objectives

On completion of this unit, the learner will be able to use a computerised accounting system to set up accounting records, enter accounting transactions, perform a bank reconciliation, correct errors and produce a range of reports. They will also be able to maintain the security of accounting information using passwords and back-up routines.

Knowledge

To perform this unit effectively you will need to know and understand the following:

		Chapter
LO1	**Learning Outcome 1**	
Enter accounting data at the beginning of an accounting period.		
1.1	Set up general ledger accounts, entering opening balances where appropriate.	7
1.2	Set up customer accounts, entering opening balances where appropriate.	6
1.3	Set up supplier accounts, entering opening balances where appropriate.	5
LO2	**Learning Outcome 2**	
Record customer transactions.		
2.1	Process sales invoices and credit notes, accounting for VAT.	8
2.2	Allocate monies received from customers in partial or full payment of invoices and balances.	8
LO3 Learning Outcome 3		
Record supplier transactions		
3.1	Process purchases invoices and credit notes, accounting for VAT	8
3.2	Allocate monies paid to suppliers in full or partial settlement of invoices and balances.	8
LO4 Learning Outcome 4		
Record and reconcile bank and cash transactions		
4.1	Process receipts and payments for non-credit transactions.	8, 10
4.2	Process recurring receipts and payments.	8, 12
4.3	Process petty cash receipts and payments, accounting for VAT.	8
4.4	Perform a periodic bank reconciliation	8, 12

		Chapter
LO5 Learning Outcome 5		
Be able to use journals for accounting transactions		
5.1	Process journals for accounting transactions.	9
5.2	Use journals to correct errors.	9
LO6 Learning Outcome 6		
Produce reports		
6.1	Produce routine reports for customers and suppliers.	5, 6, 7, 8, 11
6.2	Produce routine reports from the general ledger.	10, 11
LO7 Learning Outcome 7		
Maintain the safety and security of data held in the computerised accounting system		
7.1	Make a copy of accounting data using the bank up function of the accounting software.	1, 4
7.2	Use a software password to protect accounting information.	1, 14

THE ASSESSMENT

The purpose of the assessment is to allow the learner to demonstrate the skills and knowledge necessary to use computerised accounting software at level 2.

The assessment is designed to allow the use of any accounting software package and is in the form of a project. The assessment material will be provided by the AAT, delivered online and assessed locally.

Assessment duration: two hours.

Assessment of this unit is via a computer based project, or workplace evidence, both of which are locally assessed by the training provider.

Computer based project

AAT's two hour assessment will be based on a business organisation and comprises a series of tasks that ask the student to input data into a computerised accounting system and produce reports, allowing the student to demonstrate the skills and knowledge necessary to use computerised accounting software at Level 2.

The assessment has not been designed for use with any one particular accounting software package. It is recognised that a variety of accounting software packages are available and can be used.

The summary below describes the ability and skills students at this level must successfully demonstrate to achieve competence.

Summary

Achievement at Level 2 reflects the ability to select and use relevant knowledge, ideas, skills and procedures to complete well-defined tasks and address straightforward problems. It includes taking responsibility for completing tasks and procedures.

Knowledge and understanding

- Use understanding of facts, procedures and ideas to complete well-defined tasks and address straightforward problems.
- Interpret relevant information and ideas.
- Be aware of the types of information that are relevant to the area of study or work.

Application and action

- Complete well-defined, generally routine tasks and address straightforward problems.
- Select and use relevant skills and procedures.
- Identify, gather and use relevant information to inform actions.
- Identify how effective actions have been.

Autonomy and accountability

- Take responsibility for completing tasks and procedures.
- Exercise autonomy and judgement subject to overall direction or guidance.

STUDY SKILLS

Preparing to study

Devise a study plan

Determine which times of the week you will study.

Split these times into sessions of at least one hour for study of new material. Any shorter periods could be used for revision or practice.

Put the times you plan to study onto a study plan for the weeks from now until the assessment and set yourself targets for each period of study – in your sessions make sure you cover the whole course, activities and the associated questions in the workbook at the back of the manual.

If you are studying more than one unit at a time, try to vary your subjects as this can help to keep you interested and see subjects as part of wider knowledge.

When working through your course, compare your progress with your plan and, if necessary, re-plan your work (perhaps including extra sessions) or, if you are ahead, do some extra revision/practice questions.

Effective studying

Active reading

You are not expected to learn the text by rote, rather, you must understand what you are reading and be able to use it to pass the assessment and develop good practice.

A good technique is to use SQ3Rs – Survey, Question, Read, Recall, Review:

1 **Survey the chapter**

Look at the headings and read the introduction, knowledge, skills and content, so as to get an overview of what the chapter deals with.

2 **Question**

Whilst undertaking the survey ask yourself the questions you hope the chapter will answer for you.

3 **Read**

Read through the chapter thoroughly working through the activities and, at the end, making sure that you can meet the learning objectives highlighted on the first page.

4 **Recall**

At the end of each section and at the end of the chapter, try to recall the main ideas of the section/chapter without referring to the text. This is best done after short break of a couple of minutes after the reading stage.

5 **Review**

Check that your recall notes are correct.

You may also find it helpful to re-read the chapter to try and see the topic(s) it deals with as a whole.

Note taking

Taking notes is a useful way of learning, but do not simply copy out the text.

The notes must:

- be in your own words
- be concise
- cover the key points
- well organised
- be modified as you study further chapters in this text or in related ones.

Trying to summarise a chapter without referring to the text can be a useful way of determining which areas you know and which you don't.

Three ways of taking notes

1 **Summarise the key points of a chapter**

2 **Make linear notes**

A list of headings, subdivided with sub-headings listing the key points.

If you use linear notes, you can use different colours to highlight key points and keep topic areas together.

Use plenty of space to make your notes easy to use.

3 Try a diagrammatic form

The most common of which is a mind map.

To make a mind map, put the main heading in the centre of the paper and put a circle around it.]

Draw lines radiating from this to the main sub-headings which again have circles around them.

Continue the process from the sub-headings to sub-sub-headings.

Highlighting and underlining

You may find it useful to underline or highlight key points in your study text – but do be selective.

You may also wish to make notes in the margins.

Further reading

In addition to this text, you should also read the 'Student section' of the 'Accounting Technician' magazine every month to keep abreast of any guidance from the examiners.

An introduction to computerised accounting

1

Introduction

The aim of this manual is to guide you through the computerised accounting aspects of your studies.

To complete this manual you will need an understanding of the basics of double entry bookkeeping and you will need to be signed up to Sage One Accounts which is an online integrated computerised software system for accounting.

If you have another version of SAGE, or even another accounting package, you may not be able to use this manual efficiently.

Instructions for signing up to Sage One are provided in the next chapter.

Sage One is an online service, and will be updated on a regular basis (every 2 or 3 weeks) some updates will include minor improvements and additional features, others will be much more significant. When updates are made you will be notified with a message accessed directly from Sage One. Students are advised to read these messages and understand them. The printed copy of this text is based on the Sage One service at the point of publishing and therefore some of the screens and navigation that you see may have changed slightly.

This text uses a **case study approach** to guide you step-by-step. It assumes that you have never used a computerised accounting system before. Even if you have, it is worth starting at the beginning to ensure that you don't 'jump ahead' too quickly.

You will find 'learning objectives' detailed at the start of every chapter which are extracted from the AAT's published 'study and assessment guide' for this particular unit.

LEARNING OBJECTIVES

LO7 Maintain the safety and security of data held in the computerised accounting system.

7.1 Make a copy of accounting data using the backup function of the accounting software.

7.2 Use a software password to protect accounting information.

CONTENTS

1 Manual and computerised bookkeeping

The double entry system of bookkeeping that is still used today was developed in Italy in the fifteenth century. With the introduction of affordable and reliable information technology in the last thirty years, it was perhaps inevitable that business organisations would look to find ways to computerise their bookkeeping systems. Now it is rare to find an organisation which does not use some form of computer to aid the day-to-day record keeping that is an essential part of running a business whether large or small.

For very small organisations, a simple spreadsheet to record monies in and out of the business may suffice. However, once a business becomes larger or more complex, it may be beneficial to introduce a computerised bookkeeping system. There are many proprietary versions on the market, each of which works in a similar way. However, they will each offer different approaches to data entry, presentation of reports and so on, as well as different 'extras' such as stock management modules, budgeting and tax planning. Some systems, including Sage One, also allow a business to integrate a computerised payroll function.

2 Benefits of a computerised system

The main benefits of a computerised bookkeeping system are:

- quicker, more efficient processing of data
- fewer mathematical errors – because the system completes all the double entry and other mathematical functions (e.g. calculation of percentages) there is reduced opportunity for human error
- accounting documents (e.g. invoices, statements etc.) can be generated automatically, using tailored documents designed to incorporate company details, logos etc.
- the range of information that can be easily produced in reports is wide and varied, meaning businesses can report to various internal and external groups (e.g. management, directors, shareholders, banks etc.) in an appropriate format

- there is no need for manual processing of data – computerised bookkeeping systems complete all the double entry automatically
- hardware and software prices have fallen dramatically over the last thirty years, making a computerised system affordable to all organisations
- allow data to be easily transferred into other programs – e.g. a spreadsheet or word processing package.

3 Accounting documents

Business organisations rely on relevant documentation to record the transactions that it undertakes. Without an appropriate piece of supporting documentation, there is no way of knowing what has been bought, from whom and for how much, nor indeed what has been sold. With a high proportion of modern transactions being on credit, an accurate and comprehensive system of recording transactions is essential.

Many business documents are referred to as '**Primary Records**'. They include:

- purchase orders
- delivery notes
- purchase invoices
- credit notes
- sales invoices.

These documents are used to record business transactions in the first instance. For example, if an organisation wishes to purchase a new computer printer, it may first raise a **purchase order** which is sent to the supplier. The supplier would issue or deliver the printer along with a **delivery note**, to record the safe receipt of the goods. A **supplier invoice** requiring payment would follow. If the printer was faulty, it could be returned and a **credit note** issued.

In order for a transaction to be correctly recorded in a computerised accounting system, the appropriate documentation must first be raised and then the details entered into 'the system'; indeed, many organisations employ accounting staff whose job is primarily to enter the data accurately and completely from the source documents.

There are many other documents which are also essential in maintaining an up-to-date and accurate accounting system. Bank statements, schedules of direct debits/standing orders, supplier statements, correspondence from suppliers and customers and so on also provide invaluable information which can be used to check the computerised bookkeeping system for accuracy.

In the course of the case study which follows, you will be required to enter details from a range of source documents and use other documents to maintain a computerised bookkeeping system for a small company.

4 Coding

All computerised bookkeeping systems work by the use of codes. Each supplier and each customer must be given a unique code by which the computer software can recognise them. It is vital that there can be no confusion between two suppliers with similar names. For example, you may be fully aware that John Green and John Greenwood are entirely different people, but it could be easy for a computer to mix them up. Each must therefore be given a unique code by which they can be identified.

Similarly, each product manufactured or sold by an organisation may be given a unique code. Also, employees are usually 'coded' – you could check your pay slip to find your own Employee Reference Number.

Finally, every type of income or expense, asset or liability, is given a unique code to identify it. This makes entering transactions quite straightforward, since you need only refer to the relevant four digit code rather than a long narrative description.

Codes must be unique. However, they should also be recognisable by the person dealing with the system. For example, if a supplier was coded "SMITH006", this would be far more recognisable than a purely numeric code such as "0827329".

Care must be taken to issue codes that are not ambiguous. The use of a combination of letters and numbers (an alphanumeric code) often achieves this.

In Sage One Accounts, when you create a new customer or supplier record, you are provided with a 10 character limited alpha-numeric field to enter the customer or supplier code. The code can be whatever you require the code to be as long as it is unique within the system and 10 characters or less. Many organisations have a set structure for coding, and if this is the case in your organisation you should follow it.

5 Risks of using a computerised system

Computerised accounting systems may offer a lot of advantages to businesses, but organisations must also be aware of the potential risks posed by such systems. These risks can be categorised as:

- **Physical risks** – caused by system failure, theft, damage or loss or corruption of data and of access to systems or data by unauthorised users (e.g. by a compromise to password security)
- **Virus threats** – the risk of a computer virus (or similar) being introduced to a network, with the resultant loss of or damage to data
- **Legal threats** – from contravention of legislation such as the Data Protection Act (1998) by an organisation in the way that it stores or uses personal data.

Accounting data is particularly at risk, because it is highly confidential and potentially highly valuable to other people. Hence you must remain especially vigilant to risks to data security.

Virus threats

All computers that are linked to 'the outside world' (e.g. via a network or to the internet) are susceptible to security threats. Many people are familiar with the threat posed by viruses or other similar threats.

A virus is a piece of software that is used to maliciously infect your computer. What is more, it then has the ability to replicate itself and infect any other computer that is connected to yours. Of course, this also means that your computer is at risk of being infected by other computers as well.

Introduction of the virus to a system usually takes place when you open a file that has been deliberately infected – for example, an email attachment or a web-site, an infected piece of software, or an infected memory device (e.g. a memory stick).

The consequences of being infected by a virus are many:

- infecting all other computers you are linked to
- deleting particular files – especially files which are essential to the normal operation of your computer
- altering files so they are no longer legible

- slowing down your computer by taking up huge amounts of memory – leaving your computer extremely slow and unable to perform basic tasks
- Accessing your data and sending it to other people
- 'Reading' your passwords for essential sites such as on-line banking – enabling somebody else to access your bank account
- wiping your hard-drive – deleting everything from the computer.

Safeguards against viruses

Firewalls: these are designed to prevent hackers gaining access to a computer network via the phone line. These can be a piece of software (now often built in to operating systems such as Windows) or a hardware firewall, which is effectively a box which acts as a barrier between the modem (the phone line into your computer) and the computer itself. An effective firewall is an essential aspect of computer safeguarding, particularly where users have access to the internet.

Effective IT policies: most organisations now have clearly defined IT policies regarding the private use of the internet and e-mails, not allowing employees to install their own software (e.g. games) on work computers.

Using virus protection software: this is the most important method of protecting computer systems. It acts as a guard dog, constantly watching for suspicious files, blocking or destroying them and advising the user that there has been an attempt to compromise the security of the system. As virus protection programs are constantly being updated with details of new viruses, it is essential that it is kept updated and current at all times. An out-of-date program is no protection against the most recent viruses.

Personal vigilance: Be very wary if you receive unsolicited emails from addresses that you do not recognise. Do not open any emails that you are suspicious of – you should report these to your IT manager or your supervisor. However, you should also be wary of emails (particularly those with attachments) from addresses you **do** recognise – remember, if somebody you know has a computer which has been infected there is a high probability that their computer will then try to attack your computer as well.

Be very careful when accessing the internet. Only use sites you need for work. Be wary of links to other sites that you do not recognise. Again, if you are in any doubt, or suspect that your computer may have fallen victim to a virus, inform your supervisor.

Passwords

Passwords are one of the most common – and most abused – forms of computer security. In most businesses the access to each computer is protected by a password, as well as access to different pieces of software. Even individual files and documents can and should be protected if they contain confidential or sensitive information.

The choice of password is very important; you should be able to remember it, but it should not be easily guessed by others. Ideally, a password should:

- be at least 6–8 characters long
- contain a mixture of upper and lower case letters, numbers and symbols
- not be a recognisable word.

Under no circumstances should you choose something like your own name, you child's name or your pet dog's name – these are far too easy for someone with only a small amount of knowledge about you to guess. You should also avoid obvious combinations such as 'password' or '123456'.

You should be able to remember your own password. Do not be tempted to write it down in your diary, on a scrap of paper in your top drawer, or on a sticky note attached to the monitor!

You should also never tell anybody else your password – even your most trusted colleague. If you do suspect that somebody knows what your password is you should change it immediately.

Many systems are configured to require you to change your password every few weeks – even if yours is not, this is good practice.

Your Sage One password (if you have signed up directly – i.e. not via a 3rd party authentication service such as Google or Facebook) must have 8 characters and use both numbers and letters (Alpha-numeric).

Backups

Sage One is an internet based computer system and as such does not require the end user to perform backups. Backups are automatic and are managed by Sage.

Since the AAT Exam and syllabus is generic and not aligned to any one particular accounting system, internet based or otherwise, you can for the purposes of the exam show how you would export the audit trial report as a form of backup. How to do this will be covered in a later Chapter.

Signing up to Sage One Accounts Extra

2

CONTENTS

There are no relevant 'learning outcomes' applicable to this section of the workbook, as you will not be required to sign up Sage One Accounts Extra as part of the AAT assessment. Therefore, this particular chapter is designed to assist you with the initial set up process that will enable you to start using Sage One Accounts Extra for the first time as part of your CPAG studies.

1 Signing up to Sage One Accounts Extra

Signing up to Sage One Accounts Extra for use on your CPAG course is very straightforward.

(1) Visit the following licence redemption site:

http://info.uk.sageone.com/aat-computerised-accounting

(2) Click the option that applies to you depending on whether you are self-studying and paying for the Sage One Accounts Extra licence yourself or whether you are studying through a college that will be paying for the Sage One Accounts Extra licence on your behalf.

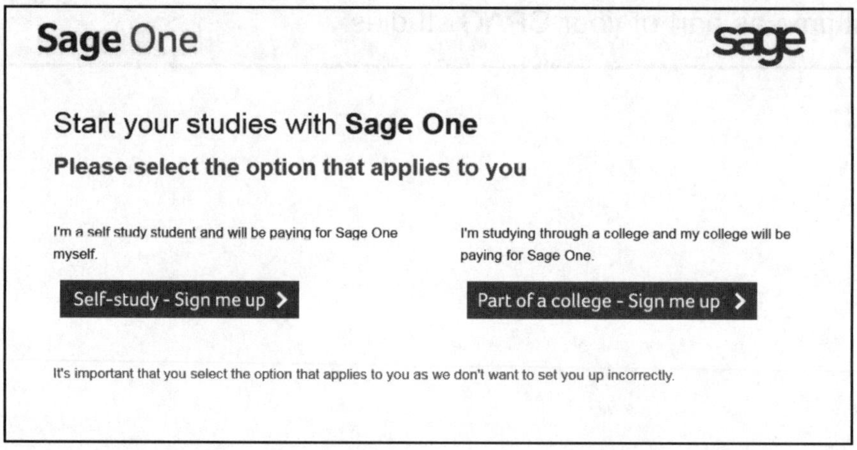

(3) Follow the instructions on the site to redeem your licence.

If you are studying though a college that is not listed within the dropdown menu, please ask your college administrator to contact Sage One educational sales directly on 0191 294 3798 for this to be rectified.

When you have signed up to Sage One Accounts Extra you can use the product again by visiting the Sage One website and clicking 'Sign In'

http://sageone.com

Setting up your company

3

CONTENTS

As with the previous chapter, there are no 'learning outcomes' associated with this chapter of the workbook.

During the AAT CPAG assessment, you will be required to enter information to match the details of the company given in the scenario within the real assessment. This will include the name and address of the company and also the details of their financial year. Please note, this is not part of the assessment process and you are allowed to ask for assistance from the invigilator of the assessment regarding this area.

1 Case Study – background to the company

You will be given a case study throughout this workbook which will form the basis for activities for you to practise on Sage One Accounts. It relates to a fictitious company called **TotalPhoto Ltd**. By completing the activities and entering the relevant transactions, you will learn how to do lots of tasks that are available on Sage One Accounts. You will also help prepare for the AAT CPAG computer based assessment as part of your AAT studies.

Background to TotalPhoto Ltd

TotalPhoto Ltd is a small company based in the market town of Miltonby, in Lancashire. It is owned by two directors, Matt Evans and Stuart Lincoln. It was established in 2004 when both Matt and Stuart left Art College. They specialise in contemporary family photography, most of which takes place in their rented studio on a small industrial estate on the outskirts of town. In addition, they also undertake a varied and increasing range of contracted photography, including weddings, dance shows, football competitions etc.

TotalPhoto Ltd has four members of staff, excluding yourself. In addition to Matt and Stuart, there is Sarala, a part-time photographer, and Michelle, the administrator for the company.

Since its inception, the company has used a manual bookkeeping system. However, the company has grown significantly in this time and Matt and Stuart now require more timely financial information with which to manage the company. They have therefore decided to implement a computerised system and to employ you as a part-time bookkeeper for the business.

We will use 1st October 2014 as '**today's date**' which is the first day of the company's financial year.

2 Setting up the company

Introduction

When you start using Sage One Accounts for your case study company, you must first enter some information about the company itself. This is important because it will identify this particular company and appear on various reports. In addition, at this stage, you must enter the dates of the company's financial year.

Data

You will need the following information for this session.

Company Name:	TotalPhoto Ltd
Company Address:	Unit 63 Bailey Industrial Estate Fornby Road Miltonby Lancashire LD37 7QZ
Telephone:	01949 969 378
Fax:	01949 969 379
E-mail:	info@totalphotoltd.webnet.uk
Website:	www.totalphotoltd.co.uk
Company Reg. Number:	734928107
VAT Number:	376 096 823
Accounting Period:	1st October – 30th September

Now we can begin entering the data for our company, TotalPhoto Ltd.

Activity

Enter the information onto the computerised system using the information provided in the previous box. Guidance follows.

From the **Summary/Getting Started** area you will notice a series of set up options.

STEP ONE Business Information – Select the 'Enter your business information' by clicking the link as shown below:

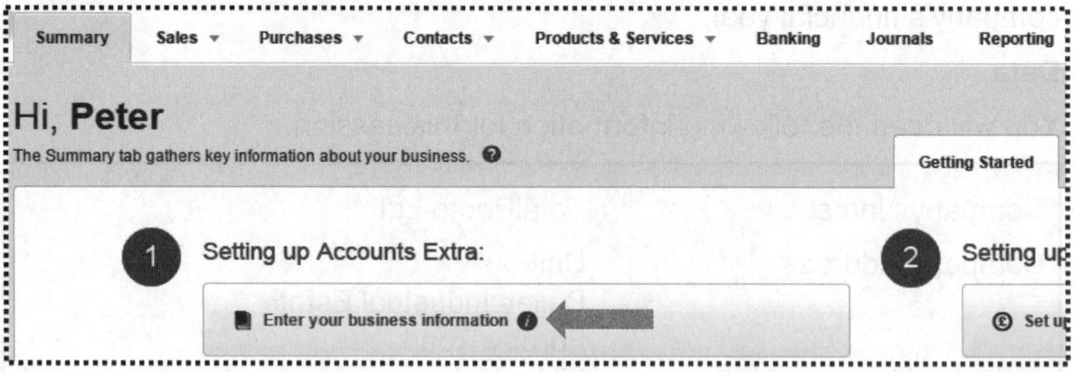

This will navigate you to the Business Settings Screen:

Be sure to check for accuracy – but don't worry if you make a mistake because you can always amend it later (we will look at how you can amend errors in a later chapter). Once you are happy with your entries click on the 

button.

You will be returned to the Getting Started Area.

STEP TWO Financial Settings – Select the 'Enter your financial settings'

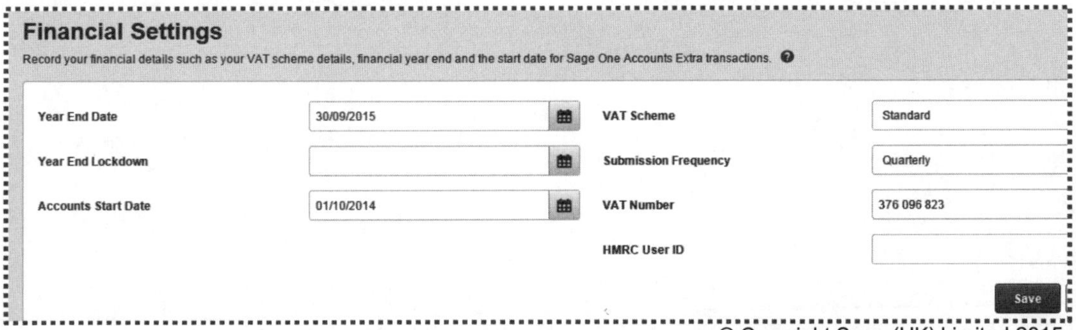
Financial Settings
Record your financial details such as your VAT scheme details, financial year end and the start date for Sage One Accounts Extra transactions.
Year End Date
30/09/2015
Year End Lockdown
Accounts Start Date
01/10/2014
VAT Scheme
Standard
Submission Frequency
Quarterly
VAT Number
376 096 823
HMRC User ID
Save

This is a really important stage. You need to enter the dates of your company's Financial Year and their VAT details. Remember, for TotalPhoto Ltd the company's Financial Year is 1st October to 30th September.

The data in this manual all refers to the year 2014-15, and so our Financial Year will start on the 1st of **October 2014** and end on **30th September 2015**.

- enter the VAT Registration Number as provided in the data (the number is 376 096 823). Select the Standard VAT scheme/ Quarterly
- enter the year end date: 30th September 2015 (next financial year)
- enter the Accounts Start Date: 1st October 2014 – which is todays date and the first day of the TotalPhoto's current financial year.

The accounts start date is the date from which the system will be used. It must be set on a date after the date of any account balances (see later chapter – opening balances)

Once you are happy with your entries click on the 
Save
button.

You will be taken to the Settings Overview area.

Navigating Sage One Accounts

4

Introduction

You have by now created your Sage One Accounts and set up the basic details of the company. The next stage is to practice navigating your way around the different sections of Sage One. Don't worry if you have never used a package like this before, it is very user-friendly and with lots of practice you will become comfortable with the different functions and areas covered.

LEARNING OBJECTIVES

LO7 Maintain the safety and security of data held in the computerised accounting system.

7.1 Make a copy of accounting data using the backup function of the accounting software.

CONTENTS

1 Menus and functions

Sage One is a web browser based system and can be securely accessed from any computer connected to the internet that is equipped with internet browser software. Microsoft Explorer, Safari and Google Chrome are examples of the browsers that can be used to access Sage One.

Sage One will operate inside a single browser tab or, if required, multiple browser tabs.

When you login to Sage One Accounts you will be directed to the Summary area. The specific tab within the summary area you will first see will depend on which one you last used when you logged out previously.

Black Navigation Bar & Feedback Tab

The black bar menu at the very top of the Sage One is used to navigate between businesses if you have more than one and also between systems such as Sage One Payroll. It also contains links to your account area and message centre. In addition you can access settings and help guides and logout from here.

Changing businesses and systems will not be required for CPAG

When we look at reporting, the black bar also will used to navigate to saved reports.

The Feedback tab allows you to send a message directly to Sage to let them know what you feel about the service.

THIS IS NOT TO BE USED TO ACCESS SUPPORT OR ASK QUESTIONS.

Top menu

Sage One Accounts features are grouped by functional area using the menu options as shown above. By hovering over each menu item you are able to view and select from the items available. To select just click the item you want, this includes the top item which is permanently displayed.

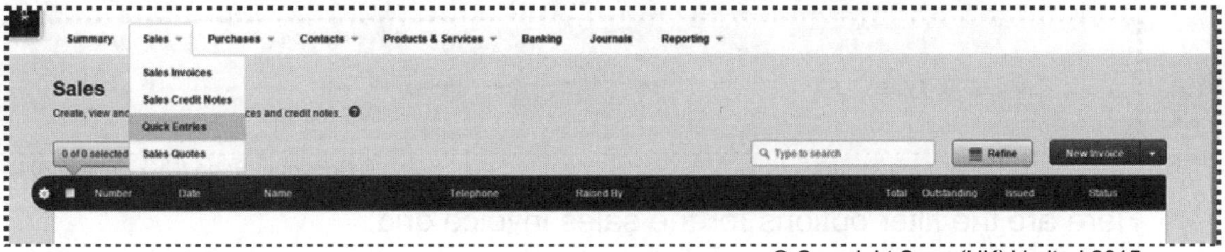

Summary screens

By selecting Summary from the top menu you will then be able to navigate to summary dashboard information about each functional area. The summary area also includes the Getting Started information described earlier

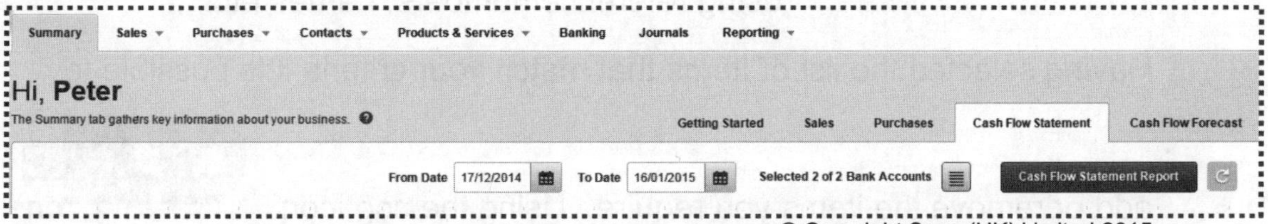

The summary screens will initially not show any data and graphs and charts will be empty. As we go through this course and enter transactions feel free to pop back to this area and have a look at how the data that you have entered has been represented.

The summary area is used by business people, bookkeepers and accountants to get quick insights into the performance of the business and understand any problems regarding debts and cash flow (for example).

Grids, filters and toolbar functions

Having selected an item from one of the top menus (e.g. sales invoices) a grid will appear listing either transactions or other things, such as contacts or products depending what has been chosen. The list content will depend on what you have chosen, based on dates and other filters/criteria used, which can be set using the 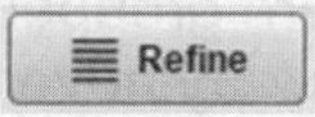
Refine
function. The filters for each type of transaction or data item will vary.

Here are the filter options for the customer grid for example:

Analysis Type
All
Analysis Category
All

Here are the filter options for the sales invoice grid:

From
01/01/2013
To
16/01/2015
Status
All

In addition to the filters, you can search the grid using the search 
Type to search
using reference numbers, names etc...

Having selected the list of items that match your criteria it is possible to add or remove the items you require. Using the cog icon  on the grid the column entries will appear and enable you to select which ones you require.

Grid tool bar

10 of 40 selected
Invoice Number
Invoice Date
Name
SI-1
31/07/2013
Age Concern
SI-2
15/07/2013
Roger Pickles
SI-3
15/07/2013
The Big Events Co
SI-4
15/07/2013
Big Strides Marke

As you select all of the items in the grid, or individual items, the grid toolbar will appear, allowing you to perform actions on the items you have selected (as indicated by the ticks). The toolbar will allow you to perform a number of actions depending on the content of the grid including; printing to pdf/csv and emailing of the list or the transactions themselves.

There are lots of different grid views and types throughout Sage One, but they are all operated more or less the same way. The differences will become more apparent as you get used to using the system.

Date

In addition the grid of data can be sorted by column headings. Click on the heading you wish to sort by and sort ascending or descending.

Online context help

Throughout Sage One you will notice the  symbol. This will allow you to access the online help system. The help page you are taken to will depend on where you were in the system when it was selected. This means you usually get the page you are looking for straight away.

From the black navigation bar, by selecting help here  you will be taken to the Sage One help centre. Using the menus and search functions contained here, you will be able to locate help content you require.

This can also be accessed using the following URL if you are not logged into Sage one. http://help.sageone.com/uk/accounts_extra/index.html. This is a great source of information and can be used alongside this text.

Drill-down enquiry

Throughout Sage One it is generally possible to click on a transaction or data item listed in a grid or a report and drill down to the next level or to a source entry. This applies to the grids described in this chapter.

2 Entering new data & editing or correcting existing data

New data

Entering transactions or other items such as customers and suppliers will be covered in detail in a later chapter. To access the input screens for a new item or transaction use the green action buttons.

Here are some examples:

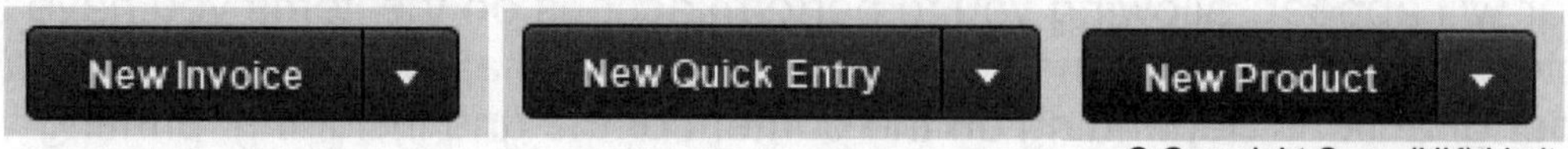

The multi-action button will allow you to perform multiple actions. As well as creating new transactions or records you will be able to use these buttons to access the import features when data is available outside of Sage One or to create other related transaction types.

You will not be required to import data as part of CPAG.

Editing & correcting data

Once a transaction such as an invoice or a bank item is entered into Sage One it can be viewed at any time. Accounting transactions appear in reports grids and if you need to look at the item you can 'click' on it and it will open in a screen very similar to the one which was used to create it.

In addition to viewing previously entered items or records it is also possible to edit them i.e. adding/deleting information. Some accounting transactions will have limitations on what can be edited depending on their status. Invoices allocated to a payment for example or banking items reconciled in the bank reconciliation module will become fully or partly locked depending on the transaction type.

There are other ways to correct accounting information if the transaction itself cannot be changed. One way is to use a journal, which will be covered in a later chapter.

3 Running reports

Reports will be covered separately in a later chapter, in terms of their content and meaning, however to access the Sage One standard reports; select the 'Reports' option from the 'Reporting' Menu and you will be presented with a series of reports to choose from.

These reports are pre-configured in terms of their data fields (columns) and format, style and layout.

To select the content or the data you require for the given report use the

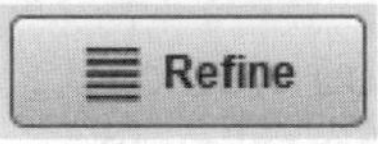

button. This will enable you to access the selection criteria and filter options such as dates, statuses, transaction types and analysis groups etc.

4 Backing up your work

It is important to guard against accidental losses which can prove very costly and time-consuming to recover or re-input. Being confident that your data is being saved regularly is critical and keeping a backup of your data should become part of your daily routine.

As we saw earlier, Sage One is an internet based computer system and does not require the end user to perform backups. Backups are automatic and are managed by Sage.

However, in the assessment you need to be able to show how you would export the audit trial report as a form of backup. Work through the following screens to learn how to do this.

Reporting menu:

Summary
Sales
Purchases
Contacts
Products & Services
Banking
Journals
Reporting
Reports
VAT Returns
Reports

From the reporting menu, select Audit Trail:

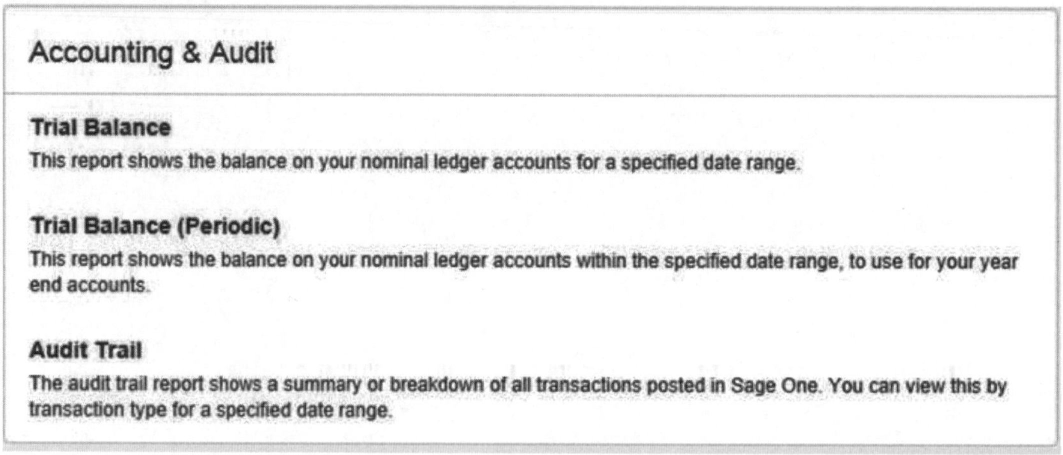
Accounting & Audit
Trial Balance
This report shows the balance on your nominal ledger accounts for a specified date range.
Trial Balance (Periodic)
This report shows the balance on your nominal ledger accounts within the specified date range, to use for your year end accounts.
Audit Trail
The audit trail report shows a summary or breakdown of all transactions posted in Sage One. You can view this by transaction type for a specified date range.

Using the  column configurator add/remove the columns of data you would like to display:

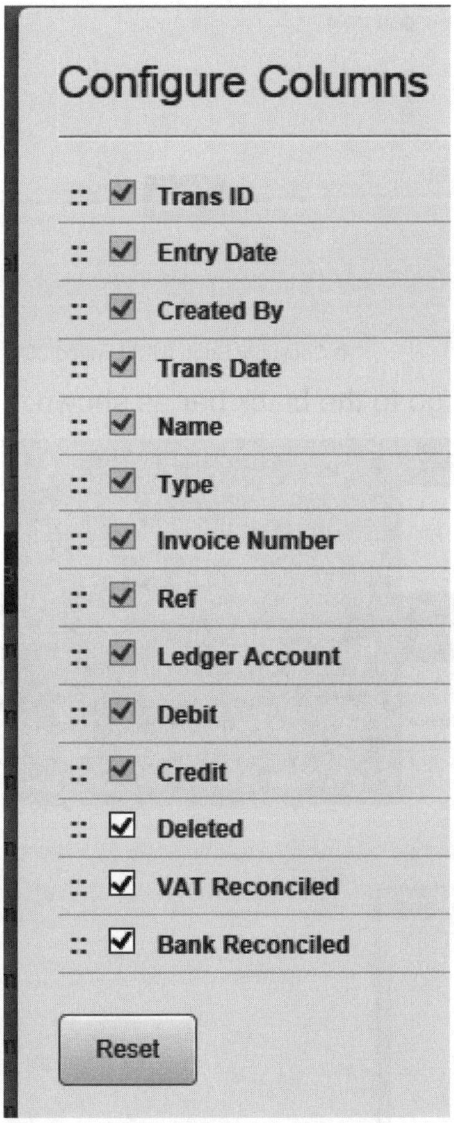
Configure Columns
Trans ID
Entry Date
Created By
Trans Date
Name
Type
Invoice Number
Ref
Ledger Account
Debit
Credit
Deleted
VAT Reconciled
Bank Reconciled
Reset

and 
Save

Using the 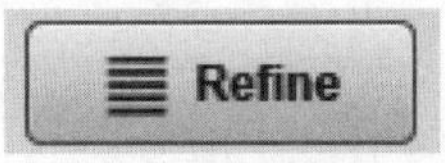
Refine
filter function, select custom reporting dates as required for all transaction types:

Reporting Period
Custom
From Date
30/09/2014
To Date
30/09/2015
Type
All

Using the 
Export
function, select CSV

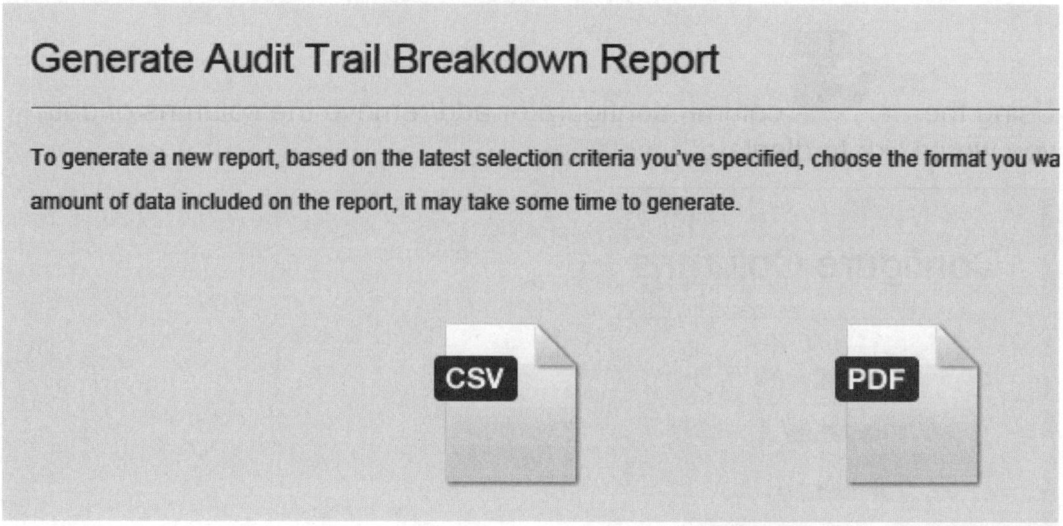
Generate Audit Trail Breakdown Report
To generate a new report, based on the latest selection criteria you've specified, choose the format you wa
amount of data included on the report, it may take some time to generate.
CSV
PDF

The report will run and to access the report go to the black bar as shown:

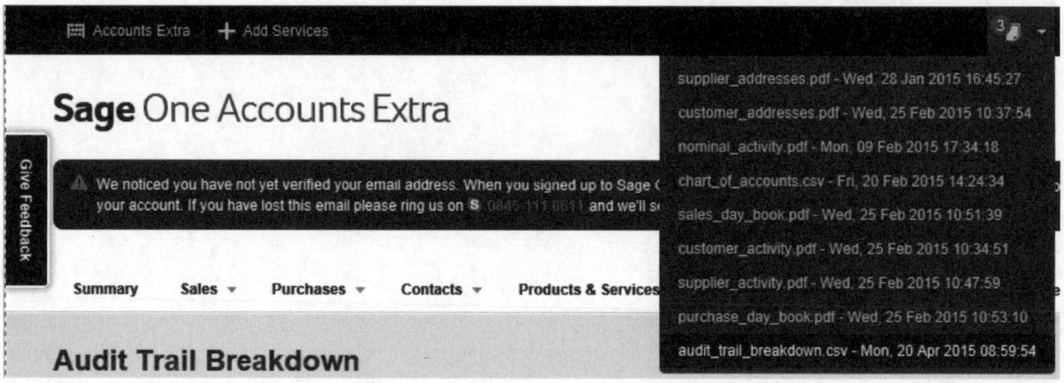
Accounts Extra
Add Services
Sage One Accounts Extra
Give Feedback
We noticed you have not yet verified your email address. When you signed up to Sage
your account. If you have lost this email please ring us on
and we'll s
Summary
Sales
Purchases
Contacts
Products & Services
Audit Trail Breakdown
supplier_addresses.pdf - Wed, 28 Jan 2015 16:45:27
customer_addresses.pdf - Wed, 25 Feb 2015 10:37:54
nominal_activity.pdf - Mon, 09 Feb 2015 17:34:18
chart_of_accounts.csv - Fri, 20 Feb 2015 14:24:34
sales_day_book.pdf - Wed, 25 Feb 2015 10:51:39
customer_activity.pdf - Wed, 25 Feb 2015 10:34:51
supplier_activity.pdf - Wed, 25 Feb 2015 10:47:59
purchase_day_book.pdf - Wed, 25 Feb 2015 10:53:10
audit_trail_breakdown.csv - Mon, 20 Apr 2015 08:59:54

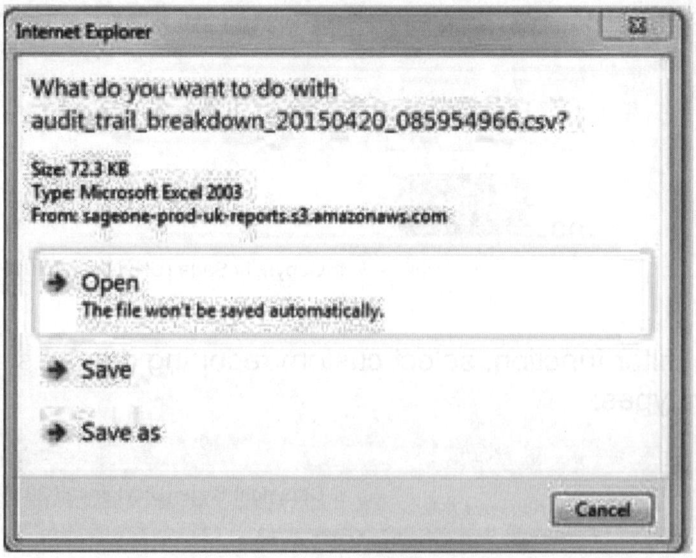
Internet Explorer
What do you want to do with
audit_trail_breakdown_20150420_085954966.csv?
Size: 72.3 KB
Type: Microsoft Excel 2003
From: sageone-prod-uk-reports.s3.amazonaws.com
Open
The file won't be saved automatically.
Save
Save as
Cancel

Select Open and Save. The file will download and the audit trail report will display in Excel.

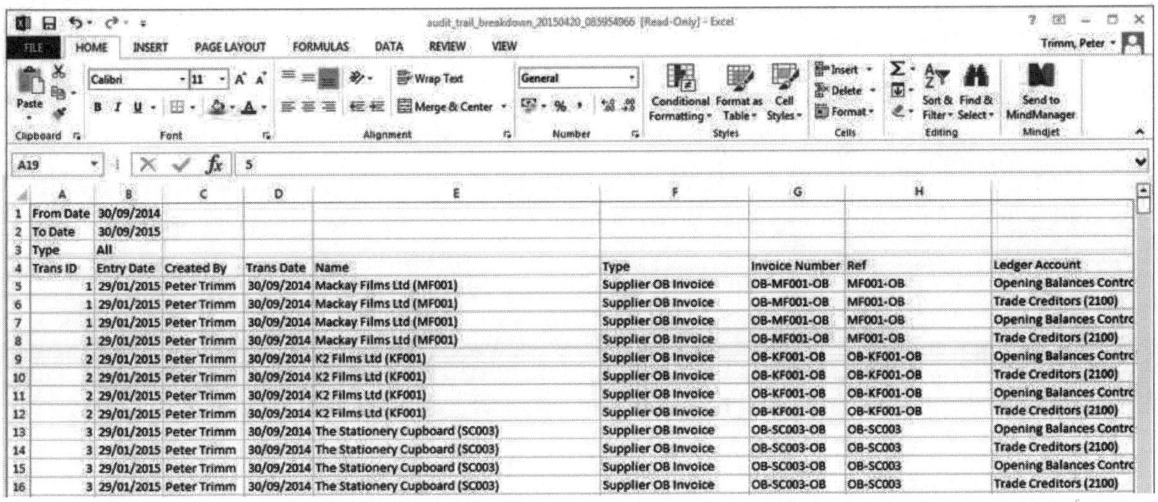

	A	B	C	D	E	F	G	H	
1	From Date	30/09/2014							
2	To Date	30/09/2015							
3	Type	All							
4	Trans ID	Entry Date	Created By	Trans Date	Name	Type	Invoice Number	Ref	Ledger Account
5	1	29/01/2015	Peter Trimm	30/09/2014	Mackay Films Ltd (MF001)	Supplier OB Invoice	OB-MF001-OB	MF001-OB	Opening Balances Contro
6	1	29/01/2015	Peter Trimm	30/09/2014	Mackay Films Ltd (MF001)	Supplier OB Invoice	OB-MF001-OB	MF001-OB	Trade Creditors (2100)
7	1	29/01/2015	Peter Trimm	30/09/2014	Mackay Films Ltd (MF001)	Supplier OB Invoice	OB-MF001-OB	MF001-OB	Opening Balances Contro
8	1	29/01/2015	Peter Trimm	30/09/2014	Mackay Films Ltd (MF001)	Supplier OB Invoice	OB-MF001-OB	MF001-OB	Trade Creditors (2100)
9	2	29/01/2015	Peter Trimm	30/09/2014	K2 Films Ltd (KF001)	Supplier OB Invoice	OB-KF001-OB	OB-KF001-OB	Opening Balances Contro
10	2	29/01/2015	Peter Trimm	30/09/2014	K2 Films Ltd (KF001)	Supplier OB Invoice	OB-KF001-OB	OB-KF001-OB	Trade Creditors (2100)
11	2	29/01/2015	Peter Trimm	30/09/2014	K2 Films Ltd (KF001)	Supplier OB Invoice	OB-KF001-OB	OB-KF001-OB	Opening Balances Contro
12	2	29/01/2015	Peter Trimm	30/09/2014	K2 Films Ltd (KF001)	Supplier OB Invoice	OB-KF001-OB	OB-KF001-OB	Trade Creditors (2100)
13	3	29/01/2015	Peter Trimm	30/09/2014	The Stationery Cupboard (SC003)	Supplier OB Invoice	OB-SC003-OB	OB-SC003	Opening Balances Contro
14	3	29/01/2015	Peter Trimm	30/09/2014	The Stationery Cupboard (SC003)	Supplier OB Invoice	OB-SC003-OB	OB-SC003	Trade Creditors (2100)
15	3	29/01/2015	Peter Trimm	30/09/2014	The Stationery Cupboard (SC003)	Supplier OB Invoice	OB-SC003-OB	OB-SC003	Opening Balances Contro
16	3	29/01/2015	Peter Trimm	30/09/2014	The Stationery Cupboard (SC003)	Supplier OB Invoice	OB-SC003-OB	OB-SC003	Trade Creditors (2100)

5 Setting up your suppliers' details

Introduction

Most business organisations will, over time, deal with a wide range of suppliers. For example, a café may have different suppliers for their meat, cheese, vegetables, wine etc. A hairdresser will buy different products from different suppliers. Sometimes supplies will be obtained from a wholesaler or a cash and carry; other supplies may be sourced directly from the manufacturers.

The organisation will need to keep very accurate and timely records of all transactions with their suppliers. These transactions will typically include:

(1) purchases and returns

(2) discounts received from the supplier

(3) payments made to the supplier by cash, cheque or bank transfer in settlement of outstanding bills.

In addition, it would be very convenient to have all the contact details of every supplier easily to hand.

Fortunately Sage One provides a comprehensive supplier management system which covers all these requirements. You will see how this works shortly, but firstly you will need to enter your suppliers' details.

LEARNING OBJECTIVES

LO1 Enter accounting data at the beginning of an accounting period.

1.3 Set up supplier accounts, entering opening balances where appropriate.

LO6 Produce reports.

6.1 Produce routine reports for customers and suppliers.

CONTENTS

1 Supplier data

We can now start inputting some data on to the computerised system using our case study firm, TotalPhoto Ltd.

Activity

TotalPhoto Ltd has six suppliers whose details are given below. Enter these onto the computerised system. Guidance on how to enter these records for suppliers follows.

Supplier details

Mackay Films Ltd **A/c Ref : MF001**
33 West Parade
Miltonby
Lancashire
LN87 7HD

Tel 01828 827493

Contact: Carl Richardson

Outstanding Balance at 30th September 2014: **£345.36**

Credit Terms: **30 days**

K2 Films Ltd **A/c Ref : KF001**
Tokyo House
72-84 Great Milne Street
London
WC4 6DD

Tel 0207 867 6599

Contact: Kim Nakajima

Outstanding Balance at 30th September 2014: **£1,726.55**

Credit Terms: **30 days**

The Stationery Cupboard **A/c Ref : SC003**
21 Potter Way
Hull
Humberside
HU87 6YY

Tel 01482 417378

Contact: Alan Pensill

Outstanding Balance at 30th September 2014: **£375.00**

Credit Terms: **14 days**

Mills Paper Products **A/c Ref : MP002**
405 Ream Road
Bradford
West Yorkshire
BD5 6QA

Tel 01726 378918

Contact: Mr Shaun Squire

Outstanding Balance at 30th September 2014: **£4,920.30**

Credit Terms: **21 days**

Octopus Inks Ltd **A/c Ref : OI001**
Unit 12
Longley Industrial Park
Gateshead
Tyne and Wear
GH77 5TG

Tel 0191 252 4132

Contact: Sheila Cribbley

Outstanding Balance at 30th September 2014: **£550.20**

Credit Terms: **30 days**

Arthur's Photographic Equipment Ltd **A/c Ref : AP004**
77 Overton Lane
Birmingham
BM97 8YK

Tel 0121 299 0192

Contact: Jennie Reeves

Outstanding Balance at 30th September 2014: **£11,275.00**

Credit Terms: **30 days**

2 Entering supplier details

Supplier Set up

The first supplier to enter is:

Mackay Films Ltd
33 West Parade
Miltonby
Lancashire
LN87 7HD

Tel 01828 827493

Fax 01828 827493

Contact: Carl Richardson **A/c Ref : MF001**

From the 'Contacts' menu, select the Suppliers option, you will be taken to the suppliers list.

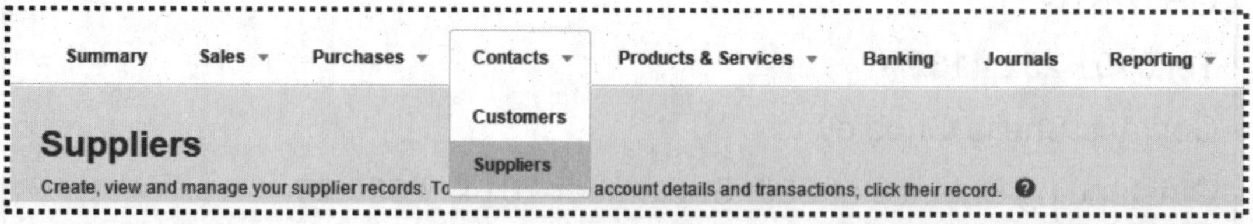
Summary
Sales
Purchases
Contacts
Products & Services
Banking
Journals
Reporting
Customers
Suppliers
Suppliers
Create, view and manage your supplier records. To
account details and transactions, click their record.

The suppliers list will display all the suppliers which have previously been set up. By default these will be sorted in alphabetical order, however it is possible to re-sort the order by clicking on the column heading you wish to sort by.

It is possible to import suppliers from a data file, this is useful in a live work situation if you are moving from another accounting system and do not wish to enter all the supplier records manually into Sage One. If you wish to experiment with this you can create a data file using Microsoft Excel by downloading the template which you can access from the help page.

To access the supplier set up use **New Supplier** button and the supplier set up page will open.

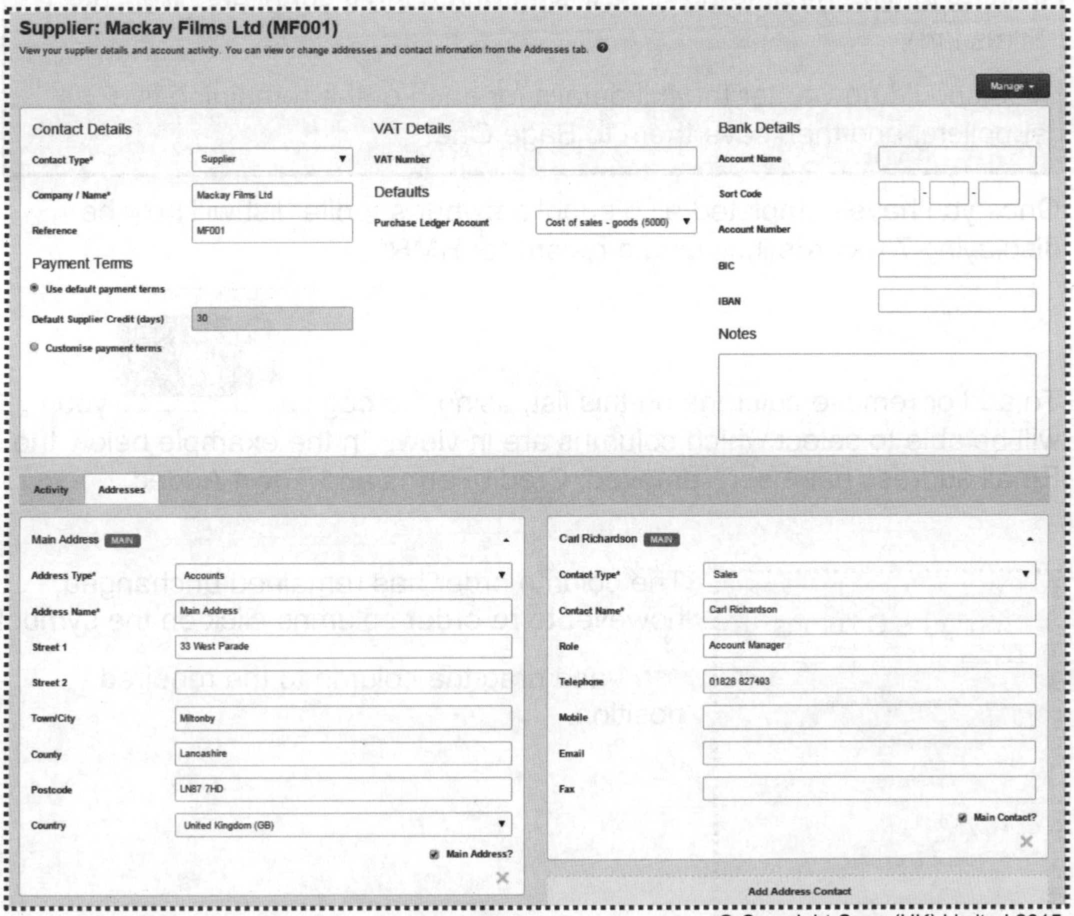

The contact type will be pre-filled 'Supplier'. Enter the business name in the Company/ Name field, the account reference and accept the default 30 days credit terms. If the credit terms are not 30 days, this can be customised by selecting the customised payment terms option.

If the supplier is VAT registered and you are aware of their VAT number this can be recorded here, as well as their bank account information. Feel free to complete these sections with some 'made up' information.

The Purchase Ledger (Nominal) Account will default to Cost of Sale Account 5000. This can be amended to the account you require but, for now, leave this unchanged.

Complete the contact information in the Addresses area as shown above. The Address Type should be amended from 'Delivery' to 'Accounts' and the Address Name can be left unchanged as 'Main Address'

Don't forget to SAVE!

Activity

You have already entered one of TotalPhoto Ltd's suppliers (Mackay Films Ltd).

You should now enter the full details for each of the remaining five suppliers, and then save them to Sage One.

Once you have completed all 6 suppliers your supplier list will now be displaying 7 records including a record for HMRC.

To add or remove columns on this list, using the cog 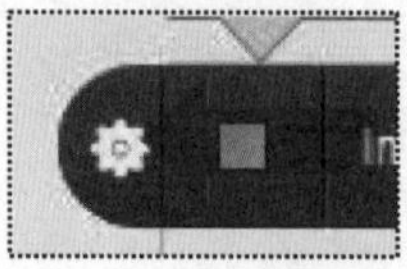 you will be able to select which columns are in view. In the example below the Email address has been removed, Credit Terms and Town Added

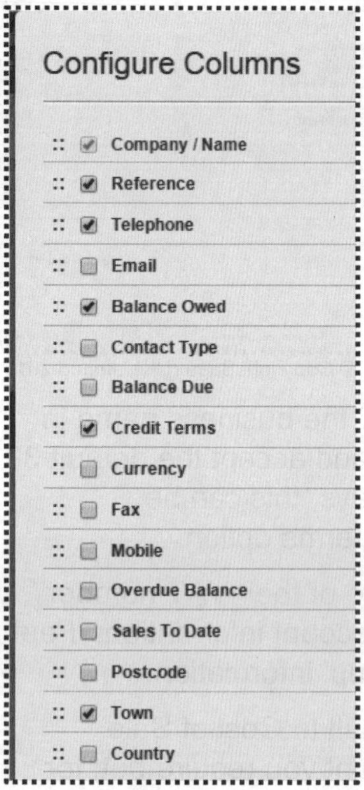

Configure Columns
Company / Name
Reference
Telephone
Email
Balance Owed
Contact Type
Balance Due
Credit Terms
Currency
Fax
Mobile
Overdue Balance
Sales To Date
Postcode
Town
Country

The column order has remained unchanged, however to re-order columns click on the symbol  and drag the column to the required position.

3 Printing supplier data reports

Supplier data reports are available from the supplier list page.

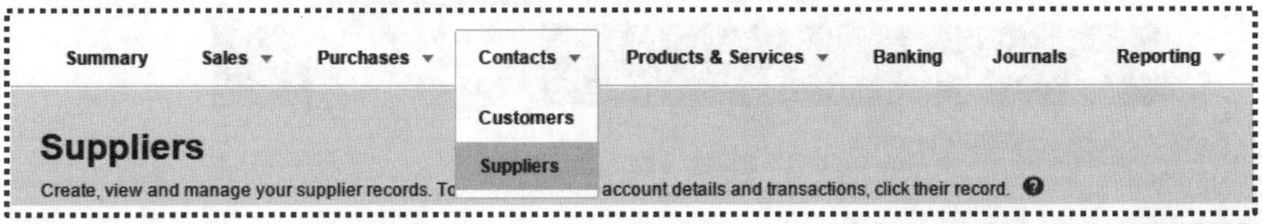
Summary
Sales
Purchases
Contacts
Products & Services
Banking
Journals
Reporting
Customers
Suppliers
Suppliers
Create, view and manage your supplier records. To
account details and transactions, click their record.

© Copyright Sage (UK) Limited 2015

From the 'Contacts' menu, select the Suppliers option. You will be taken to the suppliers list.

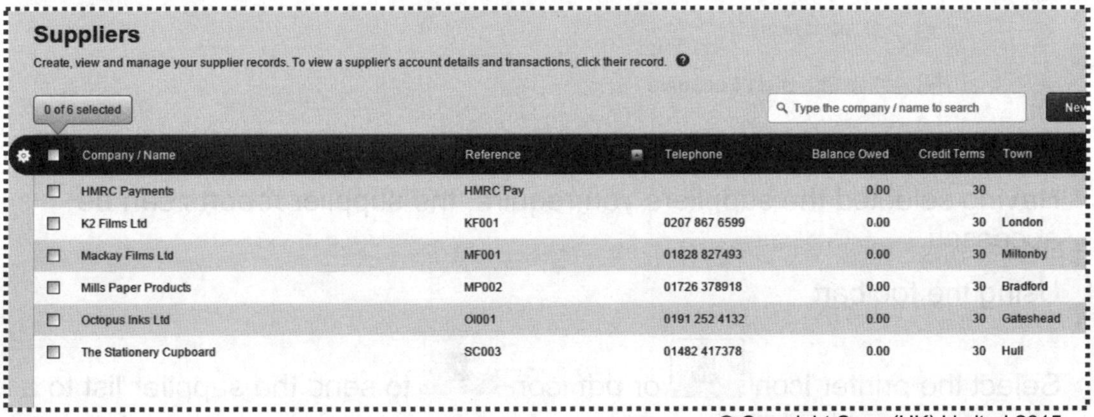
Suppliers
Create, view and manage your supplier records. To view a supplier's account details and transactions, click their record.
0 of 6 selected
Type the company / name to search
Company / Name
Reference
Telephone
Balance Owed
Credit Terms
Town
HMRC Payments HMRC Pay 0.00 30
K2 Films Ltd KF001 0207 867 6599 0.00 30 London
Mackay Films Ltd MF001 01828 827493 0.00 30 Miltonby
Mills Paper Products MP002 01726 378918 0.00 30 Bradford
Octopus Inks Ltd OI001 0191 252 4132 0.00 30 Gateshead
The Stationery Cupboard SC003 01482 417378 0.00 30 Hull

© Copyright Sage (UK) Limited 2015

To access the reports you will need to select the suppliers which are required to be included in the report. This is done by selecting them in the list using the tick boxes to the left of the supplier name. To select all suppliers select the box at the top of the grid. See below.

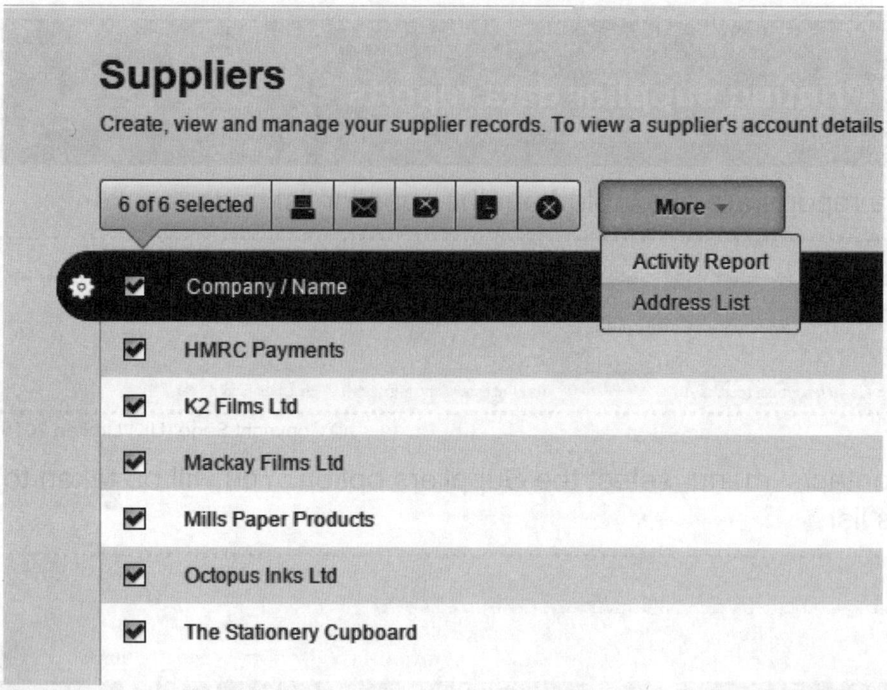
Suppliers
Create, view and manage your supplier records. To view a supplier's account details
6 of 6 selected
More
Activity Report
Address List
Company / Name
HMRC Payments
K2 Films Ltd
Mackay Films Ltd
Mills Paper Products
Octopus Inks Ltd
The Stationery Cupboard

Having selected the suppliers you require, the supplier reports can be accessed.

Using the toolbar:

Select the printer icon  or pdf icon  to send the supplier list to a printable report format:

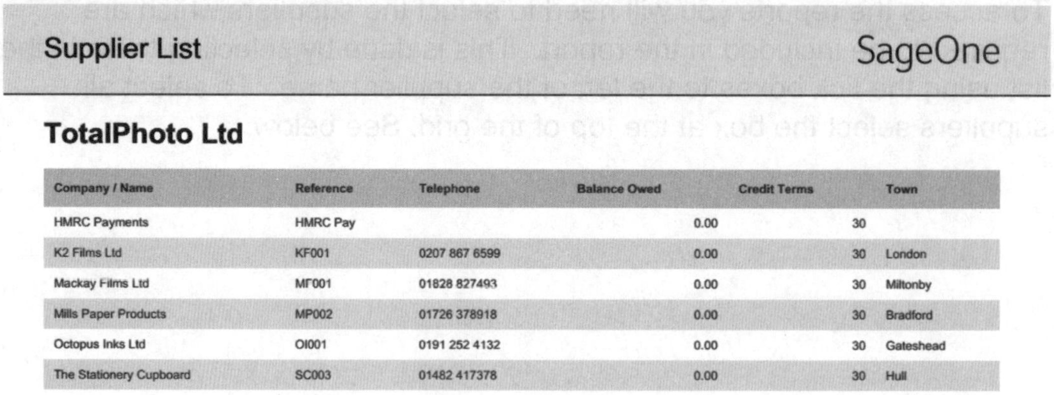

Supplier List — SageOne

TotalPhoto Ltd

Company / Name	Reference	Telephone	Balance Owed	Credit Terms	Town
HMRC Payments	HMRC Pay		0.00	30	
K2 Films Ltd	KF001	0207 867 6599	0.00	30	London
Mackay Films Ltd	MF001	01828 827493	0.00	30	Miltonby
Mills Paper Products	MP002	01726 378918	0.00	30	Bradford
Octopus Inks Ltd	OI001	0191 252 4132	0.00	30	Gateshead
The Stationery Cupboard	SC003	01482 417378	0.00	30	Hull

Select the envelope icon to send the supplier list via email:

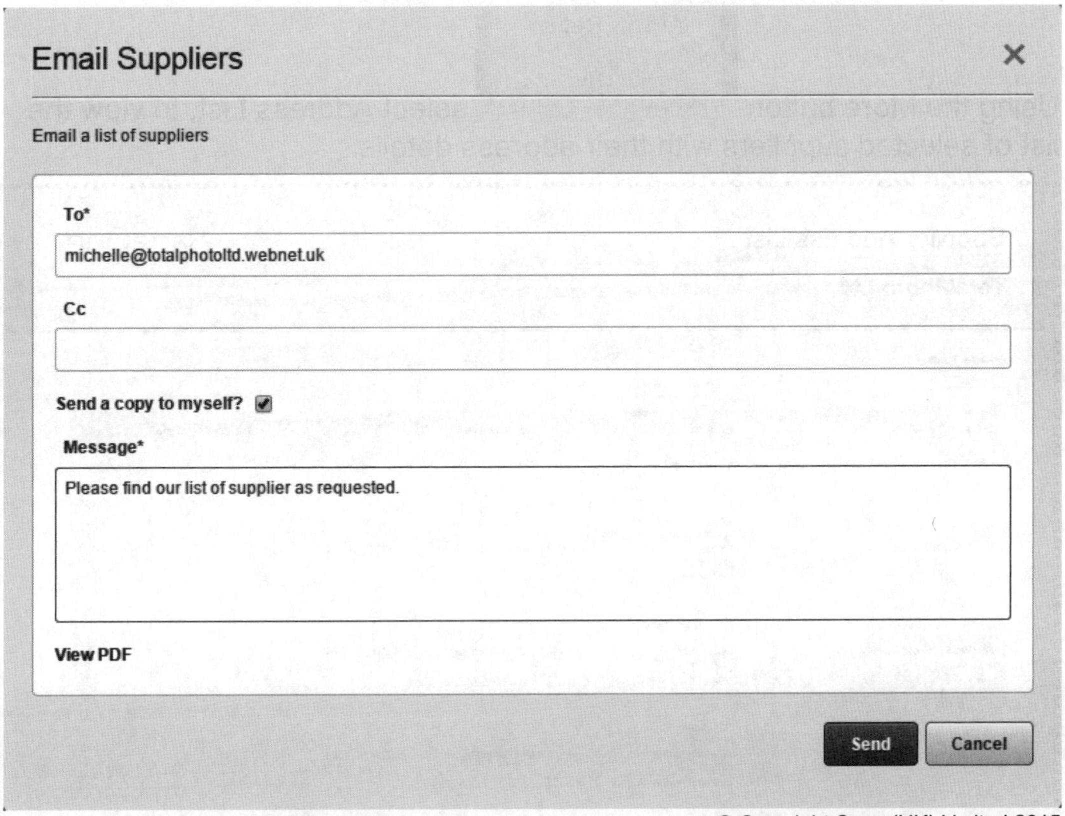
Email Suppliers
×
Email a list of suppliers
To*
michelle@totalphotoltd.webnet.uk
Cc
Send a copy to myself?
Message*
Please find our list of supplier as requested.
View PDF
Send
Cancel

Select the file icon to send the supplier list to CSV (opening in Excel).

	A	B	C	D	E	F
1	**Company / Name**	**Reference**	**Telephone**	**Balance Owed**	**Credit Terms**	**Town**
2	HMRC Payments	HMRC Pay		0	30	
3	K2 Films Ltd	KF001	0207 867 6599	0	30	London
4	Mackay Films Ltd	MF001	01828 827493	0	30	Miltonby
5	Mills Paper Products	MP002	01726 378918	0	30	Bradford
6	Octopus Inks Ltd	OI001	0191 252 4132	0	30	Gateshead
7	The Stationery Cupboard	SC003	01482 417378	0	30	Hull
8						

Using the More button 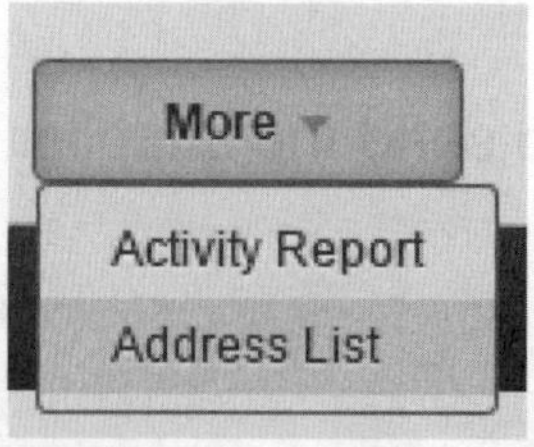

select Address List, to view the list of selected suppliers with their address details.

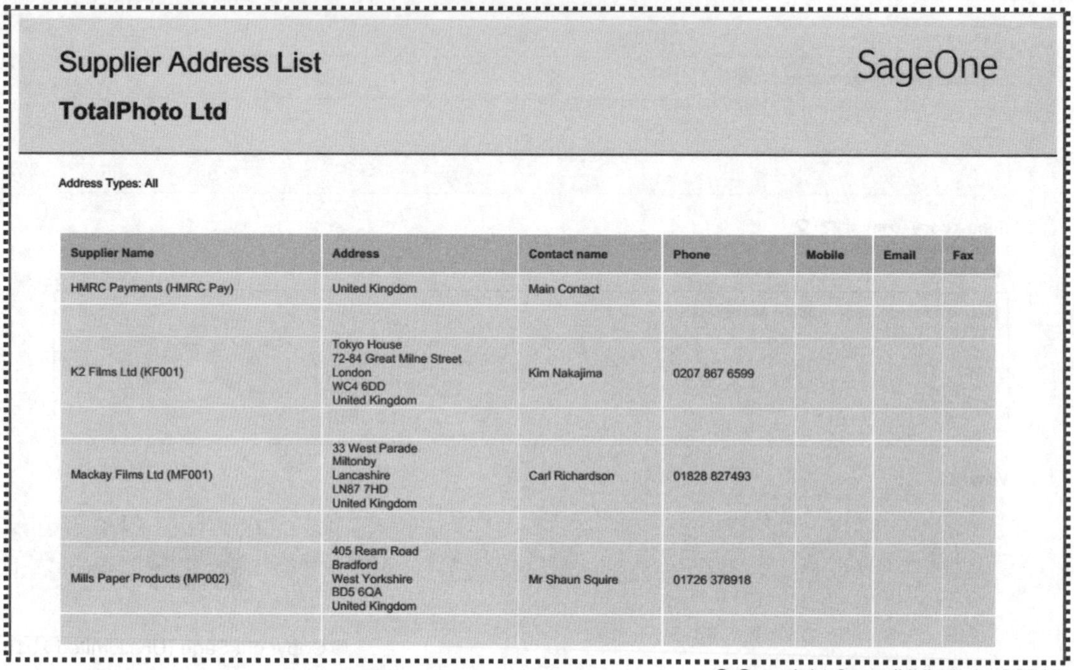

Supplier Address List

SageOne

TotalPhoto Ltd

Address Types: All

Supplier Name	Address	Contact name	Phone	Mobile	Email	Fax
HMRC Payments (HMRC Pay)	United Kingdom	Main Contact				
K2 Films Ltd (KF001)	Tokyo House 72-84 Great Milne Street London WC4 6DD United Kingdom	Kim Nakajima	0207 867 6599			
Mackay Films Ltd (MF001)	33 West Parade Miltonby Lancashire LN87 7HD United Kingdom	Carl Richardson	01828 827493			
Mills Paper Products (MP002)	405 Ream Road Bradford West Yorkshire BD5 6QA United Kingdom	Mr Shaun Squire	01726 378918			

You will be asked which address types you require. You can select 'All' and then Generate.

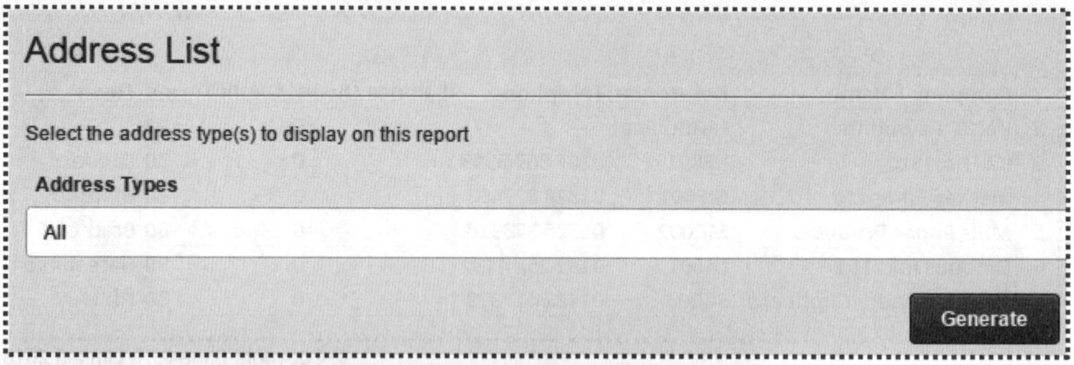

To access the report, go to the black navigation bar reports icon to display available reports and click on the supplier_addresses.pdf option.

4 Supplier opening balances

If you are operating a business and are transferring to a new accounting system, it is likely you will need to set the new system up with 'opening balances'. These include balances that are owed to suppliers.

A supplier balance is made up of all the invoices which are assigned to a supplier account which have either not be paid yet or matched/allocated with a payment on account. Occasionally invoices can be part-paid and the balance on the invoice is the unpaid part. Credit Notes and payments on account also need including as long as there is a balance outstanding on them.

In Sage One it is possible to enter all the transactions making up the opening balance on an account or with a single sum total. Having the individual amounts is often better when managing a supplier account.

In the examples we are using, we have just a single opening balance for each supplier.

Supplier opening balances

The first supplier whose outstanding balance you should enter is:

Mackay Films Ltd
33 West Parade
Miltonby
Lancashire
LN87 7HD

Tel 01828 827493

Fax 01828 827493

Contact: Carl Richardson **A/c Ref : MF001**

Outstanding Balance at 30th September 2014: **£345.36**

From the Getting Started tab, select the 'Enter outstanding supplier' transactions option.

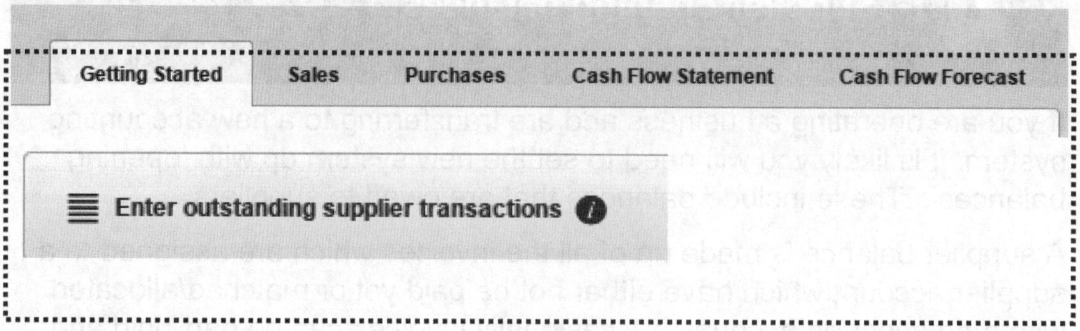

© Copyright Sage (UK) Limited 2015

After selection you will be taken to the Supplier Opening Balances page.

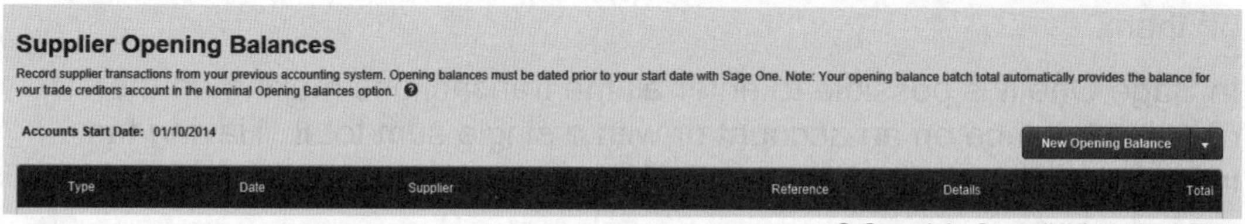

© Copyright Sage (UK) Limited 2015

You will notice the 'Accounts Start Date' was set as 01/10/14 as the first day of the accounting period for the current year.

Using the 

button – select New Opening Balance. Using the screen provided enter the opening balance for Mackay Films as shown below.

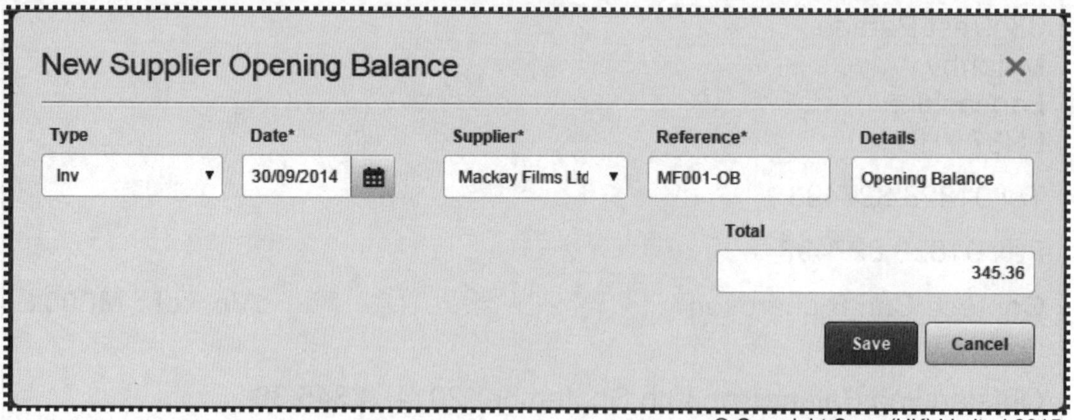

© Copyright Sage (UK) Limited 2015

Use Inv (Invoice) as the type, enter the 30th September 2014, select Mackay Films Ltd. Since we are not entering information for a particular invoice, the reference and details should be something to help you identify this as a transaction. Then save.

Activity

You have already entered one of TotalPhoto Ltd's suppliers opening balances (Mackay Films Ltd).

You should now enter the opening balance for each of the remaining five suppliers, and then save them to Sage One.

Once you are complete your list of opening balances should look like this:

Supplier Opening Balances

Record supplier transactions from your previous accounting system. Opening balances must be dated prior to your start date with Sage One. Note: Your opening balance batch total automatically provides the balance for your trade creditors account in the Nominal Opening Balances option.

Accounts Start Date: 01/10/2014

Create

	Type	Date	Supplier	Reference	Details	Total
×	Inv	30/09/2014	Mackay Films Ltd	OB-MF001-OB	Opening Balance	345.36
×	Inv	30/09/2014	K2 Films Ltd	OB-KF001-OB	Opening Balance	1,726.55
×	Inv	30/09/2014	The Stationery Cupboard	OB-SC003-OB	Opening Balance	375.00
×	Inv	30/09/2014	Mills Paper Products	OB-MP002-OB	Opening Balance	4,920.30
×	Inv	30/09/2014	Octopus Inks Ltd	OB-OI001-OB	Opening Balance	550.20
×	Inv	30/09/2014	Arthur's Photographic Equipment Ltd	OB-AP004-OB	Open Balance	11,275.00

If you now return to the supplier list you will notice the opening balance now reflects in the balanced owed column.

0 of 7 selected | Type the company / name to search | New Supplier

Company / Name	Reference	Telephone	Balance Owed	Credit Terms	Town
HMRC Payments	HMRC Pay		0.00	30	
Mackay Films Ltd	MF001	01828 827493	345.36	30	Miltonby
K2 Films Ltd	KF001	0207 867 6599	1,726.55	30	London
The Stationery Cupboard	SC003	01482 417378	375.00	30	Hull
Mills Paper Products	MP002	01726 378918	4,920.30	30	Bradford
Octopus Inks Ltd	OI001	0191 252 4132	550.20	30	Gateshead
Arthur's Photographic Equipment Ltd	AP004	0121 299 0192	11,275.00	30	Birmingham

Setting up your customers' details

6

Introduction

Now that you have successfully entered your suppliers' details you can move on to enter relevant information about your customers as well.

The process of entering your customers' details is very similar to that of entering supplier information, so you should feel confident doing this now.

It is of course vitally important that you keep accurate records for each of your customers. This information is likely to include:

(1) sales made on credit to customers, and sales returns

(2) credit terms for your customers, including any discount they may receive

(3) contact details for easy invoicing

(4) payments received from customers.

Consistent, accurate recording of information is a vital aspect of any credit management system, ensuring that your organisation gets paid as quickly as possible for its sales. This can be the difference between failure and survival for most businesses.

LEARNING OBJECTIVES

LO1 Enter accounting data at the beginning of an accounting period.

1.2 Set up customer accounts, entering opening balances where appropriate.

LO6 Produce reports.

6.1 Produce routine reports for customers and suppliers.

CONTENTS

1 Customer data

We can now start to look at the 'Customers' process and begin with entering the initial information regarding our case study firm, TotalPhoto Ltd. Again, you will find detailed step by step instructions directly after this activity.

Activity

TotalPhoto Ltd has six customers with outstanding balances as at 30th September 2014. Their details and guidance on how to enter the customer details follow.

Mr W Haslam
22 Brown Street
Miltonby
Lancashire LN87 6FD
A/c Ref : HAS004

Amount outstanding at 30th September 2010: £309.85

Credit terms: Payment in 14 days

Mrs H Poppy
120 Forrest Way
Miltonby
Lancashire LN87 9YR
A/c Ref : POP002

Amount outstanding at 30th September 2014: £220.00

Credit terms: Payment in 14 days

Mrs T Pashby
30A Andrews Street
Killington
Lancashire LN85 6TT
A/c Ref: PAS002

Amount outstanding at 30th September 2010: £89.50

Credit terms: Payment in 14 days

Campbell & Dunn Ltd
12 The Beeches
Miltonby
Lancashire LN87 9PP
A/c Ref: CAM004

Amount outstanding at 30th September 2010: £2056.85

Credit terms: 14 days

Lullabies Nursery
104 Victoria Road
Miltonby
Lancashire LN87 5PS
A/c Ref: LUL002

Amount outstanding at 30th September 2010: £726.90

Credit terms: Payment in 14 days

Miss S Pargenter
11 Alexandra Park
Miltonby
Lancashire LN87 2WD
A/c Ref: PAR006

Amount outstanding at 30th September 2010: £650.00

Credit terms: Payment in 14 days

You should now enter these six customers' details into Sage One.

2 Entering customer data

Customer Set up

The first customer to enter is:

Mr W Haslam
22 Brown Street
Miltonby
Lancashire LN87 6FD
A/c Ref : HAS004

Amount outstanding at 30th September 2010: £309.85

Credit terms: Payment in 14 days ~~Credit limit: £500~~

From the 'Contacts' menu, select the Customers option. You will be taken to the Customer list.

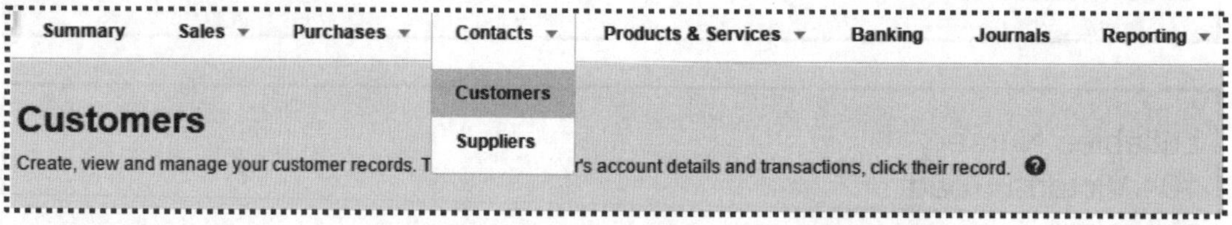
Summary
Sales
Purchases
Contacts
Products & Services
Banking
Journals
Reporting
Customers
Suppliers
Customers
Create, view and manage your customer records. T
r's account details and transactions, click their record.

The customers list will display all the customers which have previously been set up. By default these will be sorted in alphabetical order, however it is possible to re-sort the order by clicking on the column heading you wish to sort by.

It is possible to import customers from a data file, this is useful if you are moving from another accounting system and do not wish to enter all the supplier records manually into Sage One. The process to do this is not described in this book, however if you wish to experiment with this you can create a data file using Microsoft Excel by downloading the template which you can access from the help page.

To access the supplier set up use 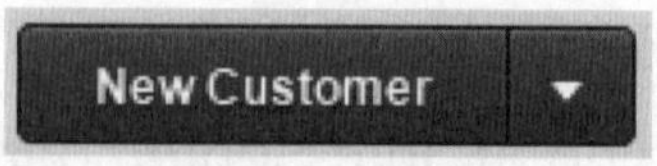
New Customer
button and the customer set up page will open.

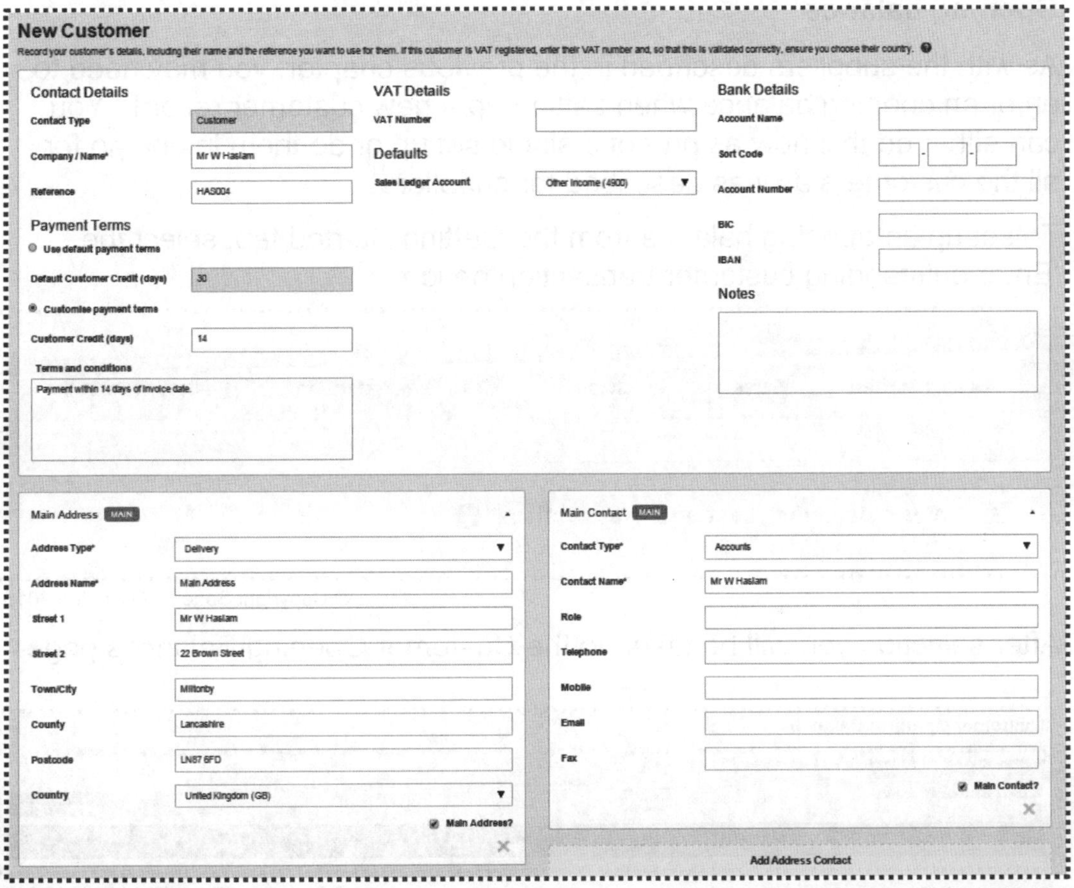
New Customer
Record your customer's details, including their name and the reference you want to use for them. If this customer is VAT registered, enter their VAT number and, so that this is validated correctly, ensure you choose their country.
Contact Details
Contact Type
Customer
Company / Name*
Mr W Haslam
Reference
HAS004
Payment Terms
Use default payment terms
Default Customer Credit (days)
30
Customise payment terms
Customer Credit (days)
14
Terms and conditions
Payment within 14 days of invoice date.
VAT Details
VAT Number
Defaults
Sales Ledger Account
Other Income (4900)
Bank Details
Account Name
Sort Code
Account Number
BIC
IBAN
Notes
Main Address
MAIN
Address Type*
Delivery
Address Name*
Main Address
Street 1
Mr W Haslam
Street 2
22 Brown Street
Town/City
Millonby
County
Lancashire
Postcode
LN87 6FD
Country
United Kingdom (GB)
Main Address?
Main Contact
MAIN
Contact Type*
Accounts
Contact Name*
Mr W Haslam
Role
Telephone
Mobile
Email
Fax
Main Contact?
Add Address Contact

The contact type will be pre-filled 'Customer'. Enter the business name in the Company/ Name field, the account reference. Using the custom payment terms enter 14 days.

If the customer is VAT registered and you are aware of their VAT number this can be recorded here, as well as their bank account information. Feel free to complete these sections with some 'made up' information.

The Sales Ledger (Nominal) Account will default to Other Income Account 4000. This can be amended to the account you require but, for now, leave this unchanged.

Complete the contact information in Addresses area as shown above. The Address Type should remain 'Delivery' in this case and the Address Name can be left unchanged 'Main Address'.

Don't forget to SAVE!

Opening balance

As with the suppliers described in the previous chapter, you may need to enter an opening balance when setting up a new customer record. You can either do this now as part of a single set up or do them in one go for all the customers as was described for suppliers.

To set up an opening balance from the Getting Started tab, select the 'Enter outstanding customer transaction option.

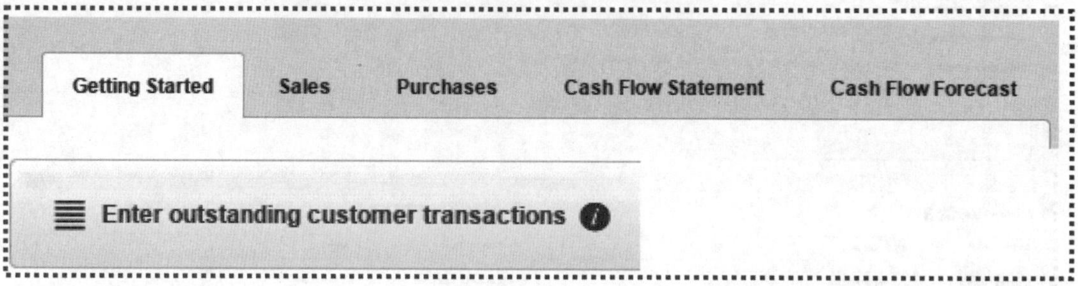

After selection you will be taken to the Customer Opening Balances page.

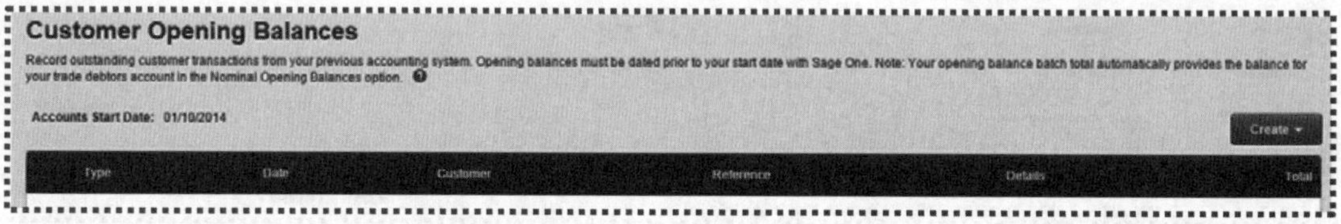

You will notice the 'Accounts Start Date' was set as 01/10/14 as the first day of the accounting period for the current year.

Using the 

button – select New Opening Balance. Using the screen provided enter the opening balance for Mackay Films as shown below.

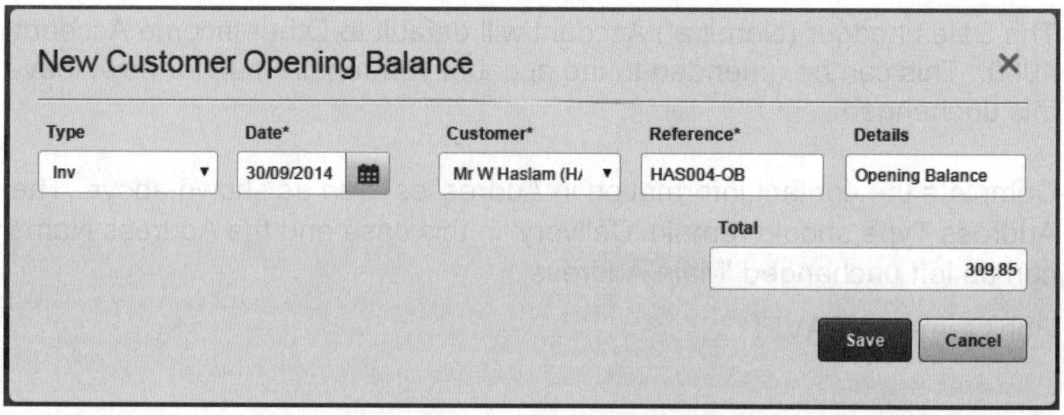

Use Inv (Invoice) as the type, enter the 30th September 2014, select Mr W Haslam. Since we are not entering information for a particular invoice, the reference and details should be something to help you identify this as a transaction. Then save.

Activity

You have already entered one of TotalPhoto Ltd's customers (Mr W Haslam).

You should now enter the full details for each of the remaining five customers, and then save them to Sage One.

When you have done this, the Customers Opening Balances page should look like this:

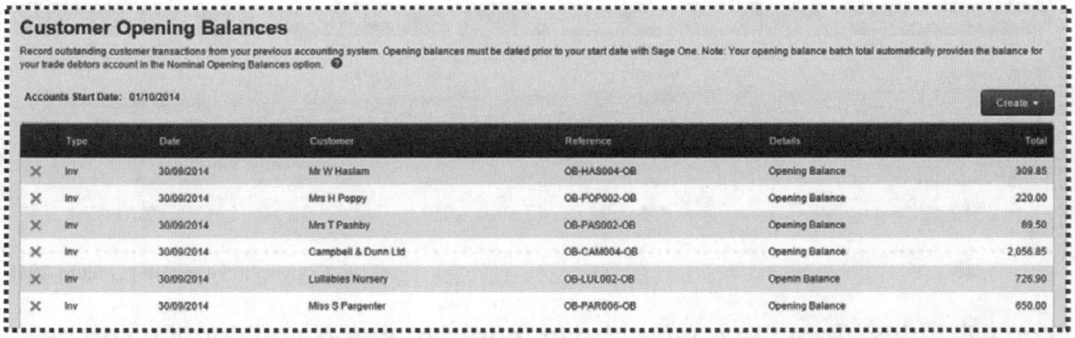

Customer Opening Balances

Record outstanding customer transactions from your previous accounting system. Opening balances must be dated prior to your start date with Sage One. Note: Your opening balance batch total automatically provides the balance for your trade debtors account in the Nominal Opening Balances option.

Accounts Start Date: 01/10/2014

Create

	Type	Date	Customer	Reference	Details	Total
X	Inv	30/09/2014	Mr W Haslam	OB-HAS004-OB	Opening Balance	309.85
X	Inv	30/09/2014	Mrs H Poppy	OB-POP002-OB	Opening Balance	220.00
X	Inv	30/09/2014	Mrs T Pashby	OB-PAS002-OB	Opening Balance	89.50
X	Inv	30/09/2014	Campbell & Dunn Ltd	OB-CAM004-OB	Opening Balance	2,056.85
X	Inv	30/09/2014	Lullabies Nursery	OB-LUL002-OB	Openin Balance	726.90
X	Inv	30/09/2014	Miss S Pargenter	OB-PAR006-OB	Opening Balance	650.00

3 Printing customer data reports

Customer data reports are available from the customer list page.

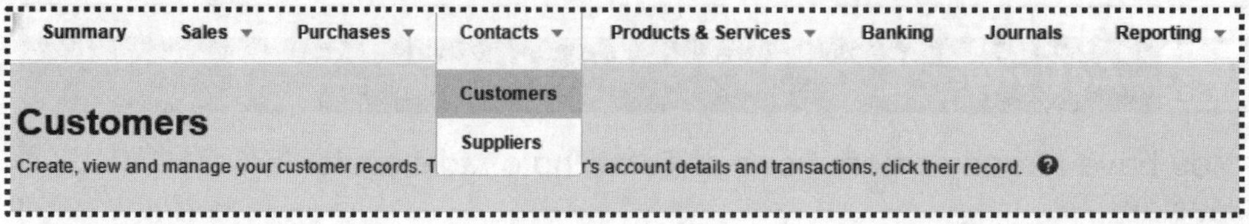
Summary
Sales
Purchases
Contacts
Products & Services
Banking
Journals
Reporting
Customers
Suppliers
Customers
Create, view and manage your customer records. T
r's account details and transactions, click their record.

From the 'Contacts' menu, select the Customers option, you will be taken to the customer list.

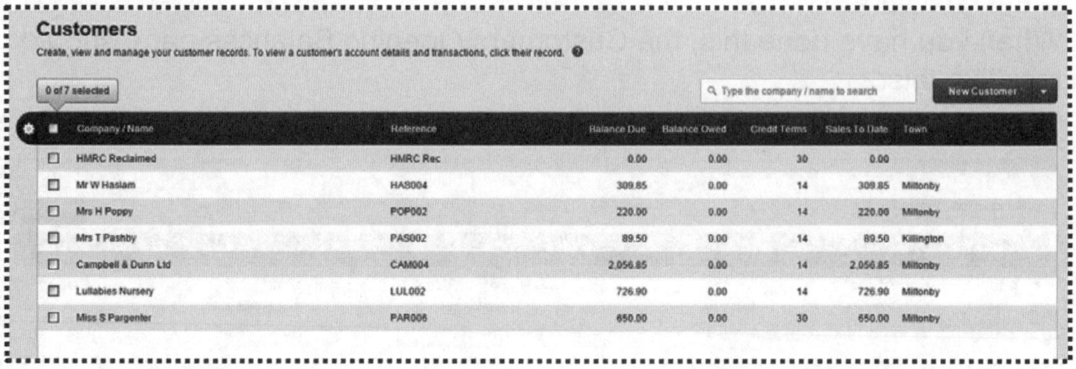
Customers
Create, view and manage your customer records. To view a customer's account details and transactions, click their record.
0 of 7 selected
Type the company / name to search
New Customer
Company / Name
Reference
Balance Due
Balance Owed
Credit Terms
Sales To Date
Town
HMRC Reclaimed HMRC Rec 0.00 0.00 30 0.00
Mr W Haslam HAS004 309.85 0.00 14 309.85 Miltonby
Mrs H Poppy POP002 220.00 0.00 14 220.00 Miltonby
Mrs T Pashby PAS002 89.50 0.00 14 89.50 Killington
Campbell & Dunn Ltd CAM004 2,056.85 0.00 14 2,056.85 Miltonby
Lullabies Nursery LUL002 726.90 0.00 14 726.90 Miltonby
Miss S Pargenter PAR006 650.00 0.00 30 650.00 Miltonby

You will notice from the image above there are some additional columns which are not displaying in your view. To add these columns using the cog 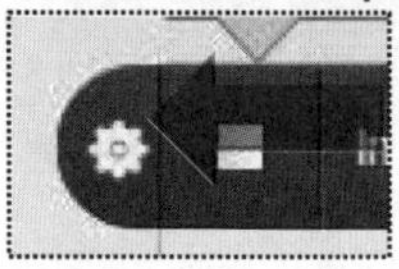 and you will be able to select which columns are in view.

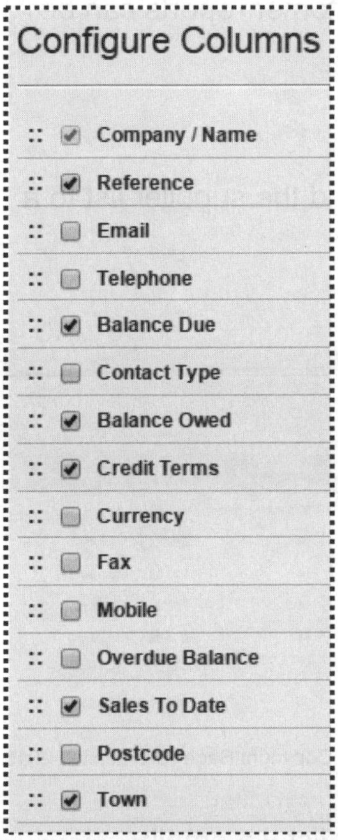

De-select Email and Telephone and select:

- Balanced Owed
- Credit Terms
- Sales To Date
- Town

The column order has remained unchanged, however to re-order columns click on the symbol :: and drag the column to the required position.

To access the reports you will need to select the suppliers which are required to be included in the report. This is done by selecting them in the list using the tick boxes to the left of the supplier name. To select all suppliers select the box at the top of the grid. See below.

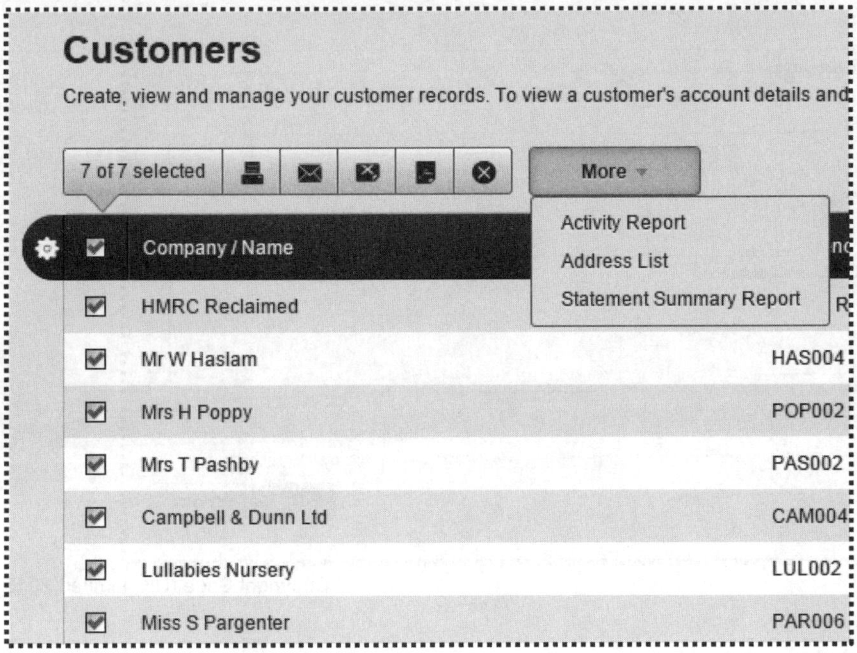

Having selected the customers you require, the customer reports can be accessed.

Using the toolbar:

Select the printer icon or pdf icon to send the supplier list to a printable report format:

Customer List SageOne

TotalPhoto Ltd

Company / Name	Reference	Balance Due	Balance Owed	Credit Terms	Sales To Date	Town
HMRC Reclaimed	HMRC Rec	0.00	0.00	30	0.00	
Mr W Haslam	HAS004	309.85	0.00	14	309.85	Miltonby
Mrs H Poppy	POP002	220.00	0.00	14	220.00	Miltonby
Mrs T Pashby	PAS002	89.50	0.00	14	89.50	Killington
Campbell & Dunn Ltd	CAM004	2,056.85	0.00	14	2,056.85	Miltonby
Lullabies Nursery	LUL002	726.90	0.00	14	726.90	Miltonby
Miss S Pargenter	PAR006	650.00	0.00	30	650.00	Miltonby

Select the envelope icon to send the supplier list via email:

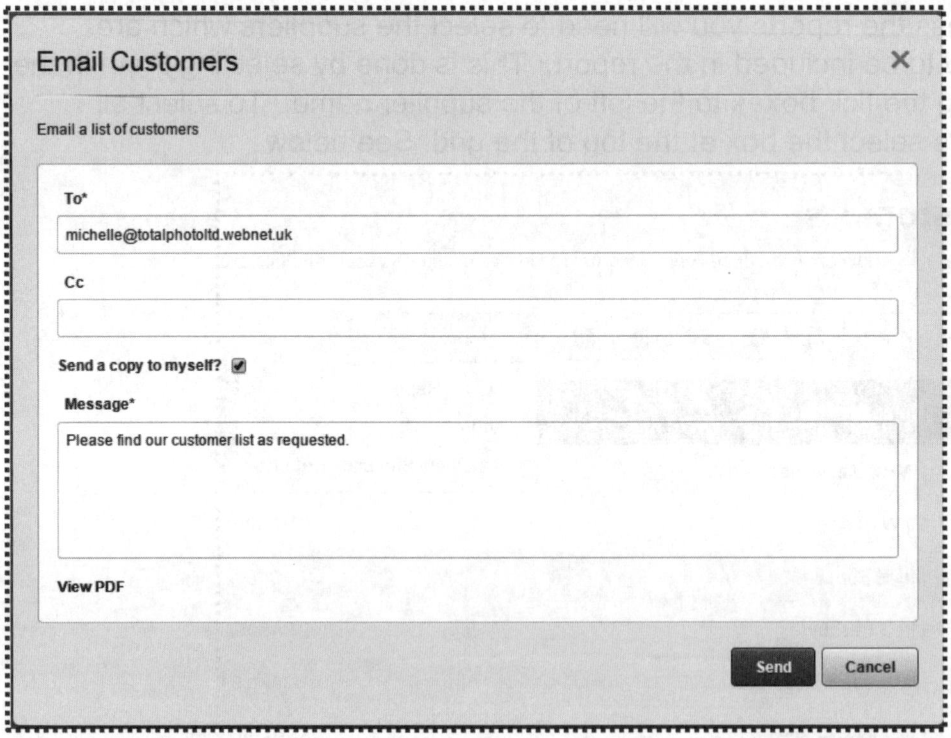
Email Customers
Email a list of customers
To*
michelle@totalphotoltd.webnet.uk
Cc
Send a copy to myself?
Message*
Please find our customer list as requested.
View PDF
Send
Cancel

Select the file icon  to send the supplier list to CSV (opening in Excel).

	A	B	C	D	E	F	G
1	**Company / Name**	**Reference**	**Balance Due**	**Balance Owed**	**Credit Terms**	**Sales To Date**	**Town**
2	HMRC Reclaimed	HMRC Rec	0	0	30	0	
3	Mr W Haslam	HAS004	309.85	0	14	309.85	Miltonby
4	Mrs H Poppy	POP002	220	0	14	220	Miltonby
5	Mrs T Pashby	PAS002	89.5	0	14	89.5	Killington
6	Campbell & Dunn Ltd	CAM004	2,056.85	0	14	2,056.85	Miltonby
7	Lullabies Nursery	LUL002	726.9	0	14	726.9	Miltonby
8	Miss S Pargenter	PAR006	650	0	30	650	Miltonby

Using the More button 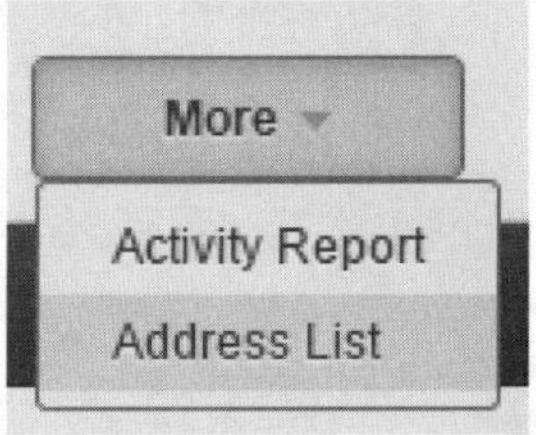
More
Activity Report
Address List
select Address List, to view the list of selected customers with their address details. You will be asked which address types you require. You can select 'All' and then Generate.

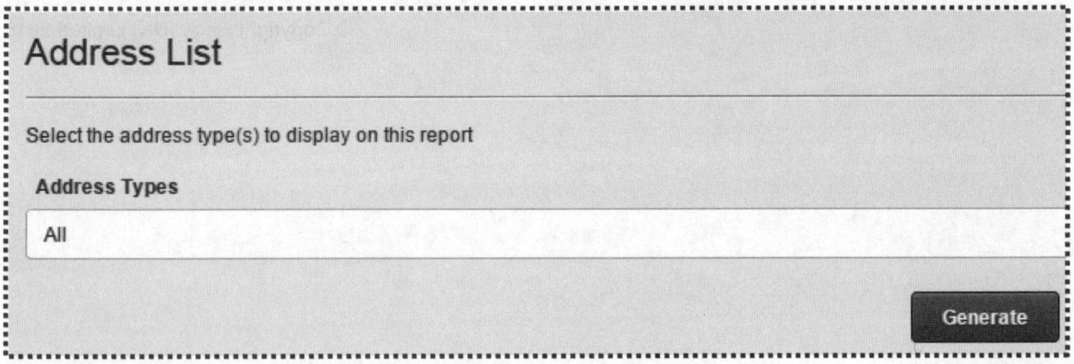
Address List
Select the address type(s) to display on this report
Address Types
All
Generate

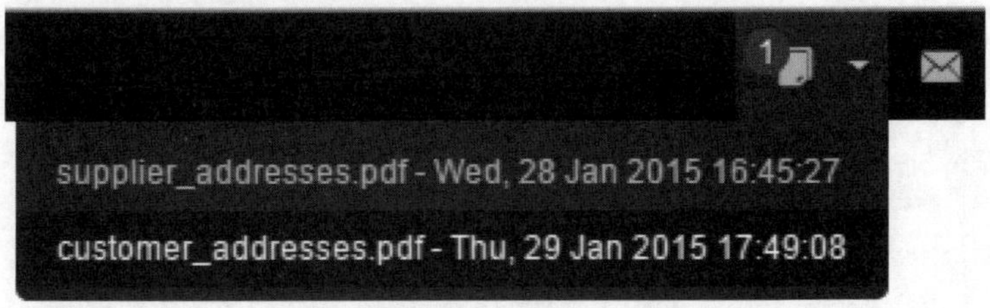
supplier_addresses.pdf - Wed, 28 Jan 2015 16:45:27
customer_addresses.pdf - Thu, 29 Jan 2015 17:49:08

To access the report, go to the black navigation bar reports icon to display available reports and click on the customer_addresses.pdf option.

Customer Address List

TotalPhoto Ltd

Sage

Address Types: All

Customer Name	Address	Contact name	Phone	Mobile	Email
HMRC Reclaimed (HMRC Rec)	United Kingdom	Main Contact			
Mr W Haslam (HAS004)	Mr W Haslam 22 Brown Street Miltonby Lancashire LN87 6FD United Kingdom	Mr W Haslam			
Mrs H Poppy (POP002)	120 Forrest Way Miltonby Lancashire LN87 9YR United Kingdom	Mrs H Poppy			
Mrs T Pashby (PAS002)	30A Andrews Street Killington Lancashire LN85 6TT United Kingdom	Mrs T Pashby			

7 The nominal ledger

LEARNING OBJECTIVES	
LO1	Enter accounting data at the beginning of an accounting period.
1.1	Set up general ledger accounts, entering opening balances where appropriate.
LO6	Produce reports.
6.1	Produce routine reports from the general ledger – trial balance.

CONTENTS

1 Introduction

The nominal ledger is probably the most important element of the Sage One (or indeed any) accounting system. The key aspect to this is the list of nominal codes. This is simply a series of different accounts which are used each time a transaction is recorded.

Each of these accounts is given a unique four digit code number. To view the list of Nominal Codes go to the **Chart of Accounts** set up and management page navigated to from either the 'Getting Started' area or via the Settings menu.

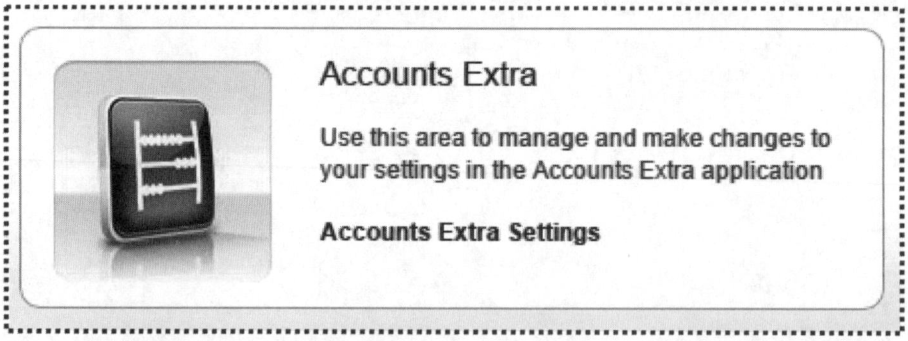

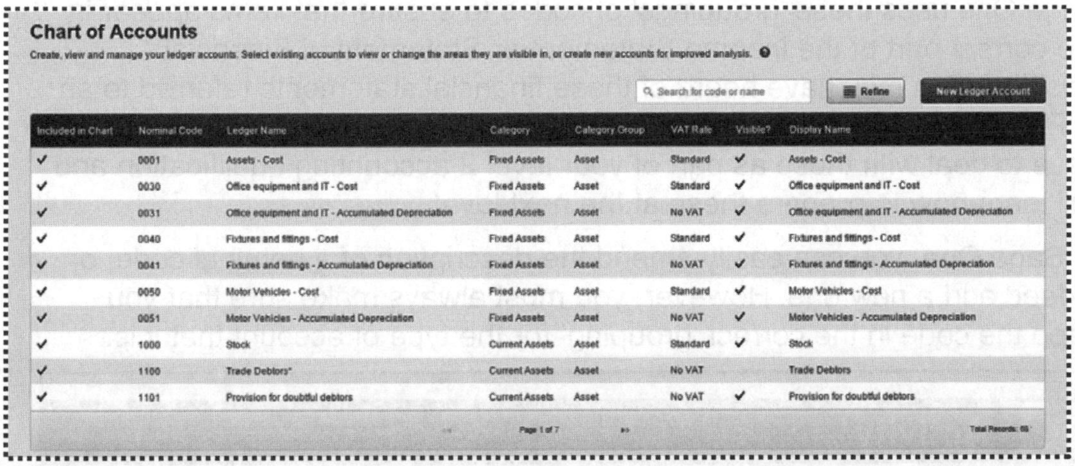
Chart of Accounts
Create, view and manage your ledger accounts. Select existing accounts to view or change the areas they are visible in, or create new accounts for improved analysis.
Search for code or name
Refine
New Ledger Account
Page 1 of 7
Total Records:

Included in Chart	Nominal Code	Ledger Name	Category	Category Group	VAT Rate	Visible?	Display Name
✓	0001	Assets - Cost	Fixed Assets	Asset	Standard	✓	Assets - Cost
✓	0030	Office equipment and IT - Cost	Fixed Assets	Asset	Standard	✓	Office equipment and IT - Cost
✓	0031	Office equipment and IT - Accumulated Depreciation	Fixed Assets	Asset	No VAT	✓	Office equipment and IT - Accumulated Depreciation
✓	0040	Fixtures and fittings - Cost	Fixed Assets	Asset	Standard	✓	Fixtures and fittings - Cost
✓	0041	Fixtures and fittings - Accumulated Depreciation	Fixed Assets	Asset	No VAT	✓	Fixtures and fittings - Accumulated Depreciation
✓	0050	Motor Vehicles - Cost	Fixed Assets	Asset	Standard	✓	Motor Vehicles - Cost
✓	0051	Motor Vehicles - Accumulated Depreciation	Fixed Assets	Asset	No VAT	✓	Motor Vehicles - Accumulated Depreciation
✓	1000	Stock	Current Assets	Asset	Standard	✓	Stock
✓	1100	Trade Debtors*	Current Assets	Asset	No VAT		Trade Debtors
✓	1101	Provision for doubtful debtors	Current Assets	Asset	No VAT	✓	Provision for doubtful debtors

The four-digit code is important, as the list is broken down into groups:

0000-0999	Fixed Assets and Depreciation (e.g. Buildings, Equipment)
1000-1999	Current Assets (e.g. Stock, Debtors, Bank)
2000-2999	Liabilities (e.g. Loans, Creditors)
3000-3999	Capital and Reserves
4000-4999	Sales & Income
5000-5999	Purchases
6000-6999	Direct Expenses (e.g. Direct Labour)
7000-7999	Miscellaneous Overheads (e.g. Phone, Rent, Postage)
8000-8999	Bad debts and Depreciation
9000-9999	Suspense and Mispostings

Sage One uses these 'groupings' of codes to ensure that items appear in the correct part of the Income Statement or Statement of Financial Position. You may have heard of these financial statements referred to as a 'Profit and Loss Account' or 'Balance Sheet'. Don't worry you will not have to deal with these as part of your level 2 accounting qualification and will learn how to prepare these at the next level.

In Sage One, you can easily amend the description of a nominal code, or indeed add a new one. However, you must always make sure that you keep the code in the correct 'grouping' for the type of account that it is.

Activity

You should now print out the list of nominal codes.

From the Reports menu – select 'Chart of Account List'

Select all Categories and click Export to PDF

Control accounts

There are some very special Nominal Codes called Control Accounts, which are essential to the running of the Sage One software. **These cannot be deleted and are always present in the Chart of Accounts.**

Control accounts are used automatically by Sage One. This means that you do not need to specify them individually when entering transactions – Sage One will work out which control account is required and apply it automatically. Other Nominal Codes (from the list you printed out) will need to be entered.

Control Accounts include Debtors Control and Creditors Control. These accounts will be used automatically when posting a sales or a purchase invoice for example, and will store the total amounts owing by customers and to suppliers.

The Bank Account is also a control account as are the accounts to which VA is posted following sales and purchases. This enables accurate recording of VAT liability for completion of VAT returns.

2 Entering a nominal code

The default Chart of Accounts contains the most common codes set up for a general business. However, you will almost certainly want to add to, or amend, these Nominal Codes to suit your business in particular.

For example, in your case study TotalPhoto Ltd you will want to be more specific when recording its sales and purchases. Before you do this, have a look at your listing of Nominal Codes. Find the 5000-5999 Range (remember, these are set aside for Purchases).

From the reports menu, select Chart of Accounts List, select Category 'Direct Expenses and the following list will appear:

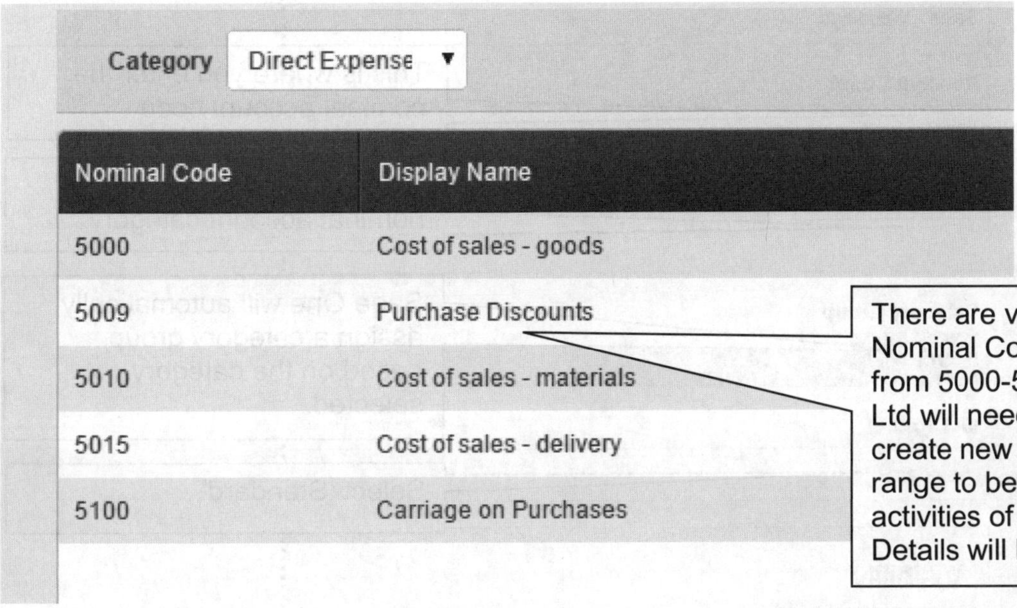
Category
Direct Expense
Nominal Code
Display Name
5000
Cost of sales - goods
5009
Purchase Discounts
5010
Cost of sales - materials
5015
Cost of sales - delivery
5100
Carriage on Purchases

There are very few, general, Nominal Codes in this range, from 5000-5999. TotalPhoto Ltd will need to be able to create new codes within this range to better reflect the activities of the business. Details will be provided later.

To create a new nominal code or amend an existing code, from the Chart of Accounts set up screen select **New Ledger Account** and the following set up screen will appear:

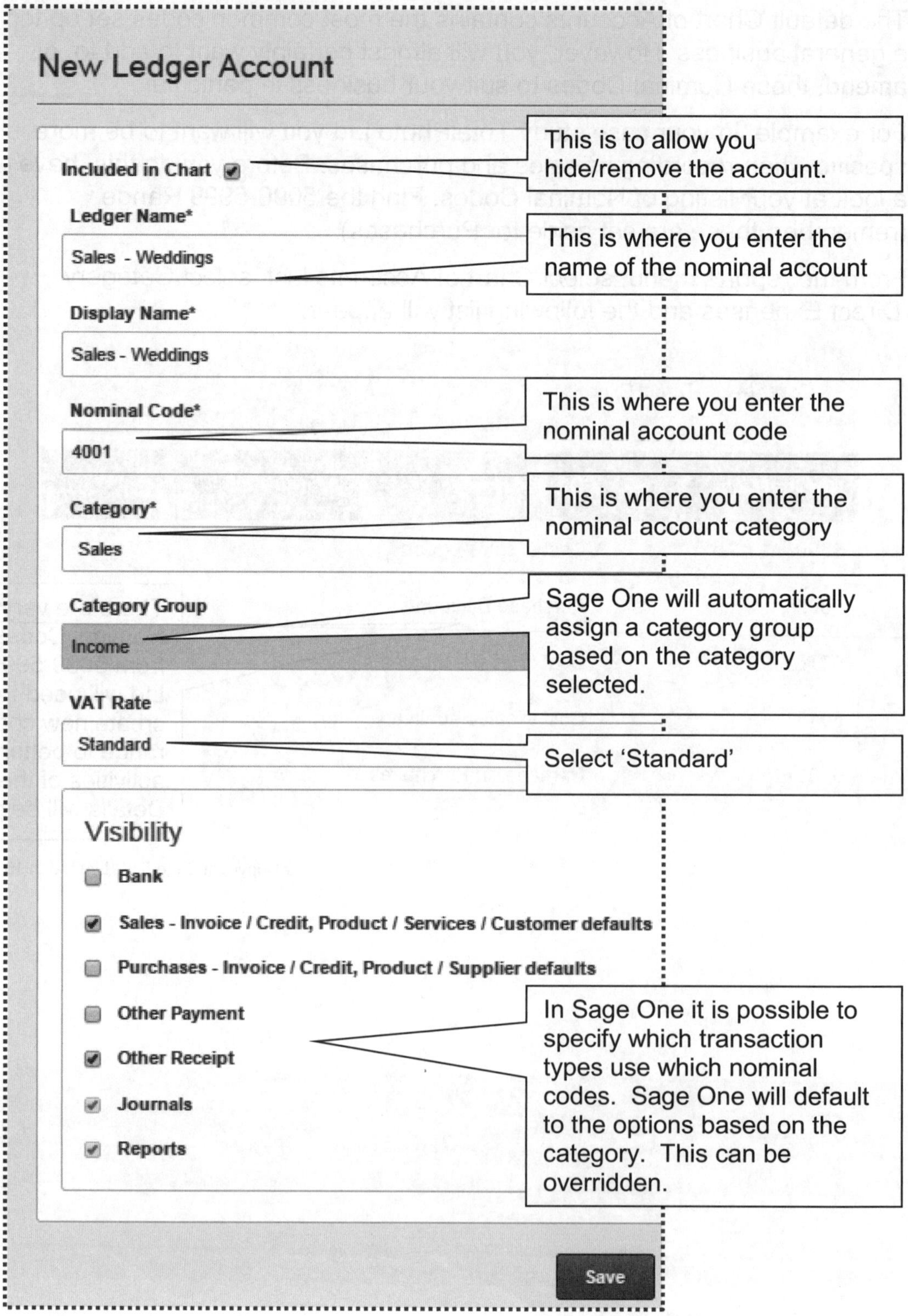
New Ledger Account
Included in Chart
This is to allow you hide/remove the account.
Ledger Name*
Sales - Weddings
This is where you enter the name of the nominal account
Display Name*
Sales - Weddings
Nominal Code*
4001
This is where you enter the nominal account code
Category*
Sales
This is where you enter the nominal account category
Category Group
Income
Sage One will automatically assign a category group based on the category selected.
VAT Rate
Standard
Select 'Standard'
Visibility
Bank
Sales - Invoice / Credit, Product / Services / Customer defaults
Purchases - Invoice / Credit, Product / Supplier defaults
Other Payment
Other Receipt
Journals
Reports
In Sage One it is possible to specify which transaction types use which nominal codes. Sage One will default to the options based on the category. This can be overridden.
Save

To amend an existing nominal account from the Chart of Accounts set up screen, select the account with a mouse click, the edit screen will appear. Make edits as required.

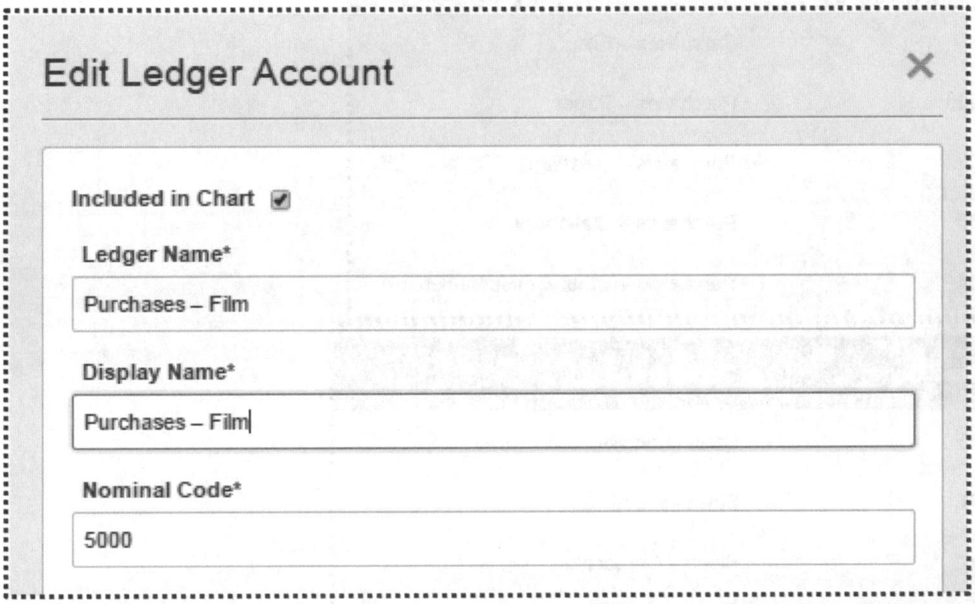
Edit Ledger Account
Included in Chart
Ledger Name*
Purchases – Film
Display Name*
Purchases – Film
Nominal Code*
5000

Activity

To practice amending and creating Nominal Codes (N/Cs), enter each of the following N/Cs and names. Do them one by one, and then save each one. These are all relevant to our case study firm – TotalPhoto Ltd.

SALES		**PURCHASES**	
Nominal Code	*Name*	*Nominal Code*	*Name*
4000	Sales – Individuals & Family	5000	Purchases – Film
4001	Sales – Weddings	5001	Purchases – Paper
4002	Sales – Corporate	5002	Purchases – Cartridges & Toner
4003	Sales – Nurseries & Schools	5003	Purchases – Stationery
4004	Other sales	5004	Purchases – Other Consumables

When you have finished; re-run the Chart of Accounts report to check that all your additions and amendments have been made correctly.

Nominal Code	Display Name
5000	Purchases – Film
5001	Purchases – Paper
5002	Purchases – Cartridges & Toner
5003	Purchases – Stationery
5004	Purchases – Other Consumables

Nominal Code	Display Name
4000	Sales – Individuals & Family
4001	Sales - Weddings
4002	Sales – Corporate
4003	Sales – Nurseries & Schools
4004	Other Sales

The next step is to post opening balances to each relevant nominal code within Sage One for your business.

Activity

You now need to enter the opening balances for each of the accounts relating to TotalPhoto Ltd. These will be the balance on each account at the end of the previous accounting period, so on 30th September 2014. The list of opening balances is shown below and **detailed guidance on how to enter these balances follow this activity.**

Important

1 You will need to create new Nominal Codes for two items: Photographic Equipment and Photographic Equipment Depreciation (use Fixed Assets the category when setting up the new codes). You may also choose to re-name the nominal account called Ordinary Shares (no 3000) to Capital – Ordinary Shares although this is optional.

2 You do not need to enter opening balances for two items, the Debtors Control Account and the Creditors Control Account. This is because these represent the total amount owed to us (debtors/receivables) and the total amount we owe (creditors/payables), made up of all of the individual balances you entered earlier. These control account balances are therefore calculated automatically by Sage One and **you do not enter them.**

3 The cash and bank balances need to be entered as part of the bank account set up. It is not possible to enter them directly in the nominal opening balances process.

4 Be very careful to enter each balance correctly as either a **debit** or a **credit** balance. Take your time to complete this activity as it will help prevent you making errors at this stage.

TotalPhoto Ltd

Opening Balances

	Nominal code	Debit	Credit
Motor vehicles (at cost)	*0050*	21800.00	
Motor Vehicles Depreciation	*0051*		5450.00
Office Equipment	*0030*	4849.00	
Office Equipment Depreciation	*0031*		921.00
Photographic Equipment	*0032*	22718.00	
Photographic Equip Depreciation	*0033*		4316.00
Stock (as at 1st October 2014)	*1000*	7403.00	
Cash in Hand	*1210*	250.00	
Bank	*1200*	10293.00	
Creditors Control Account	*2100*		19192.41
Capital – Ordinary Shares	*3000*		20000.00
Purchases – Film	*5000*	205.63	
Purchases – Paper	*5001*	1034.35	
Purchases – Cartridges & Toner	*5002*	1225.87	
Purchases – Stationery	*5003*	409.35	
Purchases – Other Consumables	*5004*	823.52	
Sales – Individuals & Families	*4000*		5401.21
Sales – Weddings	*4001*		3984.50
Sales – Corporate	*4002*		1932.09
Sales – Nurseries & Schools	*4003*		11304.20
Other Sales	*4004*		1590.30
Rent & Rates	*7100*	4280.00	
Office Costs	*7500*	603.43	
Motor expenses	*7300*	1035.64	
Travel & Entertainment	*7400*	229.39	
Debtors Control Account	*1100*	4053.10	
Profit & Loss	*3100*		5498.28
VAT	*2202*		1623.29
		81213.28	**81213.28**

Note: this is the total of the suppliers' balances that you entered earlier. This has already been entered and so will not need to be entered again

Similarly this is the total of the individual customers' accounts that you entered earlier. Again, this will not need to be entered again

Entering a new balance

Entering opening balances in Sage One is very straightforward. If you enter an opening balance incorrectly, please refer to a later chapter for detailed guidance on how to correct.

From the 'Getting Started' Area, select

Enter nominal account opening balances

And the following screen will appear. You will notice the opening balances on the debtors and creditors control account will already be entered. This has come from the opening balances entered earlier for suppliers and customers.

Ledger Account*	Details	Debit	Credit
Trade Debtors (1100)	Opening Balance	4,053.10	0.00
Trade Creditors (2100)	Opening Balance	0.00	19,192.41
Current (1200)	Opening Balance	0.00	0.00
Cash in Hand (1210)	Opening Balance	0.00	0.00
Please select	(Opening Balance)	0.00	0.00
Opening Balances Control Account (9998)	Opening Balance	15,139.31	0.00
		19,192.41	19,192.41

Accounts Start Date: 01/10/2014

Date*

30/09/2014

Reference*

Opening Balances

Enter the balances date and from the next available line select nominal Motor Vehicles – Cost (0050) and enter a

Motor Vehicles - Cost (0050)

debit value of £21,800. You will notice a balancing figure will be displayed automatically in the Opening Balances Control Account. This account will calculate automatically to keep the system 'in-balance'. This account should be zero once all the opening balances are entered.

Continue down the list of opening balances to the end. When you are complete the Opening Balances Control Account (9998) will be zero. You will not be required to enter the cash and bank balances here. This must be done as part of bank account set up.

Bank & Cash opening balances

From the Banking tab, select Current Account with a mouse click.

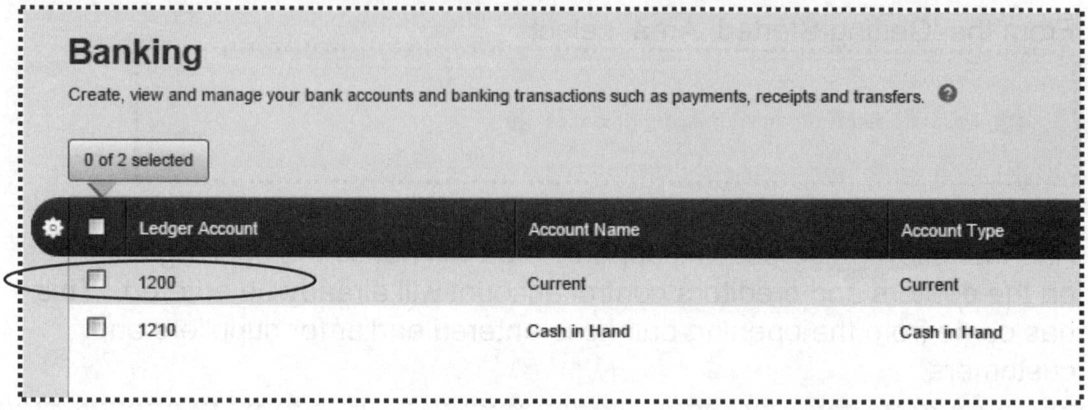
Banking
Create, view and manage your bank accounts and banking transactions such as payments, receipts and transfers.
0 of 2 selected
Ledger Account
Account Name
Account Type
1200
Current
Current
1210
Cash in Hand
Cash in Hand

From within the bank account record select Opening Balance.

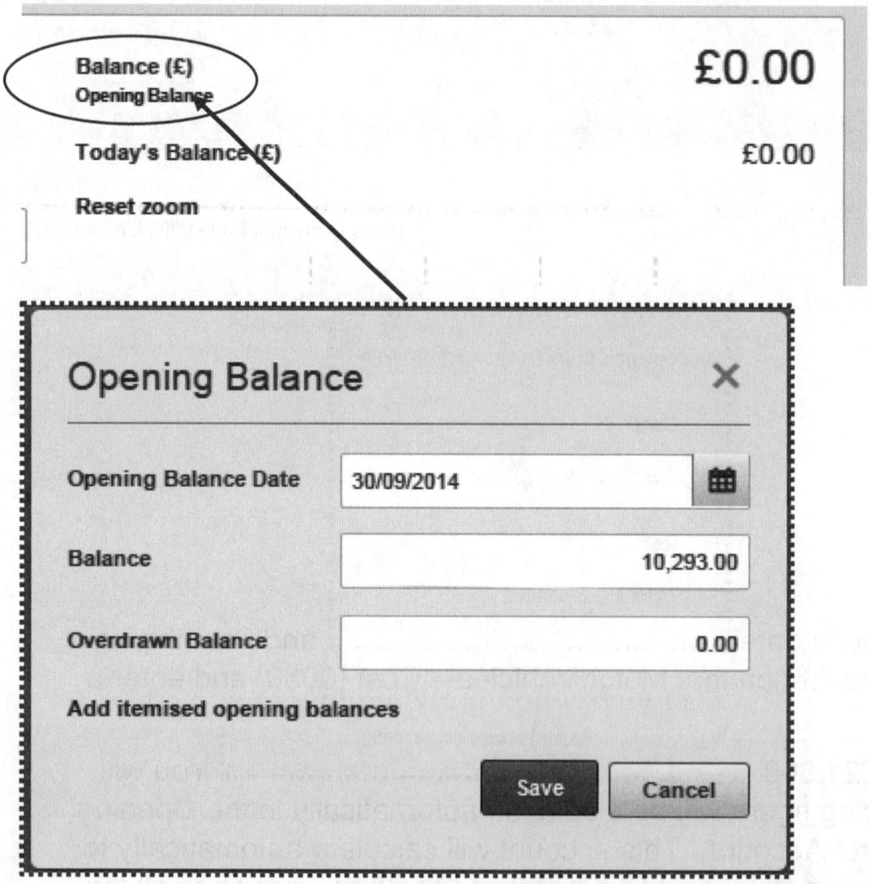
Balance (£)
Opening Balance
£0.00
Today's Balance (£)
£0.00
Reset zoom
Opening Balance
Opening Balance Date
30/09/2014
Balance
10,293.00
Overdrawn Balance
0.00
Add itemised opening balances
Save
Cancel

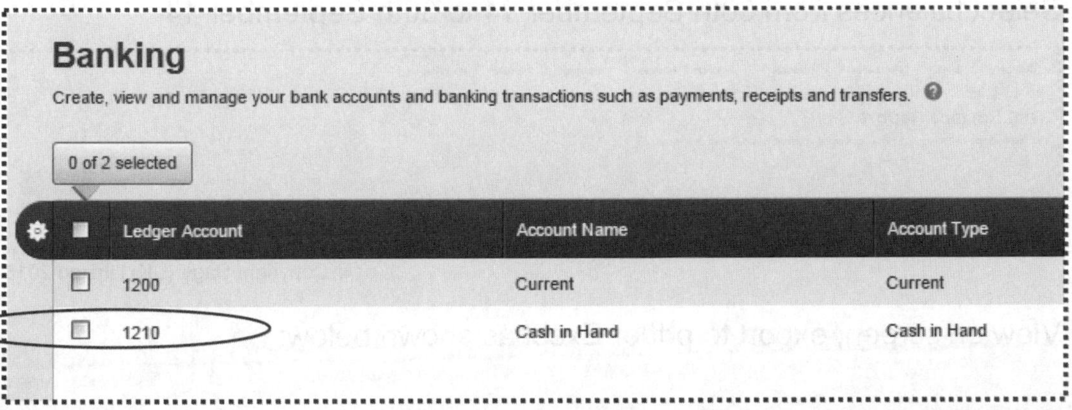
Banking
Create, view and manage your bank accounts and banking transactions such as payments, receipts and transfers.
0 of 2 selected
Ledger Account
Account Name
Account Type
1200
Current
Current
1210
Cash in Hand
Cash in Hand

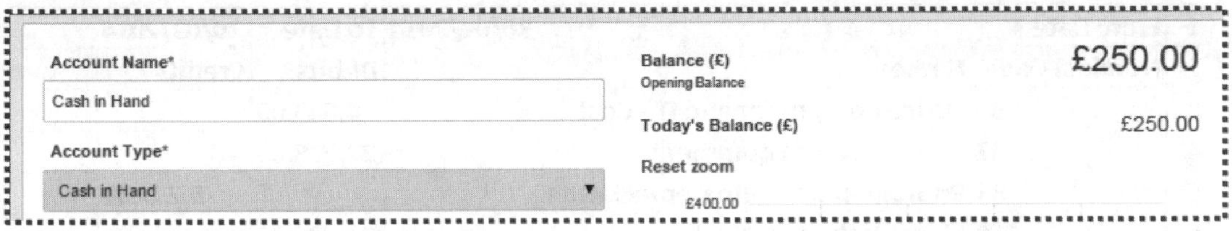
Account Name*
Cash in Hand
Account Type*
Cash in Hand
Balance (£)
Opening Balance
£250.00
Today's Balance (£)
£250.00
Reset zoom
£400.00

Once you have entered all of the nominal account opening balances, including cash and bank balances, together with the supplier and customer balances, the opening balances process is complete. Ensure the Opening Balance Control Account is zero.

3 Printing a trial balance

You should now have entered all the opening balances for TotalPhoto Ltd. You are now ready to begin entering transactions on a day to day basis. Before you do this, you should print off a Trial Balance.

Activity

Print off a trial balance for TotalPhoto Ltd as at 30 September 2014. Guidance on how to do this follows.

From the Reporting Menu/ Reports – select 'Trial Balance Report'

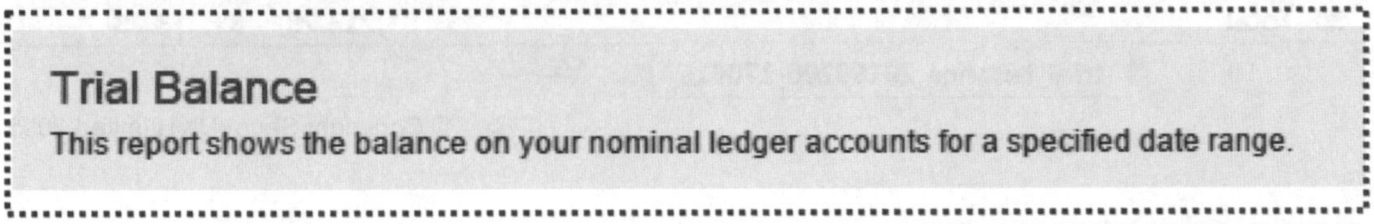
Trial Balance
This report shows the balance on your nominal ledger accounts for a specified date range.

Select balances from 30th September 14 to 30th September 14

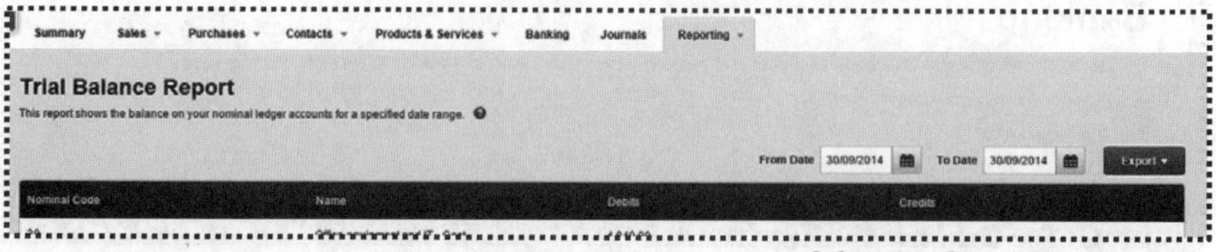
Summary
Sales
Purchases
Contacts
Products & Services
Banking
Journals
Reporting
Trial Balance Report
This report shows the balance on your nominal ledger accounts for a specified date range.
From Date 30/09/2014
To Date 30/09/2014
Export
Nominal Code
Name
Debits
Credits

View on screen, export to pdf or Excel as shown below:

	A	B	C	D	E
1	**From Date**	**30/09/2014**	**To Date**	**30/09/2014**	
2	**Nominal Code**	**Name**	**Debits**	**Credits**	
3	**30**	Office equipment and IT - Cost	4,849.00		
4	**32**	Photographic Equipment	22,718.00		
5	**33**	Photographic Equip Depreciation		5,237.00	
6	**50**	Motor Vehicles - Cost	21,800.00		
7	**51**	Motor Vehicles - Accumulated Depreciation		5,450.00	
8	**1000**	Stock	7,403.00		
9	**1100**	Trade Debtors	4,053.10		
10	**1200**	Current	10,293.00		
11	**1210**	Cash in Hand	250		
12	**2100**	Trade Creditors		19,192.41	
13	**2202**	VAT Liability		1,623.29	
14	**3000**	Ordinary Shares		20,000.00	
15	**3100**	Profit and Loss Account		5,498.28	
16	**4000**	Sales - Individuals & Family		5,401.21	
17	**4001**	Sales - Weddings		3,984.50	
18	**4002**	Sales -Corporate		1,932.09	
19	**4003**	Sales - Nurseries & Schools		11,304.20	
20	**4004**	Other Sales		1,590.30	
21	**5000**	Purchases - Film	205.63		
22	**5001**	Purchases - Paper	1,034.35		
23	**5002**	Purchases - Cartridges & Toner	1,225.87		
24	**5003**	Purchases - Stationery	409.35		
25	**5004**	Purchases - Other Consumables	823.52		
26	**7100**	Rent and rates	4,280.00		
27	**7300**	Motor Expenses	1,035.64		
28	**7400**	Travel and Entertainment	229.39		
29	**7500**	Office costs	603.43		
30	**Total**		**81,213.28**	**81,213.28**	

trial_balance_20150206_170915

How to amend an incorrect opening balance

If any of the balances are different to the ones on your printed version, you are able to amend as follows:

Firstly tick off your trial balance to determine which opening balances have been entered incorrectly and make a note of them.

If you find any errors – return to the opening balances screen and edit accordingly.

Entering transactions

8

LEARNING OBJECTIVES

LO2 Record customer transactions.

2.1 Process sales invoices and credit notes, accounting for VAT.

2.2 Allocate monies received from customers in partial or full payment of invoices and balances.

LO6 Produce reports.

6.1 Produce routine reports for customers and suppliers – statements.

LO3 Record supplier transactions.

3.1 Process purchase invoices and credit notes, accounting for VAT.

3.2 Allocate monies paid to suppliers in full or partial settlement of invoices or balances.

LO4 Record and reconcile bank and cash transactions.

4.1 Process receipts and payments for non-credit transactions.

4.3 Process petty cash receipts and payments, accounting for VAT.

CONTENTS

1 Introduction

Any business will carry out a wide range of transactions every day of the week. However, the majority of these will fall into one of the following categories:

Credit transactions

- Purchases of inventory/stock on credit.
- Sales of goods or services on credit.

Cash transactions

- Purchases made by cash/cheque/card.
- Sales made for cash/cheque/card.
- Payments made to suppliers (for goods/services bought on credit).
- Receipts from customers (for goods/services sold on credit).
- Payments made to meet other expenses.
- Payment of salaries and wages to staff.
- Petty cash transactions.
- Transactions directly through the bank account (e.g. bank charges, interest, direct debits, standing orders).

Each of these transactions will have an effect on two accounts within the Sage One system – this is the underlying principle of double-entry bookkeeping. However, Sage One simplifies this by carrying out much of the double entry automatically.

Consider first the first transactions listed above – purchases and sales made on credit. This means that a legally binding contract is established between the two parties, and (usually) the goods or services are supplied but payment is not made until some later date. The key document in this process is the **invoice** – as this is the document which demands payment and lays down the agreed terms of the transaction.

Hence, entering a credit transaction (whether a purchase or a sale) is a two stage process in Sage One.

(1) Enter the details of the invoice against the relevant supplier or customer. This will establish the presence and value of the legally binding debt.

(2) At a later date, enter the details of the payment of the debt, either the payment sent to the supplier or the receipt received from the customer.

Note that this approach is applicable for both credit sales and credit purchases – you just have to be sure to enter the details in the correct part of Sage One.

Now consider the second set of transactions listed at the start of this Chapter – each of these has a direct impact on the bank accounts within Sage One.

2 Credit sales – entering customer invoices

Our case study company TotalPhoto Ltd have had a number of credit customers. Each of these have been issued with an invoice, and these invoices now need to be entered into Sage One.

The easiest way to do this is to **batch** invoices together so that they can be input at the same time.

To enter a batch of customer (sales) invoices go to the Sales tab and select 'Quick Entries'

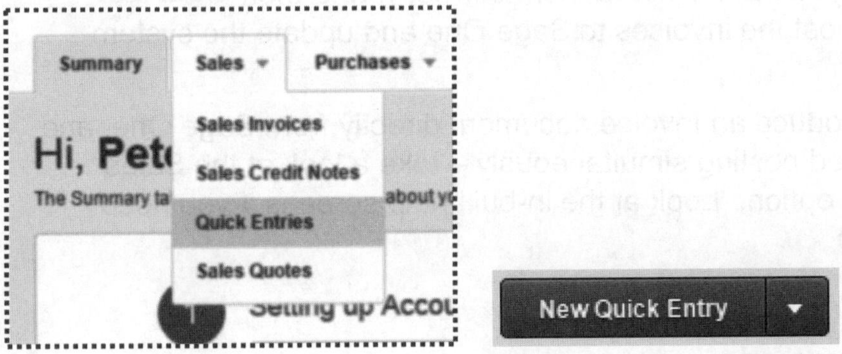

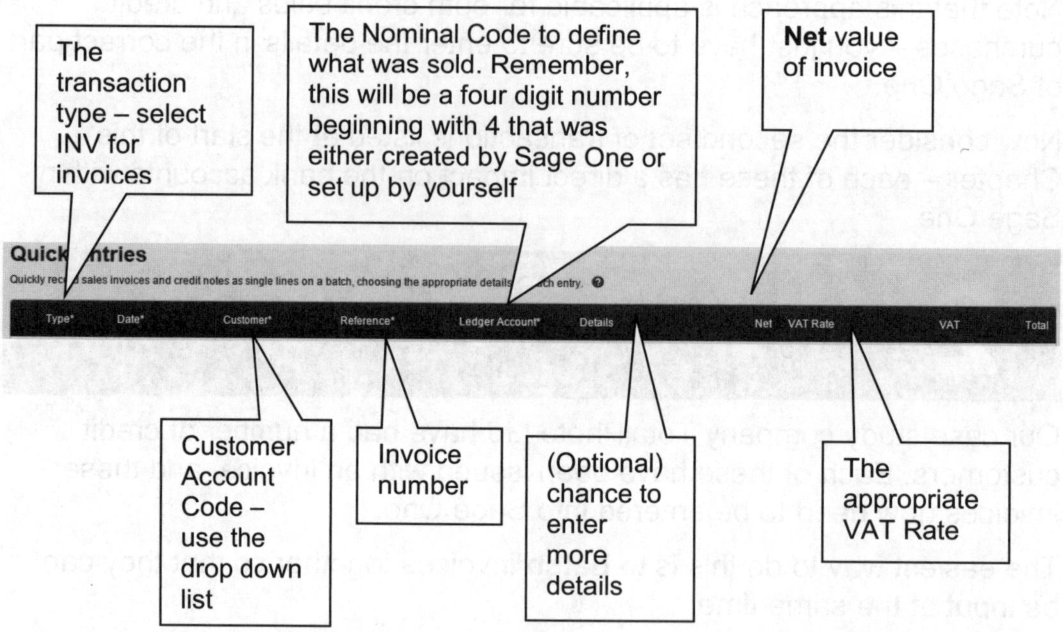
The transaction type – select INV for invoices
The Nominal Code to define what was sold. Remember, this will be a four digit number beginning with 4 that was either created by Sage One or set up by yourself
Net value of invoice
Quick ntries
Type*
Date*
Customer*
Reference*
Ledger Account*
Details
Net
VAT Rate
VAT
Total
Customer Account Code – use the drop down list
Invoice number
(Optional) chance to enter more details
The appropriate VAT Rate

Once you have entered all invoices in the batch you should then review them to ensure you have entered them correctly, and then **Save** them. This will post the invoices to Sage One and update the system accordingly.

If you wish to produce an Invoice document directly from Sage One, and make the required posting simultaneously – take a look at the Sales Invoice creation option. Look at the in-built help screens if you need further guidance.

Activity

Enter the following six invoices for TotalPhoto Ltd using the Quick-entry screen. Note that you will also have to create new customer accounts in some cases. **It is advisable to do this before you start entering details of the invoices.**

Date	Invoice No	A/c No	Customer	Nominal Code	Net Amount
01/10/2014	1	POP002	Poppy	4000	£105.00
01/10/2014	2	HAS004	Haslam	4000	£24.50
01/10/2014	3	PAR006	Pargenter	4000	£12.00
01/10/2014	4	SMI009	Smith *(see below)*	4001	£600.00
01/10/2014	5	LUL002	Lullabies Nursery	4003	£100.00
01/10/2014	6	CAM004	Campbell & Dunn	4002	£45.00
01/10/2014	7	HAS004	Haslam	4000	£12.00

All amounts in the table are **exclusive** of VAT at 20%

New Customer Details

Mr A Smith
12 Main Street
Miltonby
Lancashire
LN87 4DF

A/c Ref SMI009

Credit terms: Payment in 14 days

Credit Limit: £1000.00

Enter the details in the batch customer invoices screen as shown below. You can choose suitable wording for the 'details' field.

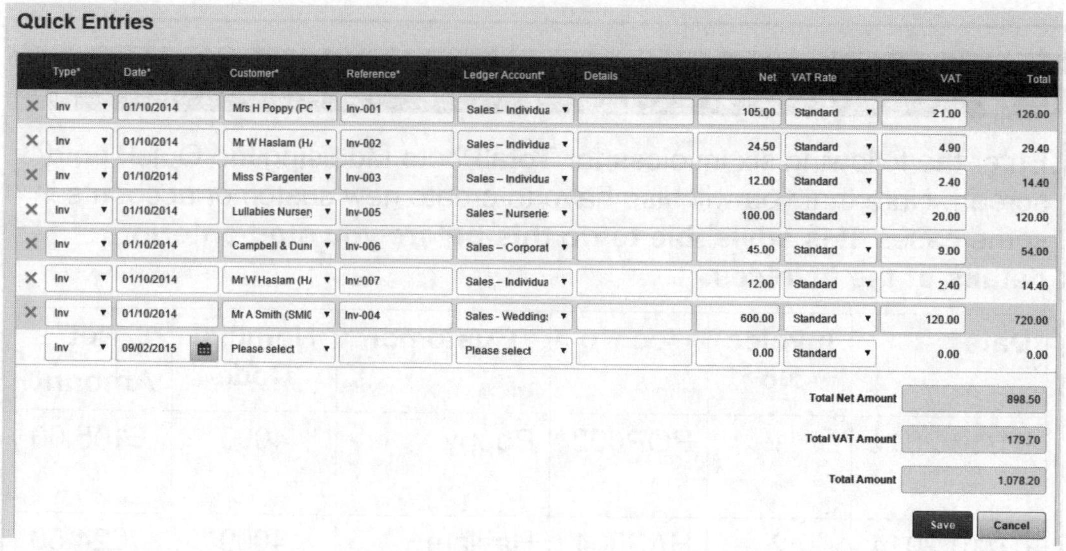

Quick Entries

	Type*	Date*	Customer*	Reference*	Ledger Account*	Details	Net	VAT Rate	VAT	Total
X	Inv	01/10/2014	Mrs H Poppy (PC	Inv-001	Sales – Individua		105.00	Standard	21.00	126.00
X	Inv	01/10/2014	Mr W Haslam (H/	Inv-002	Sales – Individua		24.50	Standard	4.90	29.40
X	Inv	01/10/2014	Miss S Pargenter	Inv-003	Sales – Individua		12.00	Standard	2.40	14.40
X	Inv	01/10/2014	Lullabies Nurser	Inv-005	Sales – Nurserie		100.00	Standard	20.00	120.00
X	Inv	01/10/2014	Campbell & Dun	Inv-006	Sales – Corporat		45.00	Standard	9.00	54.00
X	Inv	01/10/2014	Mr W Haslam (H/	Inv-007	Sales – Individua		12.00	Standard	2.40	14.40
X	Inv	01/10/2014	Mr A Smith (SMIC	Inv-004	Sales - Wedding:		600.00	Standard	120.00	720.00
	Inv	09/02/2015	Please select		Please select		0.00	Standard	0.00	0.00

Total Net Amount	898.50
Total VAT Amount	179.70
Total Amount	1,078.20

Save Cancel

When you have entered all seven invoices, your screen should look like this. Check for accuracy, and when you are happy press the

button.

You will need to set up new customers ahead of entering the invoice for new customers when using this method of entry. This can be done at any time and added to the quick-entry batch.

Activity

Print out another trial balance for 1st October 14. Compare this with one you prepared earlier and identify the changes that have occurred.

Here is a copy of how the Trial Balance should look now. Put the two reports side-by-side and note down the change on each nominal account.

Select balances from 30th September 14 to 1st October 14

Trial Balance Report

This report shows the balance on your nominal ledger accounts for a specified date range.

From Date 30/09/2014 To Date 01/10/2014 Export

Nominal Code	Name	Debits	Credits
30	Office equipment and IT - Cost	4,849.00	
32	Photographic Equipment	22,718.00	
33	Photographic Equip Depreciation		5,237.00
50	Motor Vehicles - Cost	21,800.00	
51	Motor Vehicles - Accumulated Depreciation		5,450.00
1000	Stock	7,403.00	
1100	Trade Debtors	5,131.30	
1200	Current	10,293.00	
1210	Cash in Hand	250.00	
2100	Trade Creditors		19,192.41
2200	VAT on Sales		179.70
2202	VAT Liability		1,623.29
3000	Ordinary Shares		20,000.00
3100	Profit and Loss Account		5,498.28
4000	Sales – Individuals & Family		5,554.71
4001	Sales - Weddings		4,584.50
4002	Sales – Corporate		1,977.09
4003	Sales – Nurseries & Schools		11,404.20
4004	Other Sales		1,590.30
5000	Purchases – Film	205.63	
5001	Purchases – Paper	1,034.35	
5002	Purchases – Cartridges & Toner	1,225.87	
5003	Purchases – Stationery	409.35	
5004	Purchases – Other Consumables	823.52	
7100	Rent and rates	4,280.00	
7300	Motor Expenses	1,035.64	
7400	Travel and Entertainment	229.39	
7500	Office costs	603.43	
Total		**82,291.48**	**82,291.48**

Notice which figures have changed

(1) N/C 1100 (Debtors control account) has increased from £4053.10 to £5131.30. This reflects the fact that TotalPhoto Ltd is now owed an additional £1078.20 by its debtors/receivables.

(2) N/Cs 4000, 4001, 4002 and 4003 have increased, representing the new sales that the company made on 30th September. Note that the increase in these figures (£898.50) is the **net** increase in sales.

(3) There is a new Nominal Code (2200) called 'Sales Tax Control Account'. This control account automatically records all input VAT (on purchases) and output VAT (on sales) and is used to calculate and produce the company's VAT Return. The amount on this code is currently £179.70 (a **credit** balance) – the VAT charged on all the sales invoices you have entered.

If you would like to see the 'movement' in more detail, i.e. viewing how the balances have changed from the opening balances position until now – try running the Nominal Activity Report for the same period of time – for the selected accounts. Here is the activity for the sales accounts:

Nominal Activity Report

SageOne

TotalPhoto Ltd

From Date: 30/09/2014 **To Date: 01/10/2014**

Category: Sales **Ledger Account: All**

Category	Ledger Account	Date	Reference	Type	Debit	Credit
Sales	Sales – Individuals & Family (4000)	30/09/2014	Opening Balances	Journal Opening Balance	0.00	5,401.21
Sales	Sales – Individuals & Family (4000)	01/10/2014	Inv-003	Sales QE Invoice	0.00	12.00
Sales	Sales – Individuals & Family (4000)	01/10/2014	Inv-002	Sales QE Invoice	0.00	24.50
Sales	Sales – Individuals & Family (4000)	01/10/2014	Inv-001	Sales QE Invoice	0.00	105.00
Sales	Sales – Individuals & Family (4000)	01/10/2014	Inv-007	Sales QE Invoice	0.00	12.00
Sales	Sales - Weddings (4001)	30/09/2014	Opening Balances	Journal Opening Balance	0.00	3,984.50
Sales	Sales - Weddings (4001)	01/10/2014	Inv-004	Sales QE Invoice	0.00	600.00
Sales	Sales – Corporate (4002)	30/09/2014	Opening Balances	Journal Opening Balance	0.00	1,932.09
Sales	Sales – Corporate (4002)	01/10/2014	Inv-006	Sales QE Invoice	0.00	45.00
Sales	Sales – Nurseries & Schools (4003)	30/09/2014	Opening Balances	Journal Opening Balance	0.00	11,304.20
Sales	Sales – Nurseries & Schools (4003)	01/10/2014	Inv-005	Sales QE Invoice	0.00	100.00
Sales	Other Sales (4004)	30/09/2014	Opening Balances	Journal Opening Balance	0.00	1,590.30
				Total	**0.00**	**25,110.80**

3 Customer credit notes

A credit note is essentially a 'negative invoice' and is produced and sent to customers when a refund is needed. The most likely time this will happen is when goods that the organisation has sold to a customer have been returned as faulty. However, they can also be used to correct errors.

Producing a credit note in Sage One is straightforward and can be done in three ways depending on the method the original invoice was originally created.

(1) If Invoices are created within Sage One using the 'Sales Invoice' function, whereby an invoice document is generated and sent directly from the system, a Credit Note can be made from the Invoice in question and then modified to reflect the amount of credit agreed. This could be 100% of the Invoice value or just a proportion, depending on the circumstances. By creating a Credit Note this way, the Credit Note and the Invoice to which it relates will be linked or allocated together, making the customer statements easier to understand.

(2) Credit Notes can also be created in a similar way to Invoices using the 'Sales Credit Notes' function and can either be allocated to an invoice as a later operation or just left on the account as independent transactions, forming part of the outstanding balance, or refund due.

(3) In this text we will describe Credit Note transactions, assuming the document itself has been created outside of Sage One, in the same way we posted customer invoices earlier – using the 'Sales Quick Entry' screen.

> **Activity**
>
> Let us suppose that the sale of a 6" × 4" colour print made by TotalPhoto Ltd to Miss Pargenter for £12.00 (plus VAT) (Invoice No 3) is returned as faulty. It is necessary to issue a credit note so that this debt is effectively 'removed' from Miss Pargenter's account. Enter the credit note on Sage One. Guidance on how to enter it follows. Date the Credit 8th October 2014

How to process a customer credit note

To enter a customer (sales) credit go to the Sales tab and select 'Quick Entries'

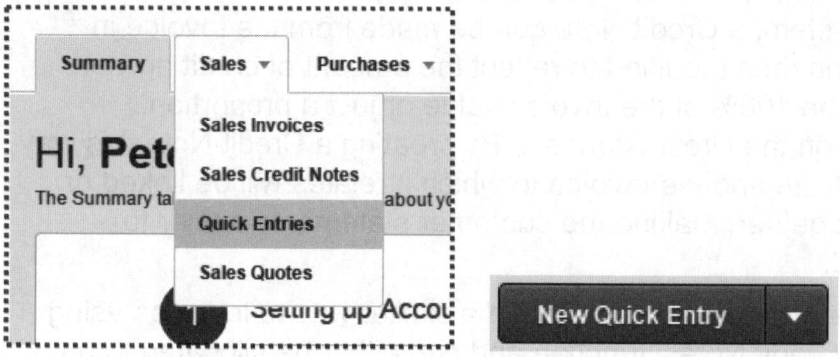
Summary
Sales
Purchases
Sales Invoices
Sales Credit Notes
Quick Entries
Sales Quotes
New Quick Entry

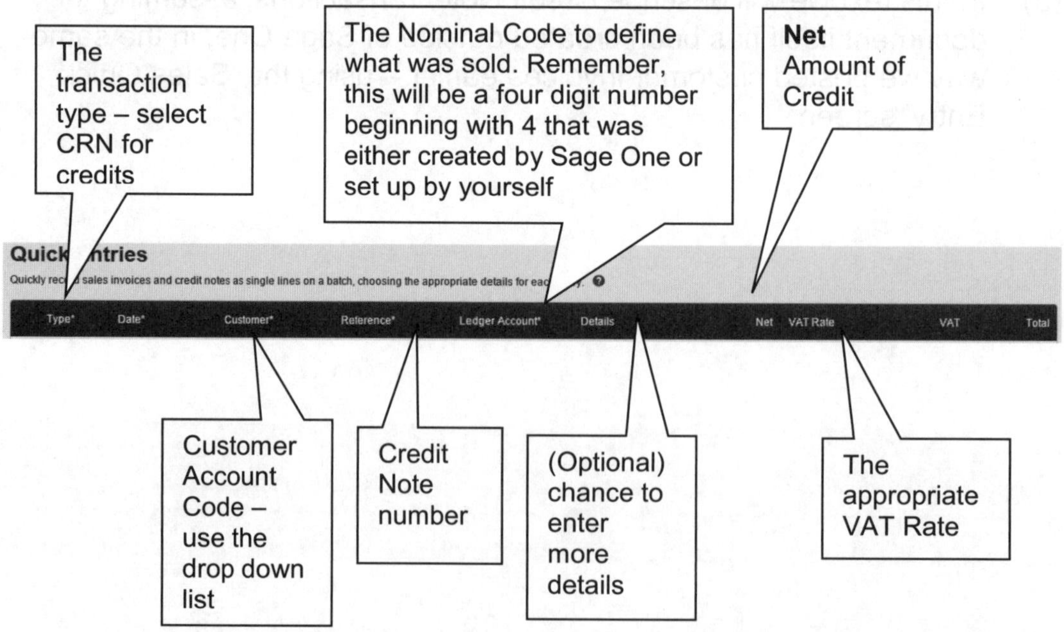
The transaction type – select CRN for credits
The Nominal Code to define what was sold. Remember, this will be a four digit number beginning with 4 that was either created by Sage One or set up by yourself
Net Amount of Credit
Type* Date* Customer* Reference* Ledger Account* Details Net VAT Rate VAT Total
Customer Account Code – use the drop down list
Credit Note number
(Optional) chance to enter more details
The appropriate VAT Rate

Once you have entered the credit, you should 
Save
. This will post the credit to Sage One and update the system accordingly.

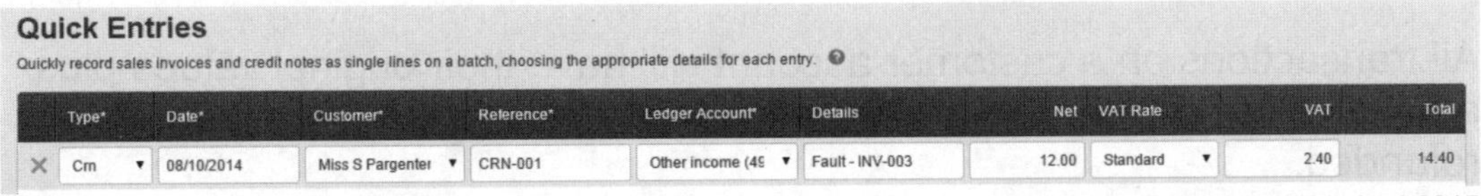
Quick Entries
Quickly record sales invoices and credit notes as single lines on a batch, choosing the appropriate details for each entry.
Type*
Date*
Customer*
Reference*
Ledger Account*
Details
Net
VAT Rate
VAT
Total
Crn
08/10/2014
Miss S Pargenter
CRN-001
Other income (4
Fault - INV-003
12.00
Standard
2.40
14.40

Viewing a Customer's Account

From the Customer List, locate 'Miss S Pargenter' either by using the search or filter features or simply visually scanning down the list.

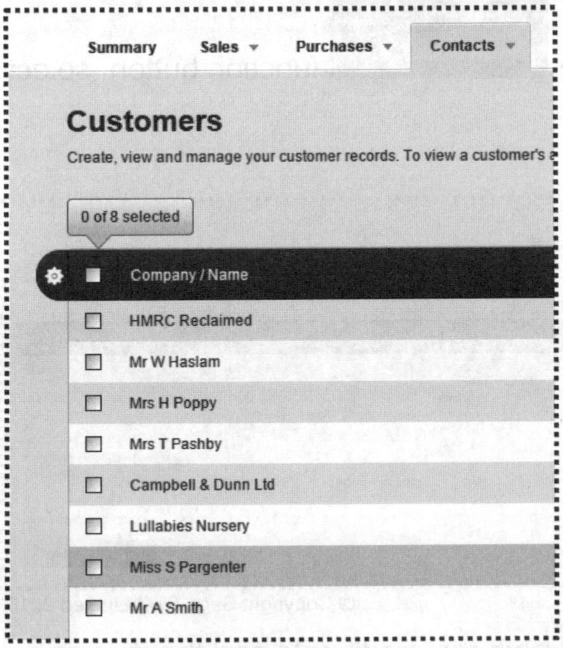
Summary
Sales
Purchases
Contacts
Customers
Create, view and manage your customer records. To view a customer's
0 of 8 selected
Company / Name
HMRC Reclaimed
Mr W Haslam
Mrs H Poppy
Mrs T Pashby
Campbell & Dunn Ltd
Lullabies Nursery
Miss S Pargenter
Mr A Smith

Using the 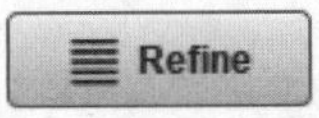
Refine
filter, on the activity grid, selecting the dates 'From:' 30/09/2014 'To:' 10/02/2015, you will be able to view all the activity that has taken place on her account between those two points in time. Additional filters around transaction types and status can also be used to refine the view and if required print or email the view displayed.

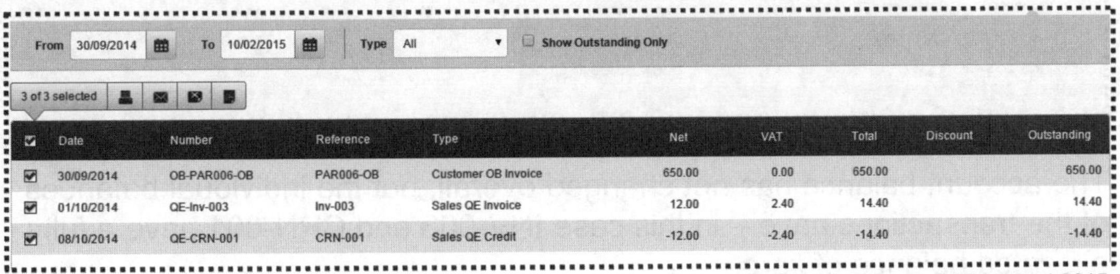
From 30/09/2014
To 10/02/2015
Type All
Show Outstanding Only
3 of 3 selected
Date
Number
Reference
Type
Net
VAT
Total
Discount
Outstanding
30/09/2014 OB-PAR006-OB PAR006-OB Customer OB Invoice 650.00 0.00 650.00 650.00
01/10/2014 QE-Inv-003 Inv-003 Sales QE Invoice 12.00 2.40 14.40 14.40
08/10/2014 QE-CRN-001 CRN-001 Sales QE Credit -12.00 -2.40 -14.40 -14.40

You will be able to see the opening balance and the invoices and credits already posted. Other transactions that could appear her include, payments received and refunds made – which will be covered later in this text.

All transactions on a customer account will have their original values plus a balance i.e. the amount of the transaction that has not been paid or refunded.

To allocate the invoice [INV-003] to the credit note [CRN-001] follow the steps described below:

From the customer record using the 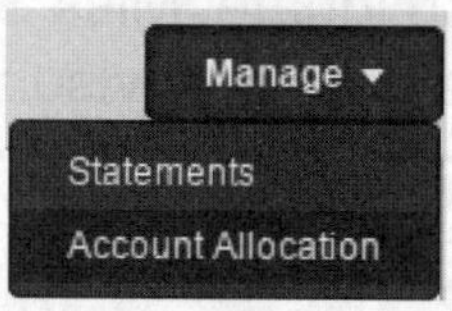
Manage
Statements
Account Allocation
function button, select Account Allocation.

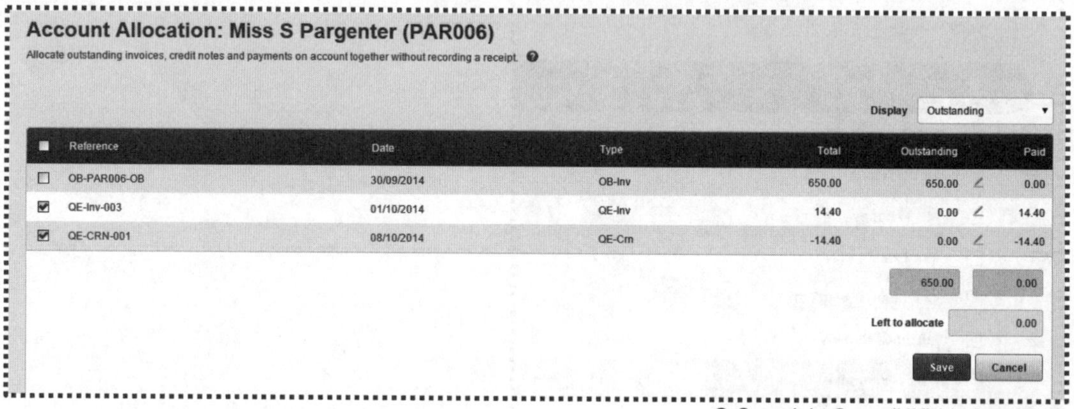
Account Allocation: Miss S Pargenter (PAR006)
Allocate outstanding invoices, credit notes and payments on account together without recording a receipt.
Display Outstanding
Reference Date Type Total Outstanding Paid
OB-PAR006-OB 30/09/2014 OB-Inv 650.00 650.00 0.00
QE-Inv-003 01/10/2014 QE-Inv 14.40 0.00 14.40
QE-CRN-001 08/10/2014 QE-Crn -14.40 0.00 -14.40
650.00 0.00
Left to allocate 0.00
Save Cancel

Using the selector tick boxes, select both the credit note and the invoice and save.

The customer activity should now look like this:

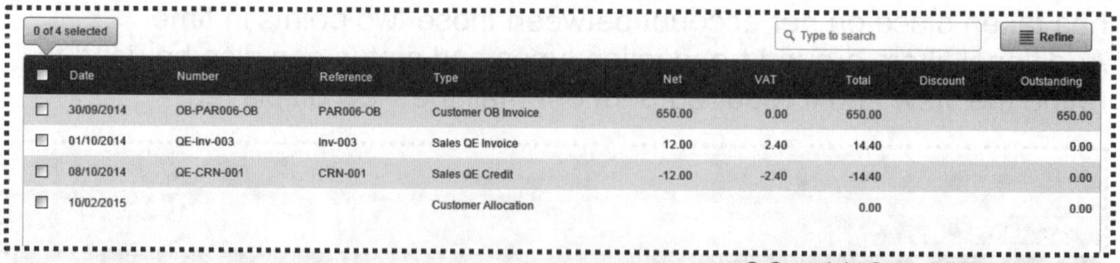
0 of 4 selected
Type to search
Refine
Date Number Reference Type Net VAT Total Discount Outstanding
30/09/2014 OB-PAR006-OB PAR006-OB Customer OB Invoice 650.00 0.00 650.00 650.00
01/10/2014 QE-Inv-003 Inv-003 Sales QE Invoice 12.00 2.40 14.40 0.00
08/10/2014 QE-CRN-001 CRN-001 Sales QE Credit -12.00 -2.40 -14.40 0.00
10/02/2015 Customer Allocation 0.00 0.00

The account balance has not changed overall, but the individual balances of the transactions have – in this case INV-003 and CRN-001 have a fully allocated balance of zero.

4 Producing customer statements

Having produced and sent invoices to customers, most businesses will also need to send periodic (usually monthly) statements to their customers which will list all new transactions – such as their new purchases, payments sent, credit notes issued to them etc.

Sage One allows the easy creation and production of customer statements.

The format of the customer statement that will be produced is based on the invoice template design style found in the settings area. The default template can be used and you do not need to change it.

From the customer list select the customer that you wish to either send a statement to or to set up periodic auto-mated email schedule for. Normally this process would be done when the customer account is initially set up.

Select Miss S Pargenter

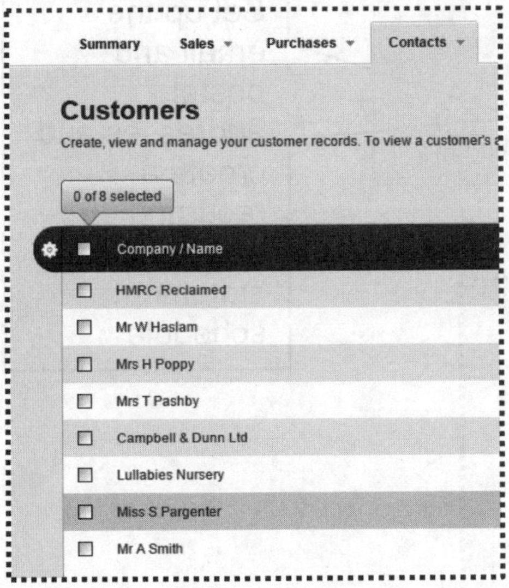

From the customer record screen, using the function button, select Statements.

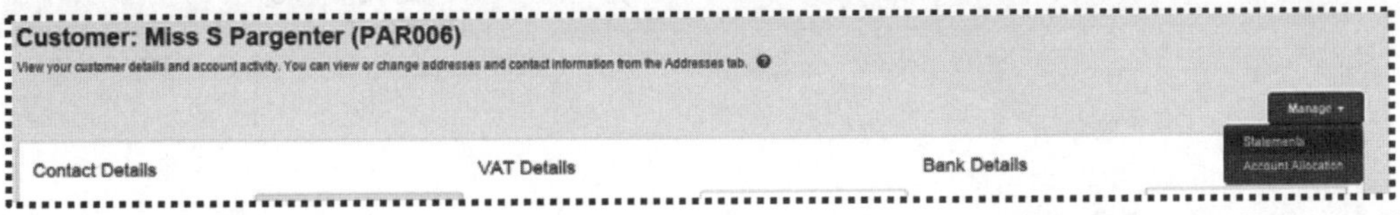

In the statements screen you will be able to see the balance owed – £650.

If you set the date range from 1st October 2014, you will see the invoice and credit note listed in the activity list as shown.

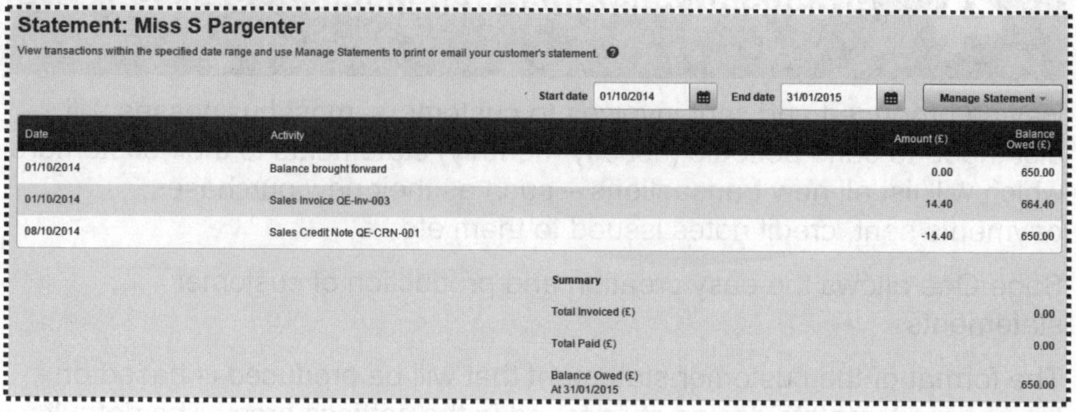

Statement: Miss S Pargenter

View transactions within the specified date range and use Manage Statements to print or email your customer's statement.

Start date 01/10/2014 End date 31/01/2015 Manage Statement

Date	Activity	Amount (£)	Balance Owed (£)
01/10/2014	Balance brought forward	0.00	650.00
01/10/2014	Sales Invoice QE-Inv-003	14.40	664.40
08/10/2014	Sales Credit Note QE-CRN-001	-14.40	650.00

Summary	
Total Invoiced (£)	0.00
Total Paid (£)	0.00
Balance Owed (£) At 31/01/2015	650.00

Using the Manage Statement function button you will be able to:

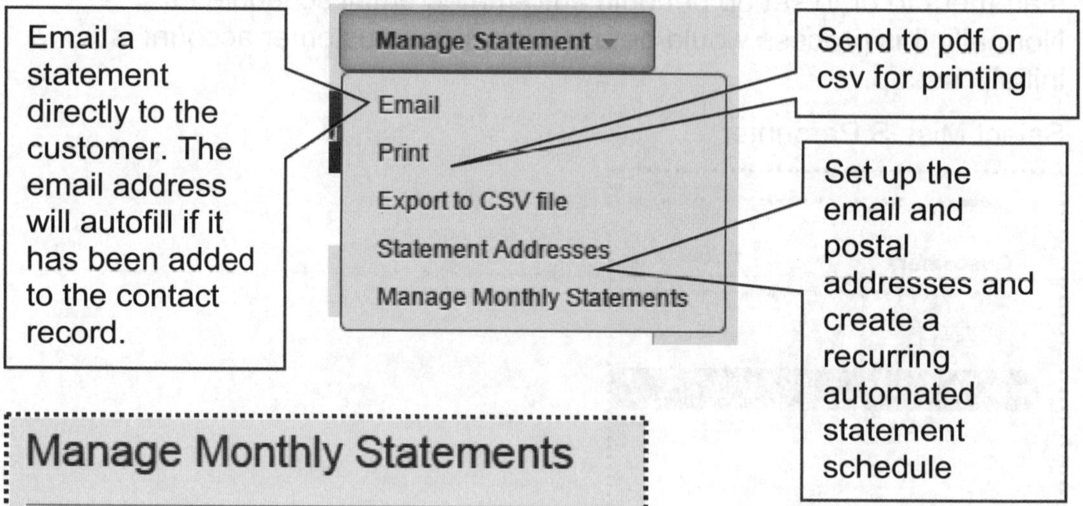
Email a statement directly to the customer. The email address will autofill if it has been added to the contact record.
Manage Statement
Email
Print
Export to CSV file
Statement Addresses
Manage Monthly Statements
Send to pdf or csv for printing
Set up the email and postal addresses and create a recurring automated statement schedule

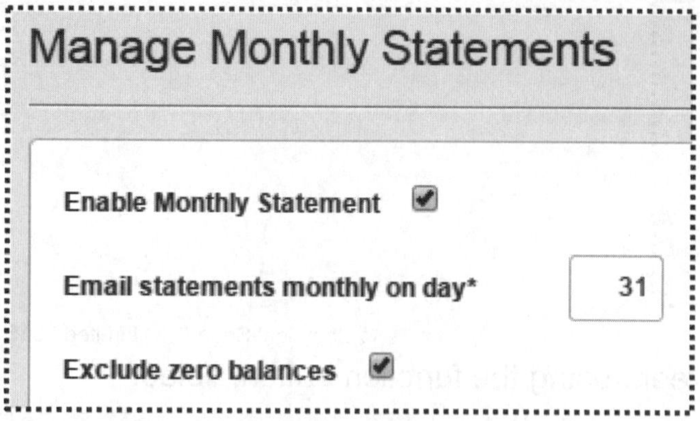
Manage Monthly Statements
Enable Monthly Statement
Email statements monthly on day*
31
Exclude zero balances

Activity

Create and print a customer statement for Miss Pargenter (Ref PAR006) It should look like this:

TotalPhoto Ltd

TotalPhoto Ltd
Unit 63 Bailey Industrial Estate Fornby Road Miltonby Lancashire
LD37 7QZ
Registered in England and Wales number 734928107

Telephone:	Website:	VAT Number
01949 969 378	www.totalphotoltd.co.uk	376 096 823

Miss S Pargenter (PAR006)

11 Alexandra Park, Miltonby, Lancashire, LN87 2WD, United Kingdom

Statement Period: 01/10/2014 to 31/01/2015

Date	Activity	Amount (£)	Balance Owed (£)
01/10/2014	Balance brought forward	0.00	650.00
01/10/2014	Sales Invoice QE-Inv-003	14.40	664.40
08/10/2014	Sales Credit Note QE-CRN-001	-14.40	650.00

Summary	
Total Invoiced (£)	0.00
Total Paid (£)	0.00
Balance Owed (£) At 31/01/2015	650.00

5 Credit purchases – entering supplier invoices

When an organisation purchases goods or services on credit, it will receive an invoice from the supplier. These must be recorded immediately in Sage One, even though they may not be paid for some time. This is when the business has purchased on credit, i.e. to pay later.

The most common way to process supplier invoices is to **batch** them (in much the same way as you did with the invoices to customers). This way, a number of invoices can be processed at the same time.

The process for entering batches of supplier statements is very similar to that for entering batches of customer invoices – except it is accessed via the Purchases tab.

Activity

TotalPhoto Ltd received the following five invoices on 1st October 2014.

Invoice Ref	Supplier	Account	Net amount	Nominal Code
1341	Mackay Films	MF001	£208.76	5000
209	The Stationery Cupboard	SC003	£14.65	5003
216	The Stationery Cupboard	SC003	£78.92	5003
2203	Octopus Inks Ltd	OI001	£309.28	5002
10092	Mills Paper Products	MP002	£162.52	5001

You should now enter the above five supplier invoices as a batch. You can choose suitable wording for the 'details' tab and a suggestion has been given for each.

When you have done the above activity the screen should look like this:

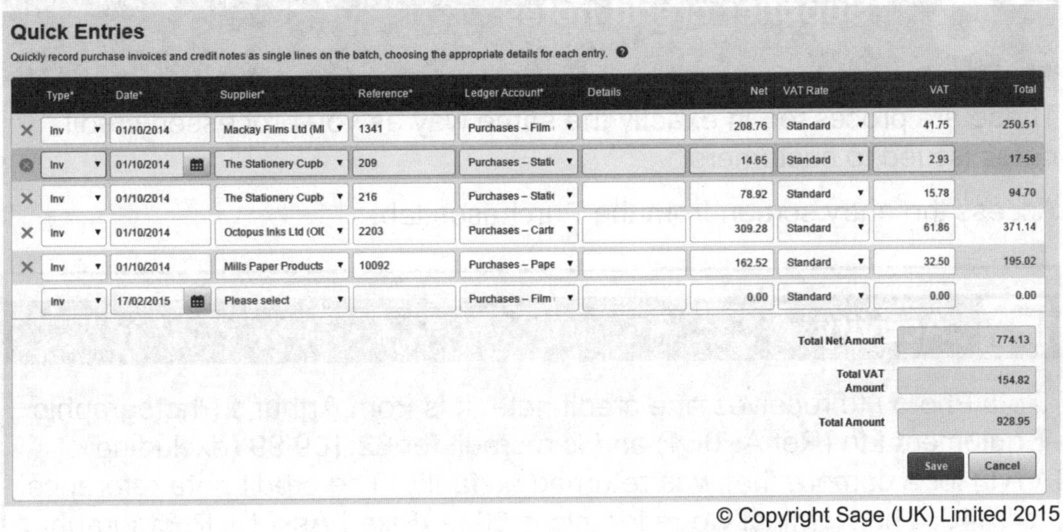
Quick Entries
Quickly record purchase invoices and credit notes as single lines on the batch, choosing the appropriate details for each entry.
Type* Date* Supplier* Reference* Ledger Account* Details Net VAT Rate VAT Total
Inv 01/10/2014 Mackay Films Ltd (MI 1341 Purchases – Film 208.76 Standard 41.75 250.51
Inv 01/10/2014 The Stationery Cupb 209 Purchases – Stati 14.65 Standard 2.93 17.58
Inv 01/10/2014 The Stationery Cupb 216 Purchases – Stati 78.92 Standard 15.78 94.70
Inv 01/10/2014 Octopus Inks Ltd (OI 2203 Purchases – Cartr 309.28 Standard 61.86 371.14
Inv 01/10/2014 Mills Paper Products 10092 Purchases – Pape 162.52 Standard 32.50 195.02
Inv 17/02/2015 Please select Purchases – Film 0.00 Standard 0.00 0.00
Total Net Amount 774.13
Total VAT Amount 154.82
Total Amount 928.95
Save
Cancel

You should verify the entries and then press the **Save** button to post your entries to Sage One.

You will be returned to the Quick Entry screen upon saving. If you wish to review the batch – refine the dates to include 1st October 2014.

NB if the supplier record is set with the default Purchase Ledger Account this will be used as the default value when entering future transactions. This will save time. This is an example for one of the TotalPhoto Suppliers.

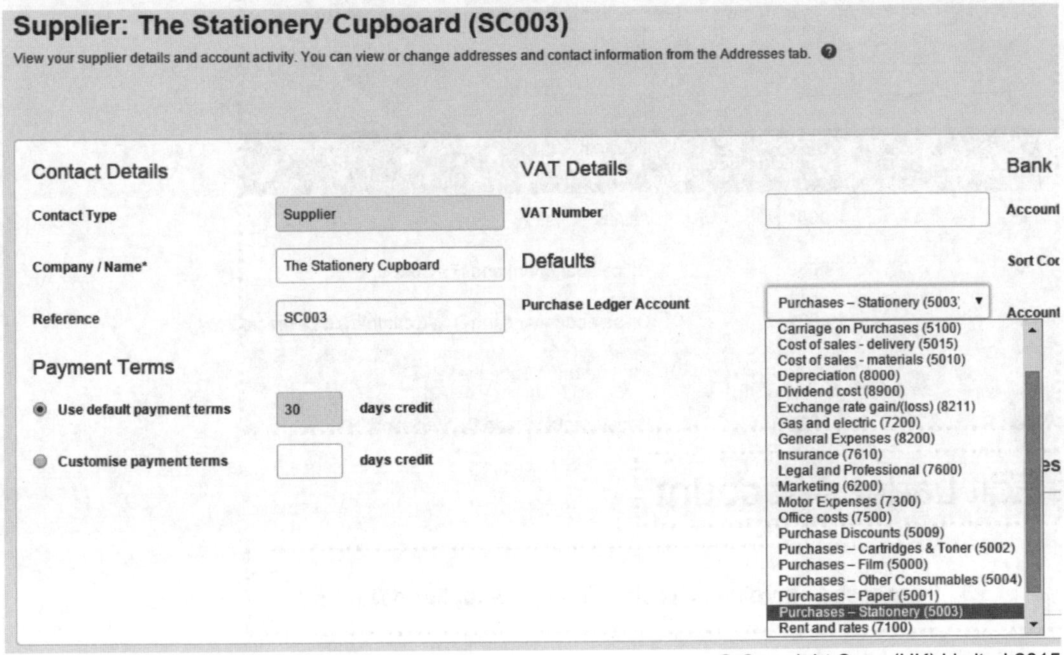
Supplier: The Stationery Cupboard (SC003)
View your supplier details and account activity. You can view or change addresses and contact information from the Addresses tab.
Contact Details
Contact Type
Supplier
Company / Name*
The Stationery Cupboard
Reference
SC003
Payment Terms
Use default payment terms
30
days credit
Customise payment terms
days credit
VAT Details
VAT Number
Defaults
Purchase Ledger Account
Purchases – Stationery (5003)
Carriage on Purchases (5100)
Cost of sales - delivery (5015)
Cost of sales - materials (5010)
Depreciation (8000)
Dividend cost (8900)
Exchange rate gain/(loss) (8211)
Gas and electric (7200)
General Expenses (8200)
Insurance (7610)
Legal and Professional (7600)
Marketing (6200)
Motor Expenses (7300)
Office costs (7500)
Purchase Discounts (5009)
Purchases – Cartridges & Toner (5002)
Purchases – Film (5000)
Purchases – Other Consumables (5004)
Purchases – Paper (5001)
Purchases – Stationery (5003)
Rent and rates (7100)
Bank
Account
Sort Coc
Account

6 Supplier credit notes

These are processed in exactly the same way as you processed credit notes issued to customers.

Access the entry screen from the Purchases tab.

Activity

TotalPhoto Ltd receives one credit note. It is from Arthur's Photographic Equipment Ltd (Ref AP004) and is a credit for £2,109.99 (excluding VAT) for a camera that was returned as faulty. The credit note reference is 134C. The Nominal Code for this is 0032 (Fixed Asset – Photographic Equipment). Process the credit note using a suitable narrative for the details section (a suggestion has been shown).

Before you carry out this activity, you need to ensure that the nominal account 0032 is **visible in the Purchases area** of Sage One. Using the Chart of Accounts set up as described earlier in this text, edit ledger account 0032 as shown below:

Chart of Accounts

Create, view and manage your ledger accounts. Select existing accounts to view or change the

Included in Chart	Nominal Code	Ledger Name
✓	0001	Assets - Cost
✓	0030	Office equipment and IT - Cost
✓	0031	Office equipment and IT - Accumulated Deprecia
✓	0032	Photographic Equipment
✓	0033	Photographic Equip Depreciation

Edit Ledger Account

☑ **Purchases - Invoice / Credit, Product / Supplier defaults**

Your entry screen for the above activity should look like this:

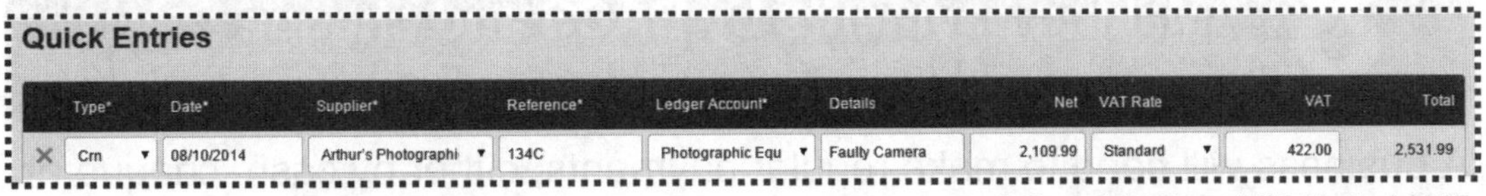

Don't forget to Save .

7 Bank transactions

Sage One allows you to run a number of 'bank accounts'. These need not necessarily all be held at a bank – they could also include cash in hand, petty cash etc.

The principles for making payments in or out of any of these accounts are the same.

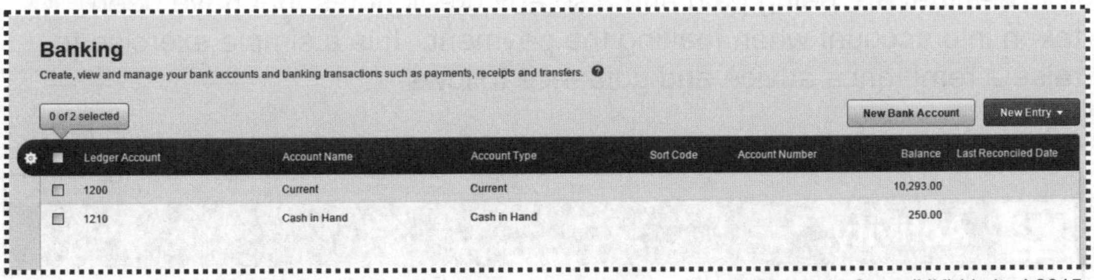

From the Banking tab, you can see that Sage One has already set up two different bank accounts, each with its own Nominal Code. You can of course amend these or add to them if you wish.

The most commonly used bank account is probably Nominal Code 1200 (Bank Current Account). This is the one that you will use in this case study for payments in and out of TotalPhoto Ltd's main current account. You can see that it has a balance at the moment of £10,293.00. You may recall that this relates to the opening balance that you entered earlier. **None of the entries that you have made since then have affected the bank balance**.

8 Making payments by BACS and cheque

A business will need to make regular payments, either by cash, cheque or by BACS payment. The most common transaction will be when a business pays its suppliers when they have previously bought on credit (promised to pay later). However, they may simply need to pay for day to day expenses. We can now look at the process of entering these types of payments in Sage One.

9 Remittance advices

It is common for businesses to produce a remittance advice when raising payments to suppliers. This document would notify the supplier of any invoices that are being paid and also any credit notes that have been taken into account when making the payment. It is a simple exercise to raise a remittance advice and guidance follows.

Activity

TotalPhoto Ltd has three payments to make on 1st October 2014. These are:

- a cheque for £107.65 (plus VAT at 20.0%) to Arrow Telecoms to pay the telephone bill
- a cheque for £55.00 to Miltonby Cricket Association for advertising in their League Handbook (no VAT on this transaction – Exempt)
- a cheque for £45.00 to Miltonby Borough Council for a parking permit (no VAT – Zero Rated).

Enter the above transactions on to Sage One and raise the relevant remittance advices. Detailed guidance follows.

Click the 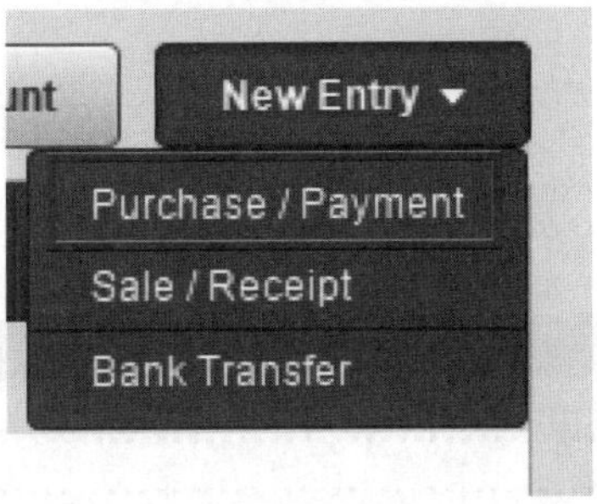
unt
New Entry
Purchase / Payment
Sale / Receipt
Bank Transfer
New Entry - Payment within the 'Bank' screen.

Using the 'Other Payment' tab area, enter the payment details one at a time for each payment. These payments are not related to a pre-existing Supplier invoice in the system and therefore the Supplier details are optional. Be careful to make sure you select the appropriate Nominal Code for the expense item, and also the correct VAT rate.

The total amount should be entered first INCLUSIVE of VAT and then analysed. The VAT will calculate automatically based on the VAT Rate selected.

[The payment amount to Arrow Telecoms is £107.65 +20% = £129.18]

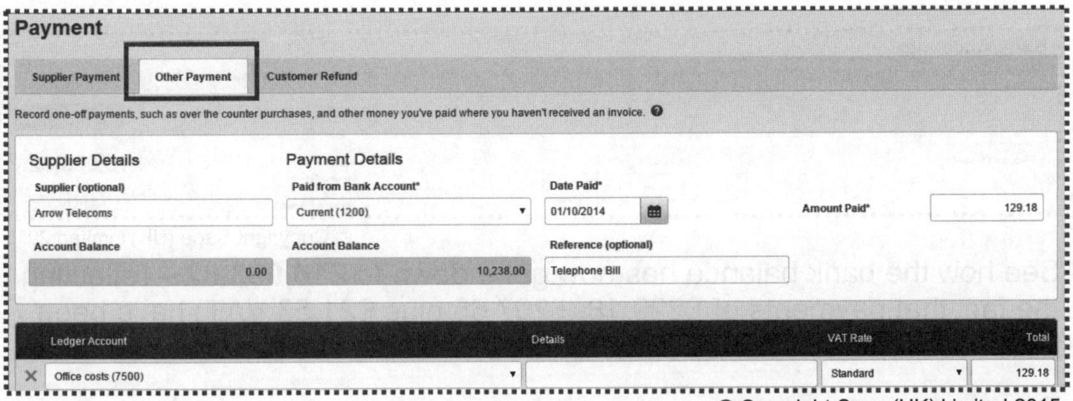
Payment
Supplier Payment
Other Payment
Customer Refund
Record one-off payments, such as over the counter purchases, and other money you've paid where you haven't received an invoice.
Supplier Details
Supplier (optional)
Arrow Telecoms
Account Balance
0.00
Payment Details
Paid from Bank Account*
Current (1200)
Account Balance
10,238.00
Date Paid*
01/10/2014
Reference (optional)
Telephone Bill
Amount Paid*
129.18
Ledger Account
Details
VAT Rate
Total
Office costs (7500)
Standard
129.18

© Copyright Sage (UK) Limited 2015

Where a payment is for more than one category of items, it is possible to analyse the payment across multiple nominal codes. In this case it's for just one – Office Costs. If there are multiple lines – Sage One will display the amount 'left to record' which must be zero before you are able to save. An example might be the purchase of fuel and food from the same supplier in one transaction. You would need to enter the fuel to one nominal code and the food to another.

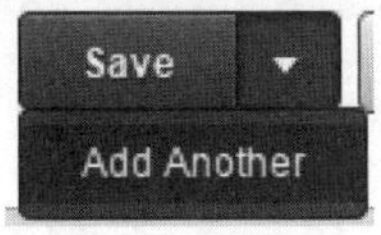
Save
Add Another
Save each transaction separately. To add a new transaction having entered one – take advantage of the 'Add Another' function.

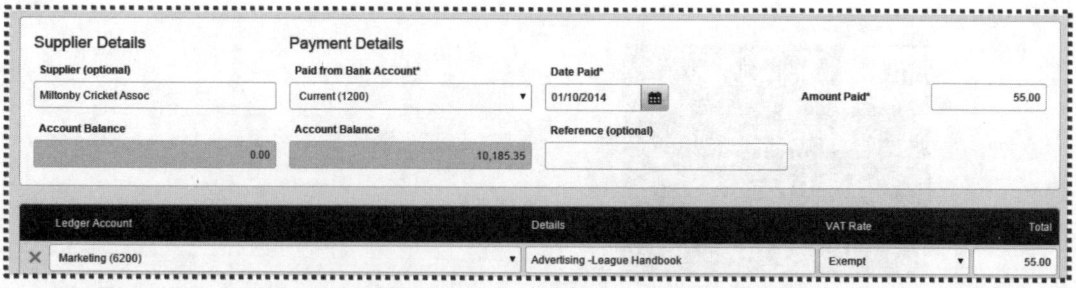
Supplier Details
Payment Details
Supplier (optional)
Milltonby Cricket Assoc
Account Balance
0.00
Paid from Bank Account*
Current (1200)
Account Balance
10,185.35
Date Paid*
01/10/2014
Reference (optional)
Amount Paid*
55.00
Ledger Account
Details
VAT Rate
Total
Marketing (6200)
Advertising -League Handbook
Exempt
55.00

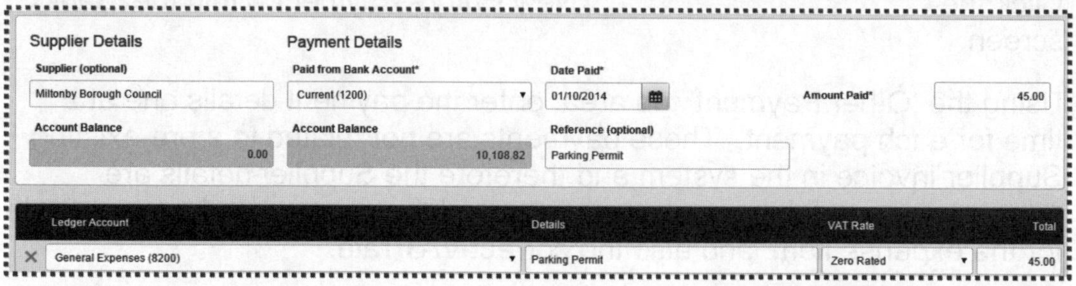
Supplier Details
Payment Details
Supplier (optional)
Miltonby Borough Council
Account Balance
0.00
Paid from Bank Account*
Current (1200)
Account Balance
10,108.82
Date Paid*
01/10/2014
Reference (optional)
Parking Permit
Amount Paid*
45.00
Ledger Account
Details
VAT Rate
Total
General Expenses (8200)
Parking Permit
Zero Rated
45.00

You could also include extra optional details such as the cheque number or BACS in the '**Ref**' box.

Now check the balance on Nominal Code 1200 (the bank current account).

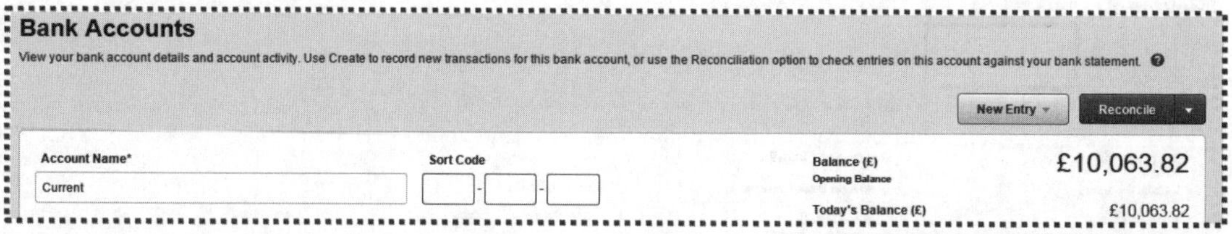
Bank Accounts
View your bank account details and account activity. Use Create to record new transactions for this bank account, or use the Reconciliation option to check entries on this account against your bank statement
New Entry
Reconcile
Account Name*
Current
Sort Code
Balance (£)
Opening Balance
£10,063.82
Today's Balance (£)
£10,063.82

See how the bank balance has now gone down to **£10,063.82** – reflecting the fact that payments of £229.18 (£207.65 plus £21.53 VAT) have been taken from it.

Paying suppliers

We can now look at the other common area for payments which is paying suppliers when the business has previously bought goods on credit. This is especially common for buying inventory/stock.

Activity

TotalPhoto Ltd also decides to pay two outstanding creditors on 1st October 14, as follows:

The Stationery Cupboard (SC003)
Amount: £375 inc VAT *Paid by cheque number 00245*

K2 Films Ltd (KF001)
Amount £1726.55 (inc VAT). *Paid by cheque number 00246*

Enter these supplier payments onto Sage One. Guidance follows.

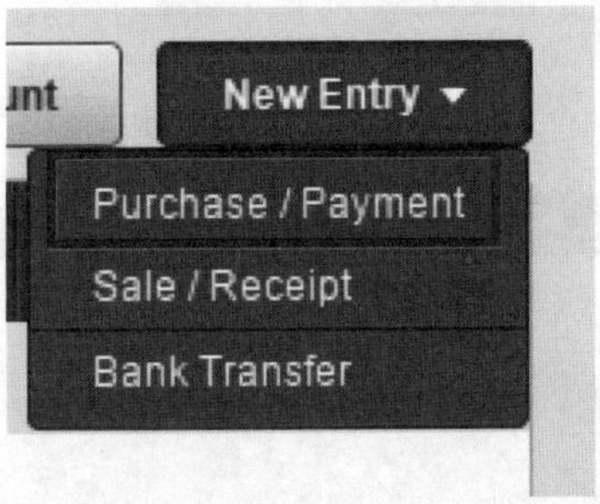

Click the New Entry - Payment within the 'Bank' screen.

Using the 'Supplier Payment' tab area, enter the payment details one at a time for each payment. These payments will be related to a pre-existing supplier invoice in the system and therefore the Supplier details are mandatory.

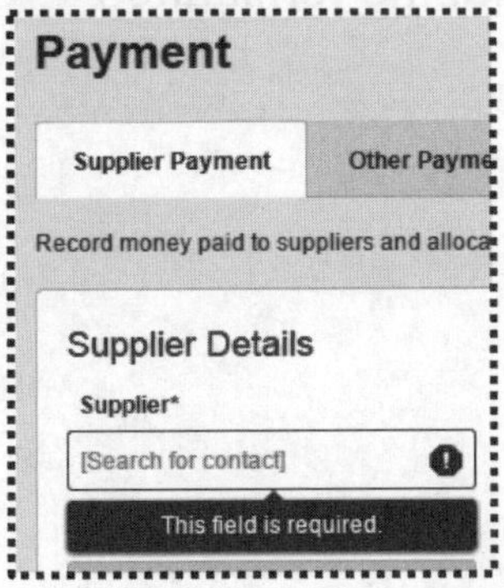

- ✓ Type 'The Stationery Cupboard' into the Supplier field.
- ✓ Select Bank Account: Current
- ✓ Enter Payment Date: 1st October 2014
- ✓ Enter the Cheque number into the reference field

The account balance (£112.28) and related outstanding invoices will appear automatically at the bottom of the screen in the activity list.

- ✓ From the activity list, select the invoices you are wishing to pay.
- ✓ Check the total amount is the amount you are wishing to pay.
- ✓ Check 'Left to allocate is zero.

NB It is also possible in Sage One to make 'payments on account' and make 'part payments' of invoices.

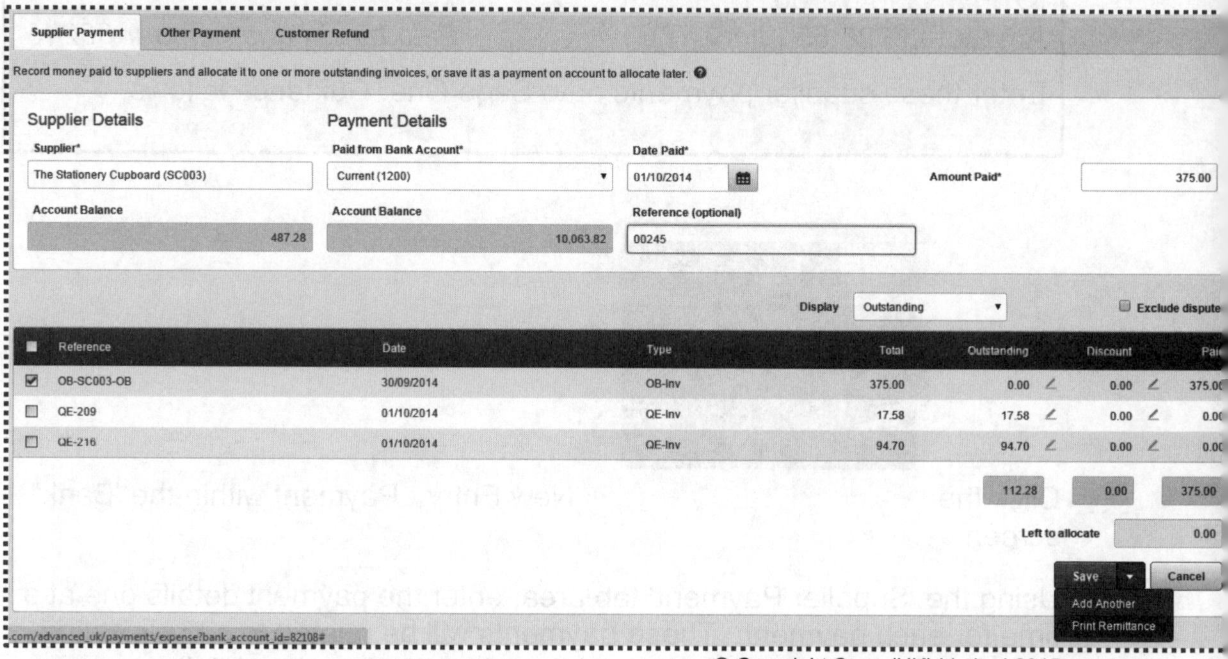

Once the payment details are entered you can either 'Save and Add Another' or 'Save and Print a Remittance'. Here is what the remittance should look like:

TotalPhoto Ltd

TotalPhoto Ltd
Unit 63 Bailey Industrial Estate Fornby Road Miltonby Lancashire
LD37 7QZ
Registered in England and Wales number 734928107

Telephone: 01949 969 378
Website: www.totalphotoltd.co.uk
VAT Number 376 096 823

The Stationery Cupboard (SC003)

21 Potter Way, Hull, Humberside, HU87 6YY, United Kingdom

Remittance Advice

Reference (optional): 00245 **Date Paid:** 01/10/2014 **Amount Paid:** 375.00

Ref	Number	Date	Total Amount	Amount Paid
SC003-OB	OB-SC003-OB	30/09/2014	375.00	375.00
			Total Paid:	**375.00**

NB: if the remittance does not appear, it is likely your browser is blocking a pop-up. To unblock:

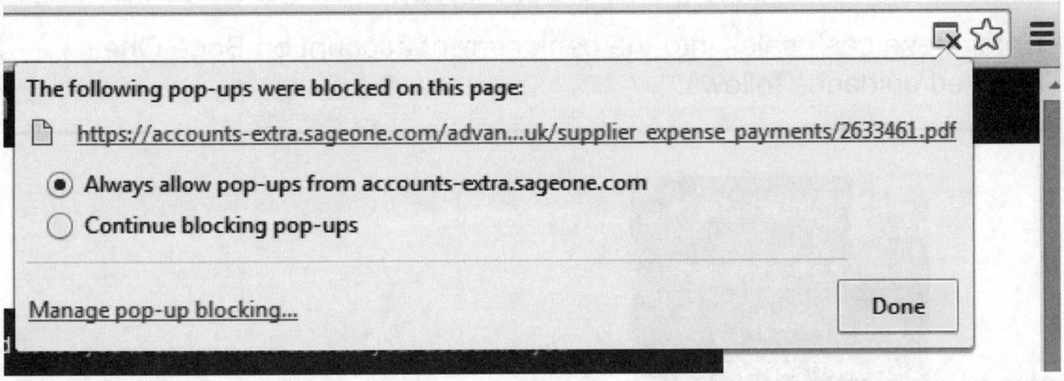
The following pop-ups were blocked on this page:
https://accounts-extra.sageone.com/advan...uk/supplier_expense_payments/2633461.pdf
Always allow pop-ups from accounts-extra.sageone.com
Continue blocking pop-ups
Manage pop-up blocking...
Done

Now enter the next payment to K2 Films Ltd, in the same way.

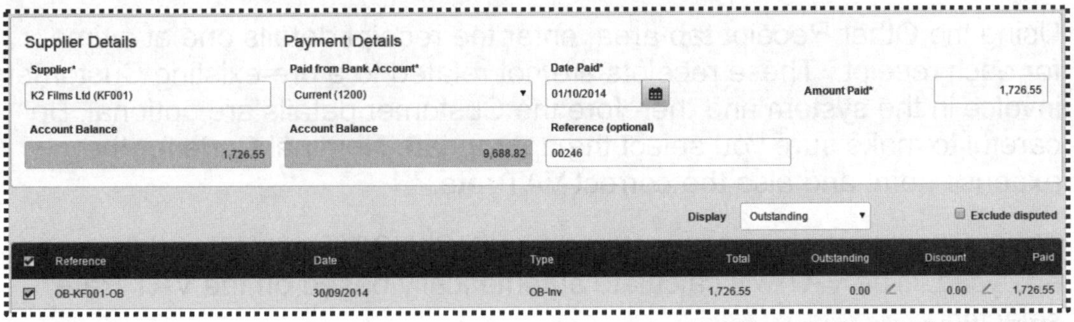
Supplier Details
Payment Details
Supplier*
K2 Films Ltd (KF001)
Paid from Bank Account*
Current (1200)
Date Paid*
01/10/2014
Amount Paid*
1,726.55
Account Balance
1,726.55
Account Balance
9,688.82
Reference (optional)
00246
Display
Outstanding
Exclude disputed
Reference
Date
Type
Total
Outstanding
Discount
Paid
OB-KF001-OB
30/09/2014
OB-Inv
1,726.55
0.00
0.00
1,726.55

10 Recording receipts

The most likely sources of receipts for most businesses are:

- cash sales
- receipts from Debtors/Receivables which are customers who have previously bought goods on credit.

We will look at these in turn.

Cash sales

These are transactions that relate to sales made for cash rather than on credit. The funds are received immediately by the business in the form of cash, cheque or card.

> **Activity**
>
> TotalPhoto Ltd also sells items to two customers who pay cash on 1st October. The first of these is a 6” × 4” Colour Print for £12.00 plus VAT (use nominal code 4000); the second is for School Photos (Set 2) for £28.00 plus VAT of 20% (nominal code 4003).
>
> Enter these cash sales into the bank current account on Sage One. Detailed guidance follows.

Click the 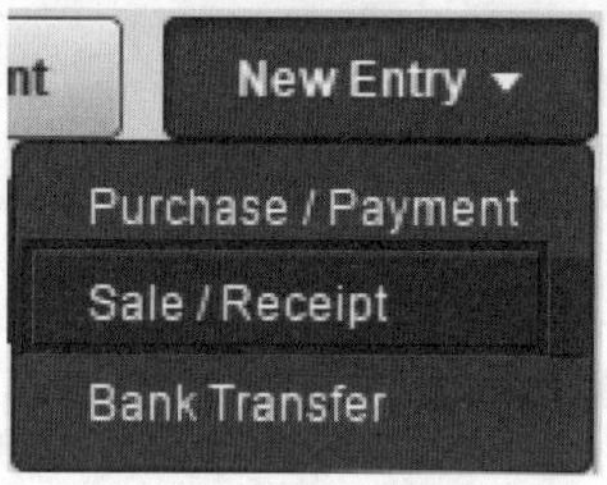

New Entry – Sale within the ‘Bank Screen’

Using the Other Receipt tab area, enter the receipt details one at a time for each receipt. These receipts are not related to a pre-existing Customer invoice in the system and therefore the Customer details are optional. Be careful to make sure you select the appropriate Nominal Code for the expense item, and also the correct VAT rate.

The total amount should be entered first INCLUSIVE of VAT and then analysed. The VAT will calculate automatically based on the VAT Rate selected.

[The receipt amount from Customer 1 is £12.00 +20% = £14.40]

[The receipt amount from Customer 2 is £28.00 +20% = £33.60]

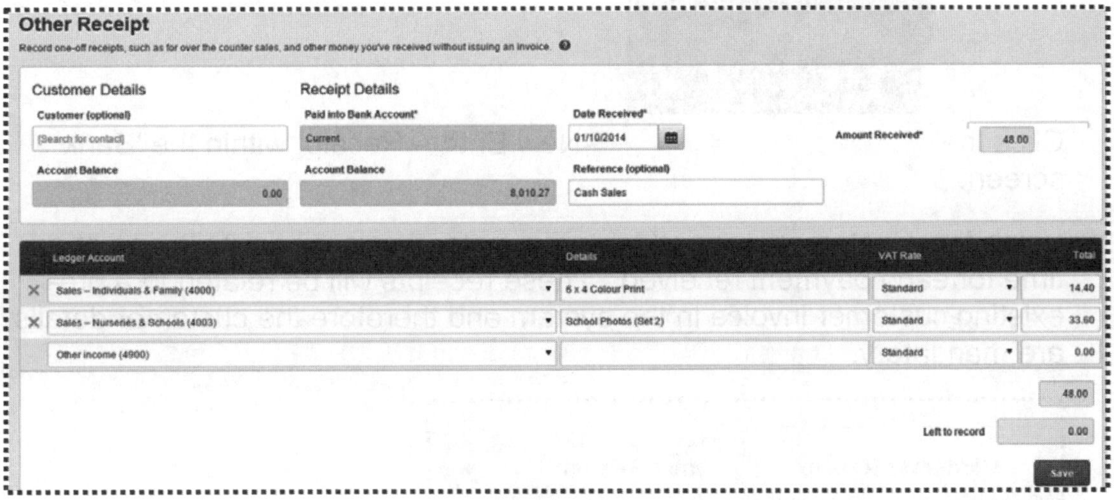

Click the **SAVE** button to post your entries to Sage One.

11 Receipts from customers

Businesses will regularly receive cheques and BACS receipts from customers that have previously bought from them on credit.

Activity

On 1st October TotalPhoto Ltd also received two amounts from customers in respect of their outstanding invoices. These were:

Lullabies Nursery (LUL002)	Cheque for £726.90
Mrs H Poppy	Cash £120.00

Enter these transactions onto Sage One. Guidance follows.

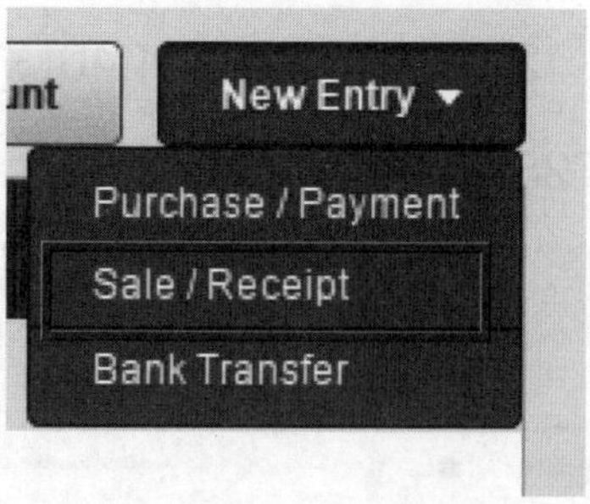
unt
New Entry
Purchase / Payment
Sale / Receipt
Bank Transfer

Click the New Entry - Receipt within the 'Bank' screen.

Using the 'Customer Receipt' tab area, enter the receipt details one at a time for each payment received. These receipts will be related to a pre-existing customer invoice in the system and therefore the customer details are mandatory.

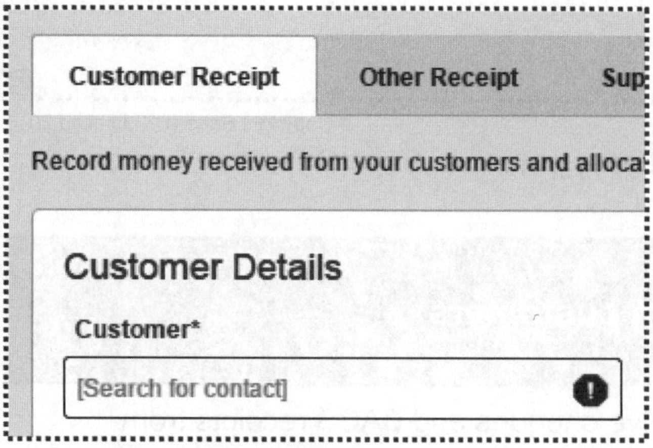
Customer Receipt
Other Receipt
Sup
Record money received from your customers and alloca
Customer Details
Customer*
[Search for contact]

- ✓ Type 'Lullabies Nursery' into the customer field.
- ✓ Select Bank Account: Current
- ✓ Enter Receipt Date: 1st October 2014
- ✓ Enter Cheque Number – *feel free to enter any 6 figure number*

The account balance (£846.90) and the related outstanding invoices will appear automatically at the bottom of the screen in the activity list.

- ✓ From the activity list, select the invoices you are wishing to pay as shown
- ✓ Check the total amount is the amount you are wishing to pay
- ✓ Check 'Left to allocate is zero

NB: It is also possible in Sage One to receive 'payments on account'.

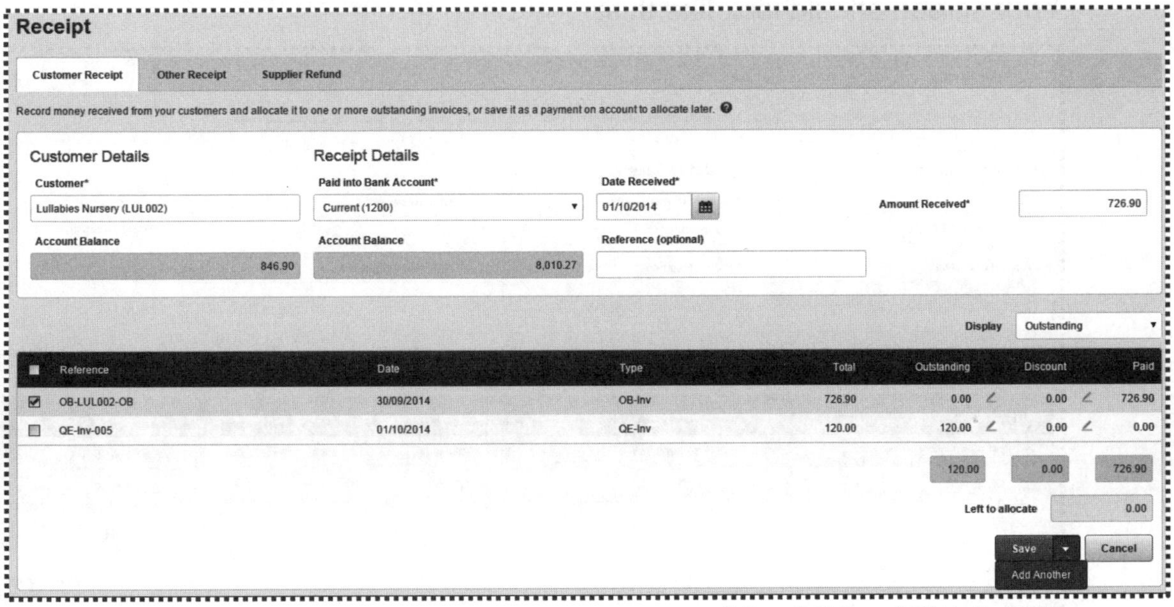
Receipt
Customer Receipt
Other Receipt
Supplier Refund
Record money received from your customers and allocate it to one or more outstanding invoices, or save it as a payment on account to allocate later.
Customer Details
Receipt Details
Customer*
Lullabies Nursery (LUL002)
Paid into Bank Account*
Current (1200)
Date Received*
01/10/2014
Amount Received*
726.90
Account Balance
846.90
Account Balance
8,010.27
Reference (optional)
Display
Outstanding
Reference
Date
Type
Total
Outstanding
Discount
Paid
OB-LUL002-OB
30/09/2014
OB-Inv
726.90
0.00
0.00
726.90
QE-Inv-005
01/10/2014
QE-Inv
120.00
120.00
0.00
0.00
120.00
0.00
726.90
Left to allocate
0.00
Save
Cancel
Add Another

Once the payment details are entered you can either 'Save' or 'Add Another'.

Now enter the second receipt, from Mrs Poppy. Note that only £120.00 has been received. This amount does not match any particular invoice, so unless notified otherwise allocate this against the oldest debt. Instead of being able to 'pay in full' you will need to enter the amount manually in the amount paid. By clicking the amount paid field the following screen will appear where you will be able to enter the amount received and check the outstanding balances now – Click **Apply**.

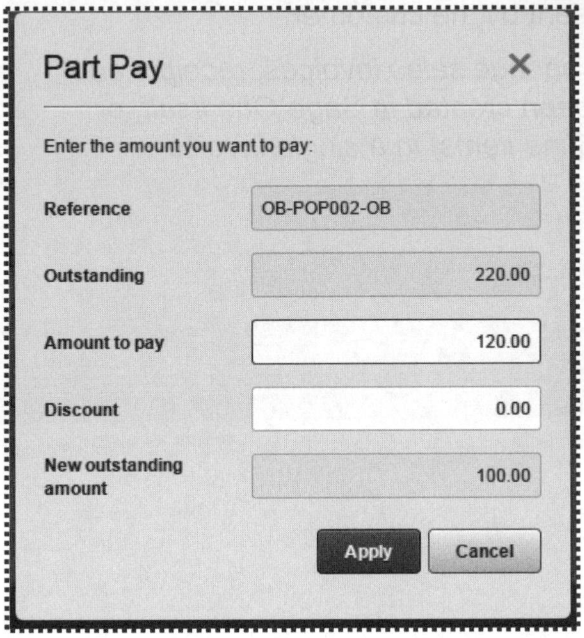
Part Pay
Enter the amount you want to pay:
Reference
OB-POP002-OB
Outstanding
220.00
Amount to pay
120.00
Discount
0.00
New outstanding amount
100.00
Apply
Cancel

Your screen should look like this:

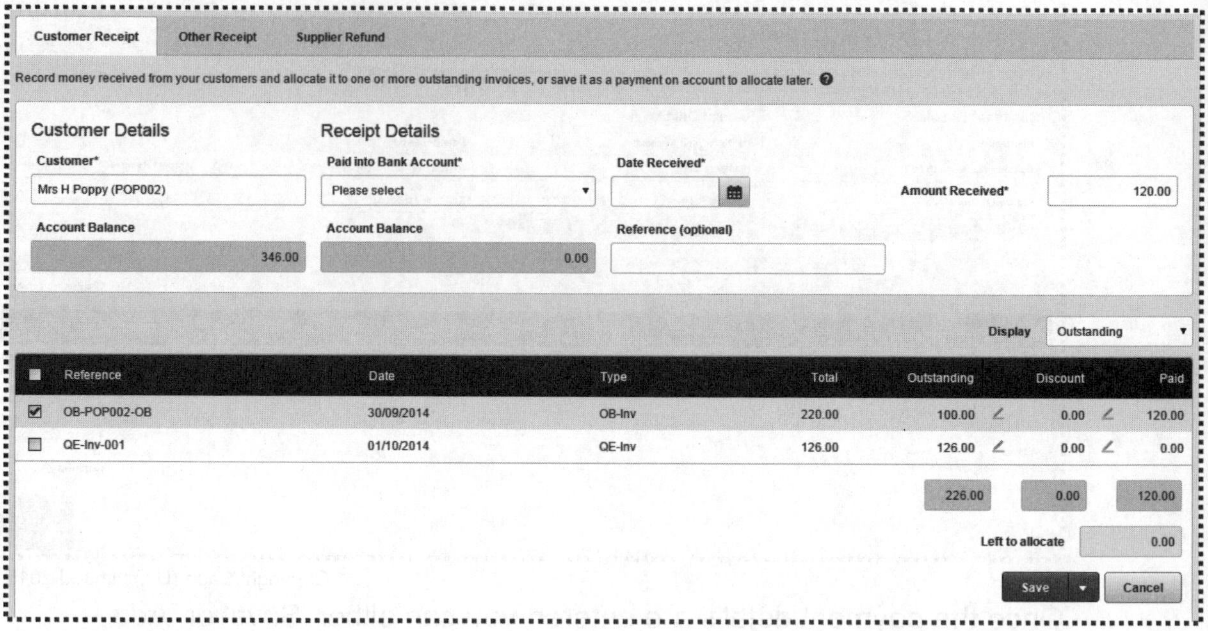
Customer Receipt
Other Receipt
Supplier Refund
Record money received from your customers and allocate it to one or more outstanding invoices, or save it as a payment on account to allocate later.
Customer Details
Receipt Details
Customer*
Mrs H Poppy (POP002)
Paid into Bank Account*
Please select
Date Received*
Amount Received*
120.00
Account Balance
346.00
Account Balance
0.00
Reference (optional)
Display
Outstanding
Reference
Date
Type
Total
Outstanding
Discount
Paid
OB-POP002-OB
30/09/2014
OB-Inv
220.00
100.00
0.00
120.00
QE-Inv-001
01/10/2014
QE-Inv
126.00
126.00
0.00
0.00
226.00
0.00
120.00
Left to allocate
0.00
Save
Cancel

The amount received and the allocation should have automatically updated. Now SAVE.

BACS receipts

When recording BACS receipts, you should follow the same process as when you record a cheque receipt from a customer. However, instead of entering the cheque number in the reference box, you will need to enter 'BACS' instead. The date entered should match the date that the BACS has appeared on the bank statement or the date given on the accompanying remittance advice sent by the customer.

In Sage One it is also possible to manage sales invoices, receipts and allocations for invoices that have been created in Sage One itself, or where there are multiple supplies (line items) in a single invoice transaction.

12 Checking bank activity

It is important for businesses to regularly check their bank transactions. There are a number of reasons for this:

- to monitor the bank balance to ensure that there is sufficient money to meet liabilities
- to monitor transactions to prevent (or identify) fraud or theft
- to ensure there is not too much money in any particular account. For example, if the balance in the current account reaches a certain level the business may decide to transfer some of it to a different account where it may earn a higher rate of interest.

In the banking tab, select the bank account you wish to check, in this case the 'Current Account:

Using the 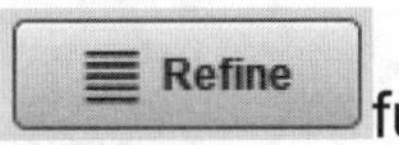

function set the 'from date' to 30th September 2014 and the 'to Date' to 30th October 2014.

From 30/09/2014 To 31/10/2014 Type All

0 of 9 selected

Date	Reference	Name	Type	Received	Paid
30/09/2014			Bank Opening Balance	10,293.00	0.00
01/10/2014			Other Payment	0.00	55.00
01/10/2014	Telephone Bill		Other Payment	0.00	129.18
01/10/2014	Parking Permit		Other Payment	0.00	45.00
01/10/2014	00245	The Stationery Cupboard	Supplier Payment	0.00	375.00
01/10/2014	00246	K2 Films Ltd	Supplier Payment	0.00	1,726.55
01/10/2014	Cash Sales		Other Receipt	48.00	0.00
01/10/2014		Lullabies Nursery	Customer Receipt	726.90	0.00
01/10/2014		Mrs H Poppy	Customer Receipt	120.00	0.00

You will notice the current bank balance is now showing £8,857.17 made up of an opening balance of £10,293 with receipts of £894.90 and payments of £2330.73.

NB Sage One supports a full 'bank reconciliation' function.

Activity

You should now produce a revised Trial Balance as at 31st October.

Your Trial Balance should now look like this.

TotalPhoto Ltd

Period Trial Balance

TotalPhoto Ltd

Trial Balance Report

From Date: 30/09/2014 **To Date: 31/10/2014**

Nominal Code	Name	Debits	Credits
0030	Office equipment and IT - Cost	4,849.00	
0032	Photographic Equipment	20,608.01	
0033	Photographic Equip Depreciation		5,237.00
0050	Motor Vehicles - Cost	21,800.00	
0051	Motor Vehicles - Accumulated Depreciation		5,450.00
1000	Stock	7,403.00	
1100	Trade Debtors	4,270.00	
1200	Current	8,857.17	
1210	Cash in Hand	250.00	
2100	Trade Creditors		15,487.82
2200	VAT on Sales		185.30
2201	VAT on Purchases		245.65
2202	VAT Liability		1,623.29
3000	Ordinary Shares		20,000.00
3100	Profit and Loss Account		5,498.28
4000	Sales – Individuals & Family		5,554.71
4001	Sales - Weddings		4,584.50
4002	Sales – Corporate		1,977.09
4003	Sales – Nurseries & Schools		11,432.20
4004	Other Sales		1,590.30
5000	Purchases – Film	414.39	
5001	Purchases – Paper	1,196.87	

5002	Purchases – Cartridges & Toner	1,535.15	
5003	Purchases – Stationery	502.92	
5004	Purchases – Other Consumables	823.52	
6200	Marketing	55.00	
7100	Rent and rates	4,280.00	
7300	Motor Expenses	1,035.64	
7400	Travel and Entertainment	229.39	
7500	Office costs	711.08	
8200	General Expenses	45.00	
Total		**78,866.14**	**78,866.14**

13 Transfers

Sometimes a business may transfer money from one account to another. For example, it may deposit money from 'Petty Cash' to the 'Bank Current Account' or vice versa. Alternatively, it may transfer an amount from the current account to a deposit account.

Activity

TotalPhoto Ltd currently have £250.00 in their petty cash tin and think this is too much. Therefore, they want to deposit £150.00 from the petty cash account to the bank current account. They take £150 out of the tin, then take it to the bank and pay it into the bank current account.

Process this transaction onto Sage One. Guidance follows.

When 'transferring' cash from a Cash in Hand or Petty Cash account the process in Sage One is called a 'Bank Deposit'. All other bank account to bank account transfers are called 'Bank Transfers'.

From the banking tab, select the Cash in Hand account by clicking on the name description.

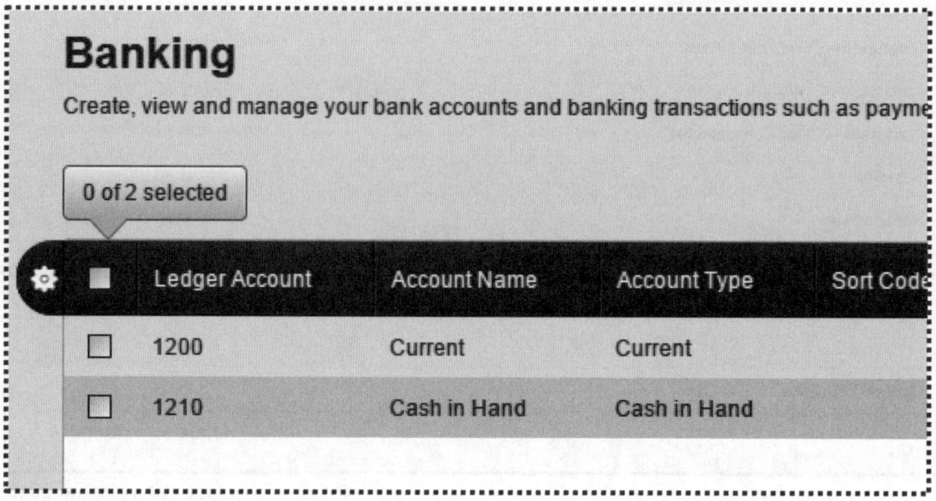
Banking
Create, view and manage your bank accounts and banking transactions such as payme
0 of 2 selected
Ledger Account
Account Name
Account Type
Sort Code
1200
Current
Current
1210
Cash in Hand
Cash in Hand

Once on the Cash in Hand Account record, using the New Entry drop down, chose 'Bank Deposit.

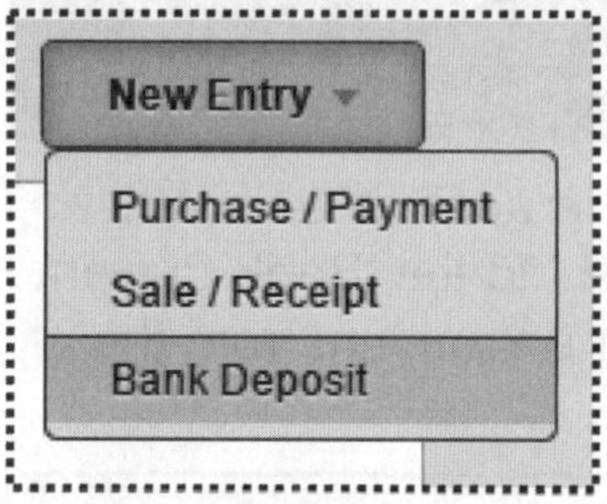
New Entry
Purchase / Payment
Sale / Receipt
Bank Deposit

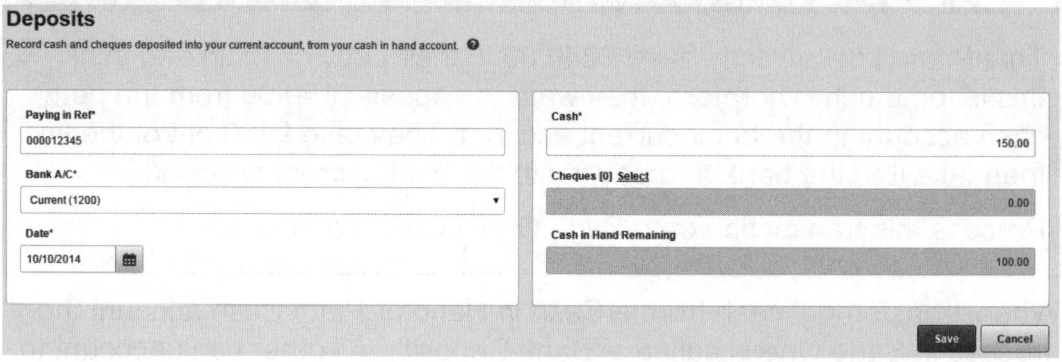
Deposits
Record cash and cheques deposited into your current account, from your cash in hand account.
Paying in Ref*
000012345
Bank A/C*
Current (1200)
Date*
10/10/2014
Cash*
150.00
Cheques (0) Select
0.00
Cash in Hand Remaining
100.00
Save
Cancel

Enter a paying in slip / deposit slip reference or a meaningful reference to help you track this transaction at a later date.

Enter the bank account into which the deposit will be made. (10th Oct 2014).

Enter £150 into the Cash field and SAVE.

The Cash in Hand account can be used to record receipts ahead of depositing a cheque into an actual bank account. This will make sure a customer account or a sales balance is correct without having to go to the bank. When the deposit is made into the bank, this can be recorded using the cheques function in the deposits screen.

14 Petty cash

Most businesses use petty cash as a way of paying for minor expenses such as taxi fares, tea, milk and coffee, window cleaning etc.
Payments out of petty cash are recorded in exactly the same way as any other payments made from a bank account. Remember to make sure that you use the correct account number (1210).

Also be sure to enter the correct VAT rate for each transaction. Many items commonly paid for out of petty cash are zero-rated, exempt or the supplier is not registered for VAT.

Use the VAT status as shown below but note that a window cleaner or taxi firm could have supplied a VAT receipt in a real business setting and, if so, this should be reflected in the entry to Sage One.

Activity

TotalPhoto Ltd makes the following payments out of petty cash on 10th October 2014.

Voucher No	Description	Amount	VAT?
11762	Window cleaner	£4.00	No
11763	Tea and milk	£2.65	No
11764	Newspapers	£3.00	No
11765	Stamps	£3.60	No
11766	Pens	£1.99	Inclusive at 20.0%
11767	Taxi fare	£8.00	No
	Total for Day	**£23.24**	

Enter the above transactions onto Sage One. Guidance follows.

From the banking tab, select the Cash in Hand account by clicking on the name description.

Once on the Cash in Hand Account record, using the New Entry drop down, chose Payment.

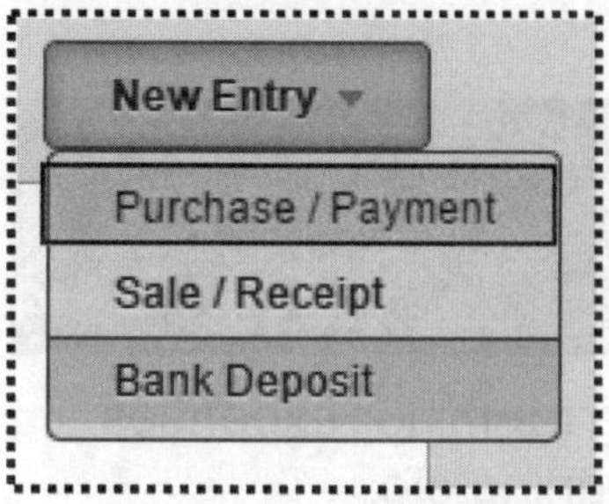
New Entry
Purchase / Payment
Sale / Receipt
Bank Deposit

From the Payment area – use the 'Other Payment' tab.

Supplier Payment
Other Payment
Customer Refund

Since these payments are not being assigned to a supplier's account and are on the same date, these can be added as a single transaction with multiple lines.

It may be preferable however to post them separately if you require the voucher numbers to be displayed in other reports and list views.

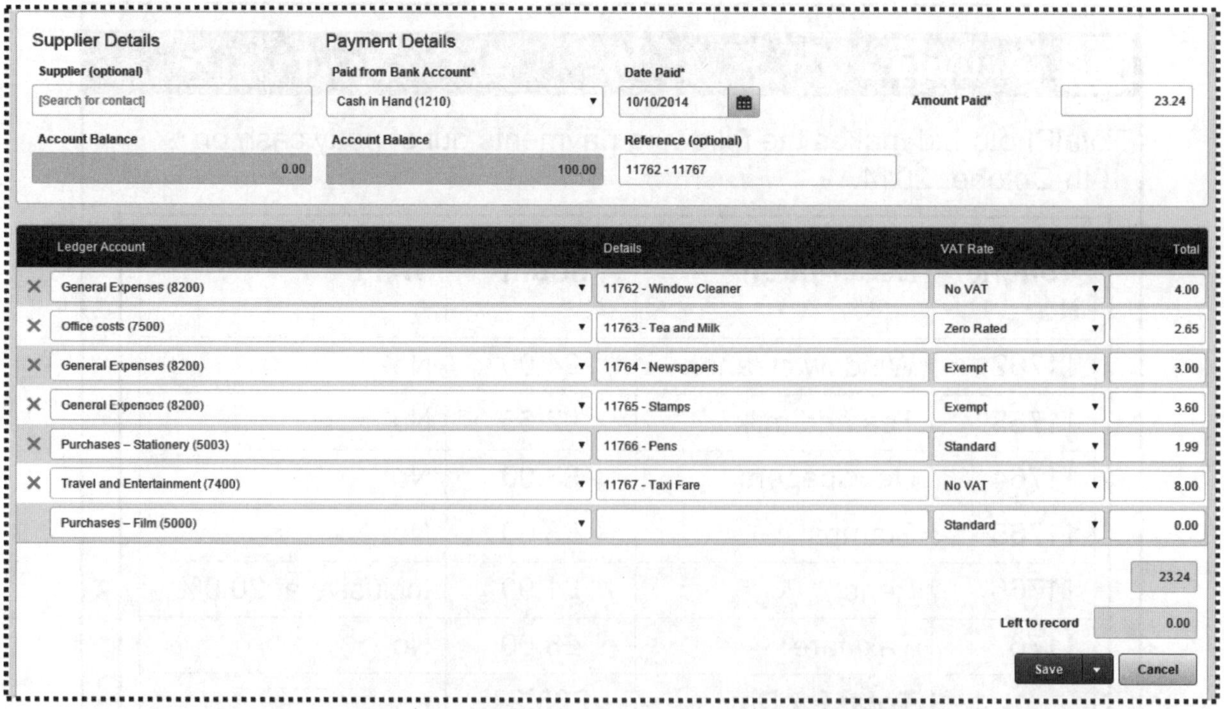
Supplier Details
Payment Details
Supplier (optional)
[Search for contact]
Paid from Bank Account*
Cash in Hand (1210)
Date Paid*
10/10/2014
Amount Paid*
23.24
Account Balance
0.00
Account Balance
100.00
Reference (optional)
11762 - 11767
Ledger Account
Details
VAT Rate
Total
General Expenses (8200)
11762 - Window Cleaner
No VAT
4.00
Office costs (7500)
11763 - Tea and Milk
Zero Rated
2.65
General Expenses (8200)
11764 - Newspapers
Exempt
3.00
General Expenses (8200)
11765 - Stamps
Exempt
3.60
Purchases – Stationery (5003)
11766 - Pens
Standard
1.99
Travel and Entertainment (7400)
11767 - Taxi Fare
No VAT
8.00
Purchases – Film (5000)
Standard
0.00
23.24
Left to record
0.00
Save
Cancel

NB ensure the Amount Paid is manually entered. It will be the sum of the items entered for that day. Then SAVE. All items are entered INCLUSIVE of VAT.

The activity for the Cash in Hand account should now look like this:

Date	Reference	Name	Type	Received	Paid
30/09/2014			Bank Opening Balance	250.00	0.00
10/10/2014	000012345		Deposit: Current	0.00	150.00
10/10/2014	Petty Cash: 11762 - 11767		Other Payment	0.00	23.24

Reimbursing the petty cash account

To reimburse the petty cash account, simply transfer the money from one account to the petty cash account.

Activity

TotalPhoto Ltd reimbursed their petty cash tin at the end of 13th October with the amount necessary to bring the float back to £100.00. The amount spent during the 10th October was £23.24 and so this is the amount to be reimbursed. (nothing was spent on the 13th October). This money was taken from the 'Bank Current Account'

Process the above transaction onto Sage One. Guidance follows.

Step 1

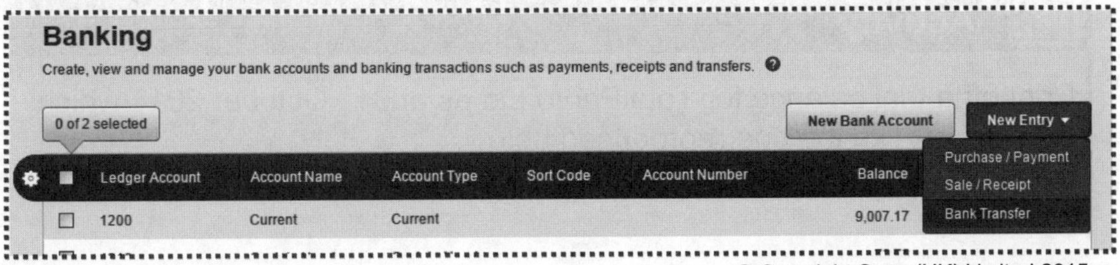

Step 2

Bank Transfer
Record the transfer of money between your bank accounts. This includes payments from your bank account to a credit card or loan account.
Paid from Bank Account*
Current (1200)
Paid into Bank Account*
Cash in Hand (1210)
Amount Transferred*
23.24
Date Transferred*
13/10/2014
Reference (optional)
Description
Reimburse Fri 10th Oct 14
Save
Cancel

You have now learnt how to process the vast majority of transactions that most businesses will deal with on a day to day basis.

Activity

Print off a trial balance for TotalPhoto Ltd as at 31st October 2014 which should look like the one reproduced below.

This one was exported to Excel:

	A	B	C	D
1	From Date	30/09/2014	To Date	31/10/2014
2	Nominal Code	Name	Debits	Credits
3	30	Office equipment and IT - Cost	4,849.00	
4	32	Photographic Equipment	20,608.01	
5	33	Photographic Equip Depreciation		5,237.00
6	50	Motor Vehicles - Cost	21,800.00	
7	51	Motor Vehicles - Accumulated Depreciation		5,450.00
8	1000	Stock	7,403.00	
9	1100	Trade Debtors	4,270.00	
10	1200	Current	8,983.93	
11	1210	Cash in Hand	100	
12	2100	Trade Creditors		15,487.82
13	2200	VAT on Sales		185.3
14	2201	VAT on Purchases		245.32
15	2202	VAT Liability		1,623.29
16	3000	Ordinary Shares		20,000.00
17	3100	Profit and Loss Account		5,498.28
18	4000	Sales & Individuals & Family		5,554.71
19	4001	Sales - Weddings		4,584.50
20	4002	Sales & Corporate		1,977.09
21	4003	Sales & Nurseries & Schools		11,432.20
22	4004	Other Sales		1,590.30
23	5000	Purchases & Film	414.39	
24	5001	Purchases & Paper	1,196.87	
25	5002	Purchases & Cartridges & Toner	1,535.15	
26	5003	Purchases & Stationery	504.58	
27	5004	Purchases & Other Consumables	823.52	
28	6200	Marketing	55	
29	7100	Rent and rates	4,280.00	
30	7300	Motor Expenses	1,035.64	
31	7400	Travel and Entertainment	237.39	
32	7500	Office costs	713.73	
33	8200	General Expenses	55.6	
34	Total		78,865.81	78,865.81

Journals

9

LEARNING OBJECTIVES

LO5 Be able to use journals to enter accounting transactions.

5.1 Process journals for accounting transactions.

5.2 Use the journal to correct errors.

CONTENTS

1 Introduction

So far you have learnt how to process day-to-day transactions through Sage One. These have included recording sales and purchases and making and receiving payments.

Sometimes, however, a business will need to record an accounting transaction that falls outside the 'norm'. In these instances, a **journal** is required to correct errors or make adjustments.

Common reasons for journals include:

- correction of errors – for example, amending opening balances or removing duplicate entries
- writing off irrecoverable debts.

  Year end adjustments such as depreciation, accruals and prepayments ***(you do not need to be aware of these areas for the CPAG assessment as they will be covered at a higher level).***

2 Correction of errors

You may find that you enter a transaction incorrectly and post it to Sage One before you have noticed. In certain circumstances you will need to correct the error by producing a journal.

Quite often the incorrect transaction can just simply be edited, however if for example the transaction is locked – as possibly it is included as part of a reconciliation or VAT return, a compensating journal will be required.

Activity

Earlier, you entered a payment from the bank for £55.00 to Miltonby Cricket Association for advertising in their handbook.

It has now come to light that the amount actually owed to Miltonby Cricket Association is £85 – an underpayment of £30 has been made.

You do not have time to make the additional payment of £30 ahead of a meeting where you need to present the accounts, however you want to make sure this is accounted for in the reports you are presenting.

Using a journal, reference JNL01 post a journal. Guidance follows.

The problem – At the moment, the marketing costs are understated by £30, as we have only paid £55 instead of the correct amount of £85.

The solution – From the Journals tab, using the 'New Journal' function, open the journal screen.

Journals
Reporting
Type reference to search
Refine
New Journal

Enter the details as below:

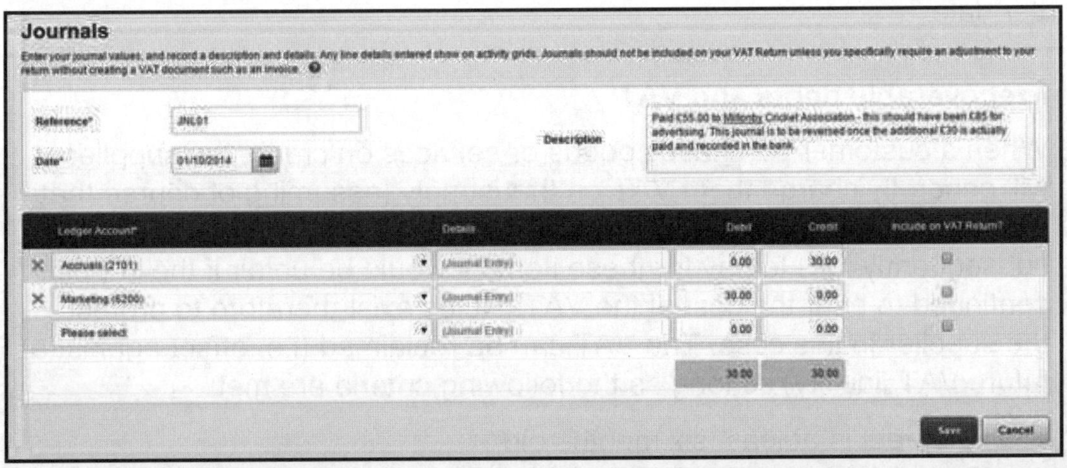
Journals
Reference*
JNL01
Date*
01/10/2014
Description
Ledger Account*
Details
Debit
Credit
Include on VAT Return?
Accruals (2101)
Marketing (6200)
Please select
Save
Cancel

Date
Reference
Description
01/10/2014
JNL01
Paid £55.00 to Miltonby Cricket Association - this should have been £85 for advertising. This journal is to be reversed once the additional £30 is actually paid and recorded in the

Press**Save.**

You have credited the accruals account by £30 and debited the marketing account by the same amount. When you run reports, you will notice as a result of this journal posting the marketing costs will be correct and increased by £30. Although this £30 will not as yet be reflected in the bank account the credit will however be included on the Accruals Account.

At a future date, when you have time, you can make the actual bank payment, but instead of debiting Marketing costs you will debit the Accruals Account.

3 Irrecoverable debts

A bad or irrecoverable debt arises when a customer (debtor/receivable) fails to make payment on their debt. At some point the organization will need to judge that the debt is no longer likely to be recovered and will need to write off the debt. This has the effect of decreasing the total receivables/debtors (as detailed in the sales ledger control account) and creating an irrecoverable debt expense that will reduce profits.

To write off an irrecoverable debt in Sage One you will need to perform a credit note exactly as was shown earlier using the Quick Entries function. This will ensure that the bad debt is written off against your profits for the current year.

The Credit Note should NOT be sent to the customer as they may pay at a later date.

Irrecoverable debts and VAT

When a customer purchases goods or services on credit, the supplier will generally charge them VAT on that supply (assuming of course that they are VAT registered and the supplies attract VAT). If the customer subsequently fails to pay for these items it would be unfair if the supplier continued to bear the cost of the VAT. Rules exist therefore to protect the supplier in this case. The VAT can be reclaimed (i.e. offset against a future VAT liability) so long as the following criteria are met:

- the debt is at least six months old
- genuine attempts have been made to recover the debt
- the debt has been written off in the accounts.

Activity

TotalPhoto Ltd is currently has a debtor T Pashby (A/c Ref PAS002). This debt relates to photographs sold almost a year ago. A number of letters have been sent to the given address but have been returned as 'not living at this address anymore'. There have been numerous attempts to contact the customer without any response.

A decision has now been taken to write off the bad debt (£89.50 including VAT). Process this transaction in Sage One. Guidance follows.

Before you start this activity, you need to ensure the 'Bad Debts' nominal account is visible in the Sales area of Sage One. From the settings area, Chart of Accounts set up – Edit Ledger Account – 8100. Tick Sales – Invoice

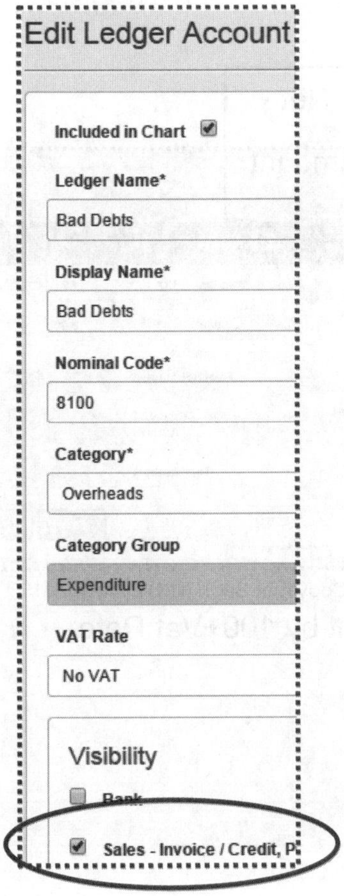
Edit Ledger Account
Included in Chart
Ledger Name*
Bad Debts
Display Name*
Bad Debts
Nominal Code*
8100
Category*
Overheads
Category Group
Expenditure
VAT Rate
No VAT
Visibility
Bank
Sales - Invoice / Credit, P

The bad debt write off process follows:

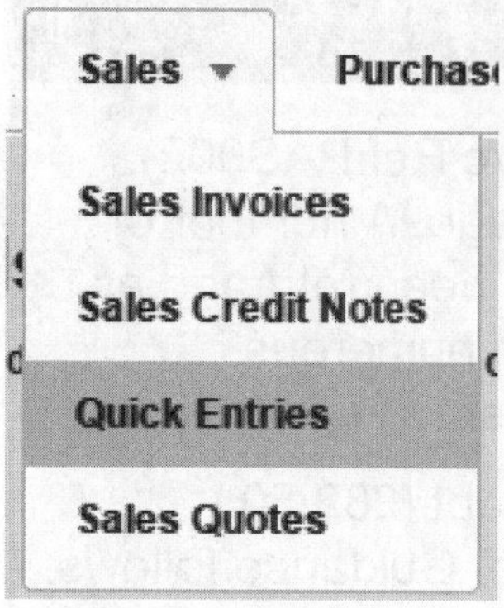
Sales
Purchas
Sales Invoices
Sales Credit Notes
Quick Entries
Sales Quotes

From the Sales tab, navigate to 'Quick Entries'

Click the 
New Quick Entry
function button

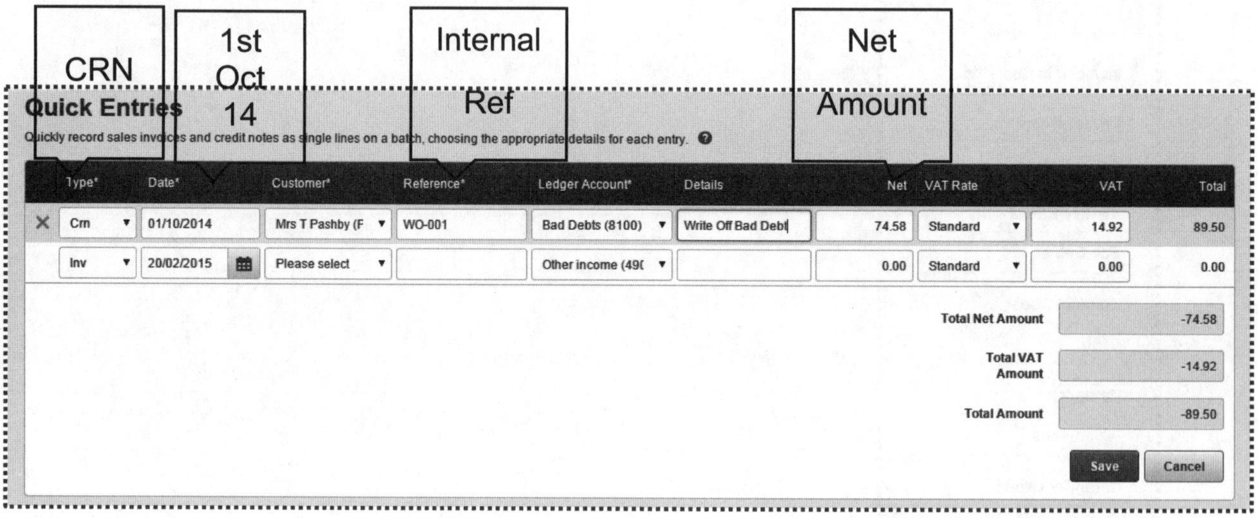
CRN
1st Oct 14
Internal Ref
Net Amount
Quick Entries
Quickly record sales invoices and credit notes as single lines on a batch, choosing the appropriate details for each entry.
Type*
Date*
Customer*
Reference*
Ledger Account*
Details
Net
VAT Rate
VAT
Total
Crn
01/10/2014
Mrs T Pashby (F
WO-001
Bad Debts (8100)
Write Off Bad Debt
74.58
Standard
14.92
89.50
Inv
20/02/2015
Please select
Other income (49
0.00
Standard
0.00
0.00
Total Net Amount
-74.58
Total VAT Amount
-14.92
Total Amount
-89.50
Save
Cancel

To calculate the net amount, divide the gross amount by 100+Vat Rate (120) and multiply by 100.

Activity

Run a Profit and Loss report for the period 30th September 2014 until **31st October 2014**. The report can be found in the Reporting/Reports tab.

Profit and Loss Report

Look out for the Bad Debt write off and marketing costs.

The report should look like this:

TotalPhoto Ltd

Profit and Loss Report

30 September, 2014 - 31 October, 2014

Sales		
Sales – Individuals & Family (4000)	5,554.71	
Sales - Weddings (4001)	4,584.50	
Sales – Corporate (4002)	1,977.09	
Sales – Nurseries & Schools (4003)	11,432.20	
Other Sales (4004)	1,590.30	
	Total Sales	**25,138.80**
Direct Expenses		
Purchases – Film (5000)	414.39	
Purchases – Paper (5001)	1,196.87	
Purchases – Cartridges & Toner (5002)	1,535.15	
Purchases – Stationery (5003)	504.58	
Purchases – Other Consumables (5004)	823.52	
	Total Direct Expenses	**4,474.51**
	GROSS PROFIT / LOSS	**20,664.29**
Overheads		
Marketing (6200)	85.00	
Rent and rates (7100)	4,280.00	
Motor Expenses (7300)	1,035.64	
Travel and Entertainment (7400)	237.39	
Office costs (7500)	713.73	
Bad Debts (8100)	74.58	
General Expenses (8200)	55.60	
	Total Overheads	**6,481.94**
	NET PROFIT / LOSS	**14,182.35**

Bank reconciliation

10

LEARNING OBJECTIVES

LO4 Record and reconcile bank and cash transactions.

4.1 Process receipts and payments for non-credit transactions.

4.4 Perform a periodic bank reconciliation.

LO6 Produce reports

6.2 Produce routine reports from the nominal ledger – Account activity.

CONTENTS

1 Introduction

A useful exercise for all businesses to undertake on a regular basis is to reconcile their bank account. In essence this means checking the company's own records with the bank statement received from their bank.

We need to review the bank reconciliation process for our case study business. TotalPhoto Ltd received the following statement from their bank.

STATEMENT No 10

15th October 2014

Account number

Sort code

Date		*Payments*	*Receipts*	*Balance*
30/09/14	Op Bal			10293.00C
01/10/14	Counter credit		14.40	10307.40C
01/10/14	Counter credit		33.60	10341.00C
01/10/14	Counter credit		726.90	11067.90C
01/10/14	Counter credit		120.00	11187.90C
01/10/14	Interest		11.22	11199.12C
01/10/14	Bank Charges	31.41		11167.71C
06/10/14	DD North West Radio	240.00		10927.71C
10/10/14	Bank transfer		150.00	11077.71C
13/10/14	Bank transfer	23.24		11054.47C
13/10/14	Chq 242	55.00		10999.47C
14/10/14	Chq 243	129.18		10870.29C
14/10/14	Chq 244	45.00		10825.29C

D = Debit

C = Credit

The bank statement will rarely agree exactly with the company's own records, for three reasons. Let's think about what these are:

1 **Items on the bank statement not yet recorded in Sage One**

There may be some items on the bank statement which do not yet appear in the company's records. Here, there is interest which has been credited to the business' account of £11.22, and also bank charges of £31.41 which have been debited from the account. There is also a direct debit for £240.00. It is likely that the company would not know the exact amount or date of the first of these receipts/payments from the bank account until the statement is actually received – further ones however can be scheduled – see recurring payments and receipts in a later chapter. You should always check however that all standing orders/direct debits/BACS transfers etc. have been fully recorded in the company's records and have been processed by the bank.

Discrepancies between the bank statement and the company's own records of this nature should be dealt with by updating the company's records.

2 **Timing differences**

This is a very common cause of discrepancies between the bank statement and the company's own records. Timing differences occur because the company will generally update its records before the bank has had the opportunity to process all transactions.

Imagine the scenario where a company writes a cheque to a supplier on 1st March. The accounts clerk is likely to update the company's records (i.e. Sage One) on that day. However, if the cheque was produced late in the afternoon it may not actually be posted until the following day and may not arrive at the supplier's address until two or three days after that. Weekends and public holidays can delay this further. It may then not be banked immediately by the supplier; it may take them two or three days to actually bank the cheque in their own branch. The cheque must then go through the banks' clearing system which may take 3–5 working days. Therefore the funds associated with that cheque (written on 1st March) may not actually be cleared out of the bank account until say 10th March or maybe later.

If a bank statement is sent to the company in this time it will not show the cheque payment, as it will not have been fully processed at the time the statement is produced. It will, however, have been recorded in the company's own accounts.

It is important therefore to undergo a process of bank reconciliation regularly to ensure that the only differences between the bank statement and the company's own records are caused by these timing differences (which can easily be accounted for), and not by the third reason for discrepancies, where an error has occurred.

3 **Errors**

It is perfectly possible for either the bank or (more likely) the company to have made an error in the course of producing their figures.

2 Performing a bank reconciliation using Sage One

Activity

Perform a bank reconciliation for TotalPhoto Ltd using the bank statement provided at the start of this chapter. Guidance follows.

From the **Banking tab/area**, select the current account and open the bank record.

Using the 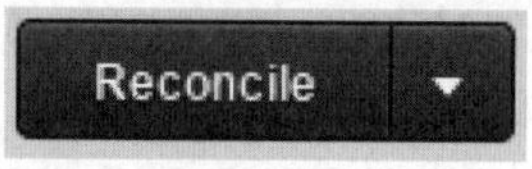
Reconcile
function button, navigate to the Bank Reconciliation page.

(Do not use the drop down option to import the bank statement – we will manually reconcile the statement.)

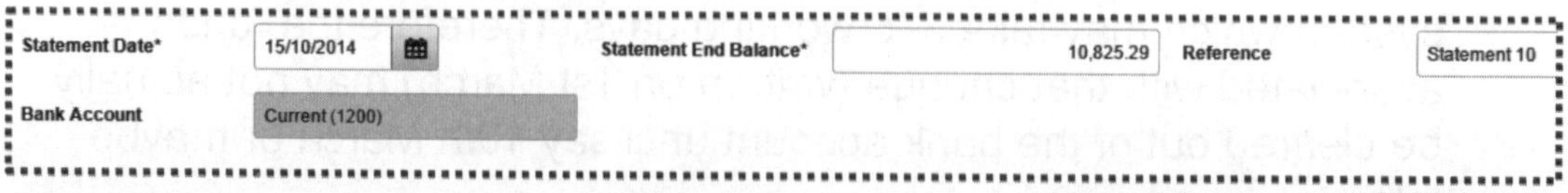
Statement Date*
15/10/2014
Statement End Balance*
10,825.29
Reference
Statement 10
Bank Account
Current (1200)

Enter the Statement date 15th Oct 14, closing balance £10825.29 and statement number 10 and 
Apply

Working down the bank statement, 'tick' Reconciled? when the item appears on the bank activity at the bottom of the Bank Reconciliation page. The page supports 10 lines per page, it is likely there will be more than one page of transactions available for matching/reconciling.

It is useful to also manually 'tick' using a pencil any item matched on the bank statement within Sage One.

In this example we combined the Cash Sales deposit into a single receipt of £48.00

Other Receipt
48.00
0.00
Mouse –Click- Tick

Date		Payments	Receipts	Balance
30/09/14	Op Bal			✓10293.00C
01/10/14	Counter credit	✓	14.40	10307.40C
01/10/14	Counter credit		33.60	10341.00C
01/10/14	Counter credit		726.90✓	11067.90C
01/10/14	Counter credit		120.00✓	11187.90C
01/10/14	Interest		11.22	11199.12C
01/10/14	Bank Charges	31.41		11167.71C
06/10/14	DD North West Radio	240.00		10927.71C
10/10/14	Bank transfer		150.00✓	11077.71C
13/10/14	Bank transfer	23.24✓		11054.47C
13/10/14	Chq 242	55.00✓		10999.47C
14/10/14	Chq 243	129.18✓		10870.29C
14/10/14	Chq 244	45.00✓		10825.29C

The above bank statement is showing all transactions as already posted in Sage One – indicated by a tick ✓

The following items have not been posted in Sage One:

01/10/14	Interest		11.22	11199.12C
01/10/14	Bank Charges	31.41		11167.71C
06/10/14	DD North West Radio	240.00		10927.71C

The 'Interest and Charges' can be added directly into the Sage One reconciliation system using the **Interest and Charges** function.

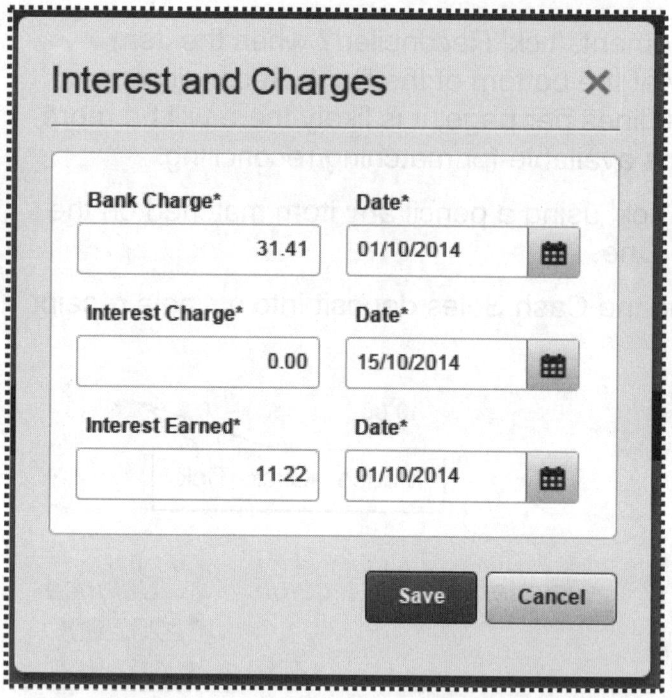
Interest and Charges
Bank Charge*
31.41
Date*
01/10/2014
Interest Charge*
0.00
Date*
15/10/2014
Interest Earned*
11.22
Date*
01/10/2014
Save
Cancel

The bank charge transactions will appear at the bottom of the activity list, showing as reconciled.

This is how the reconciliation activity list should appear, depending on how it has been sorted. It may be easier to sort by date by clicking on the date columns header.

Date	Reference	Name	Category	Received	Paid	Reconcile
30/09/2014			Bank Opening Balance	10,293.00	0.00	☑
01/10/2014	Cash Sales		Other Receipt	48.00	0.00	☑
01/10/2014		Lullabies Nursery	Customer Receipt	726.90	0.00	☑
01/10/2014		Mrs H Poppy	Customer Receipt	120.00	0.00	☑
10/10/2014	000012345		Deposit Cash in Hand	150.00	0.00	☑
13/10/2014			Transfer: Cash in Hand	0.00	23.24	☑
01/10/2014	Chq 242		Other Payment	0.00	55.00	☑
01/10/2014	Chq 243		Other Payment	0.00	129.18	☑
01/10/2014	Chq 245	The Stationery Cupboard	Supplier Payment	0.00	375.00	☐
01/10/2014	Chq 244		Other Payment	0.00	45.00	☑

Date	Reference	Name	Category	Received	Paid	Reconcile
01/10/2014	Bank Charge		Bank Payment	0.00	31.41	☑
01/10/2014	Chq 246	K2 Films Ltd	Supplier Payment	0.00	1,726.55	☐
01/10/2014	Interest Earned		Bank Receipt	11.22	0.00	☑

At the bottom of the screen is a reconciliation summary.

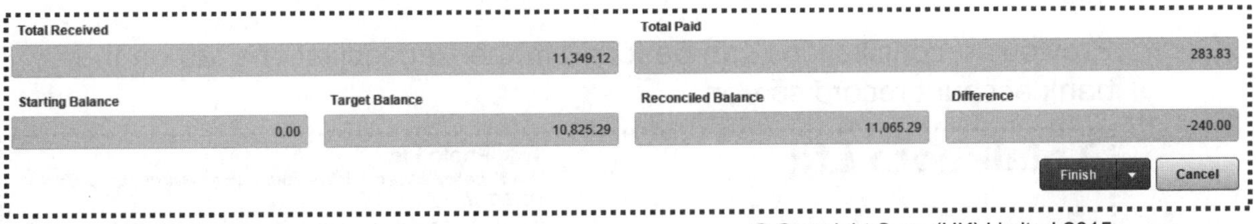
Total Received
11,349.12
Total Paid
283.83
Starting Balance
0.00
Target Balance
10,825.29
Reconciled Balance
11,065.29
Difference
-240.00
Finish
Cancel

The target balance is the statement balance and the reconciled balance is the sum of all bank transactions reconciled. The difference between the two is the 'unreconciled balance' described as 'difference'.

You will notice the difference is £240 which is the Direct Debit to North West Radio. This has not yet been posted in Sage One but is included in the target balance. This can be done either after or before finalising the reconciliation – if after, the difference will be carried forward to the next reconciliation and dealt with there. Normally, to keep things less complicated it is better to make all known postings as soon as possible and not carry them forward.

Enter as an 'Other Payment':

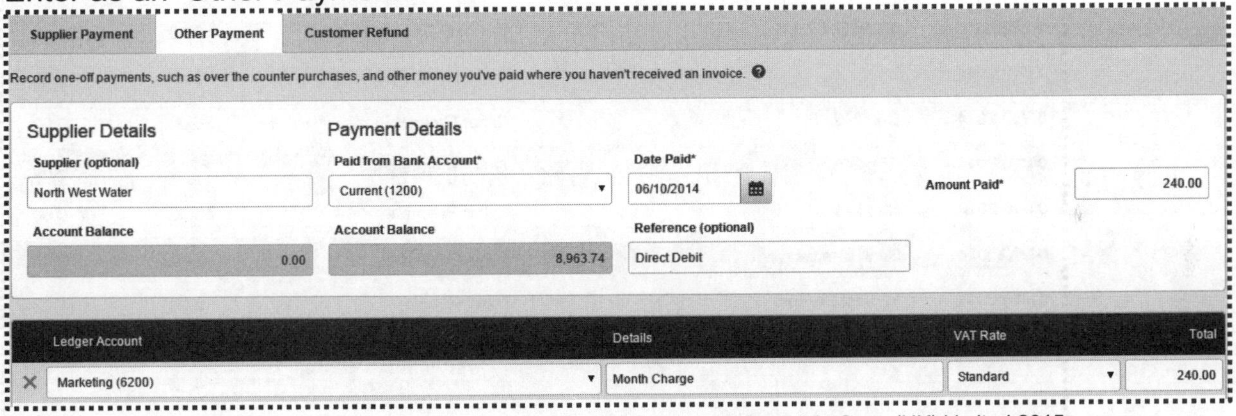
Supplier Payment
Other Payment
Customer Refund
Record one-off payments, such as over the counter purchases, and other money you've paid where you haven't received an invoice.
Supplier Details
Supplier (optional)
North West Water
Account Balance
0.00
Payment Details
Paid from Bank Account*
Current (1200)
Account Balance
8,963.74
Date Paid*
06/10/2014
Reference (optional)
Direct Debit
Amount Paid*
240.00
Ledger Account
Details
VAT Rate
Total
Marketing (6200)
Month Charge
Standard
240.00

Return to the Bank Reconciliation, locate the £240 transaction and tick as reconciled.

The Un-reconciled difference will now be zero.

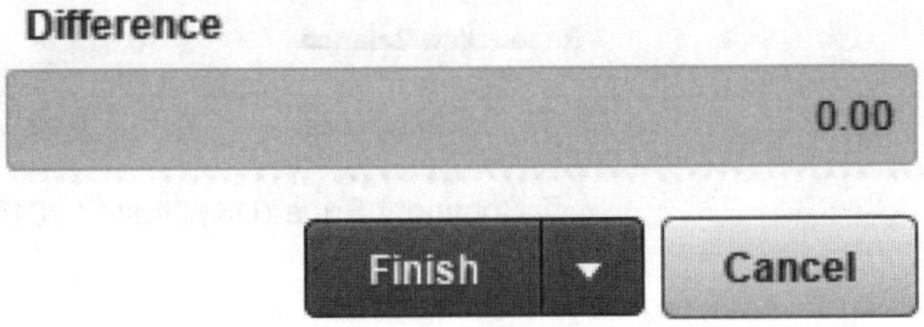
Difference
0.00
Finish
Cancel

Click FINISH.

Using the print function, your reconciliation report should now look like this:

Previous reconciliations can be found in the Reconciliations tab on the bank account record screen.

TotalPhoto Ltd

TotalPhoto Ltd
Unit 63 Bailey Industrial Estate Fornby Road Miltonby Lancashire LD37 7QZ
Registered in England and Wales number 734928107

Telephone: 01949 969 378 **Website:** www.totalphotoltd.co.uk **VAT Number** 376 096 823

Bank Account	Current (1200)	**Statement Date**	15/10/2014
Reference	Statement 10	**Reconciled By**	Pierre Trimm

Date	Reference	Name	Category	Paid	Received
30/09/2014			Bank Opening Balance	0.00	10,293.00
01/10/2014	Cash Sales		Other Receipt	0.00	48.00
01/10/2014		Lullabies Nursery	Customer Receipt	0.00	726.90
01/10/2014		Mrs H Poppy	Customer Receipt	0.00	120.00
10/10/2014	000012345		Deposit: Cash in Hand	0.00	150.00
13/10/2014			Transfer: Cash in Hand	23.24	0.00
01/10/2014	Chq 242		Other Payment	55.00	0.00
01/10/2014	Chq 243		Other Payment	129.18	0.00
01/10/2014	Chq 244		Other Payment	45.00	0.00
01/10/2014	Bank Charge		Bank Payment	31.41	0.00
01/10/2014	Interest Earned		Bank Receipt	0.00	11.22
06/10/2014	Direct Debit		Other Payment	240.00	0.00

Total Received	11,349.12
Total Paid	523.83
Starting Balance	0.00
Statement End Balance	10,825.29
Reconciled Balance	10,825.29
Difference	0.00

The purpose of a bank reconciliation is to identify:

- transactions which have been posted in the accounting system which have not appeared on the bank statement
- transactions which appear on the bank statement which have not been accounted for in the accounting system.

The sum of these items will enable you to reconcile the actual bank balance with the balance of the back account according to the accounting system.

Following a bank reconciliation process in Sage One Accounts, it is possible to run a report to list and total bank account postings which have not appeared on the bank statement. See Unreconciled Bank Transactions report.

The items on this report will continue to grow until a bank reconciliation process has been carried out again. When a new unreconciled bank statement is available and a new reconciliation is carried out, the available items for reconciliation/matching will be all transactions in the accounting system which have yet to be reconciled previously – per the report.

Normally all transactions which appear on the bank statement, which have not been accounted for in the accounting system, will be created and posted/matched at the time of processing the reconciliation. Very rarely there may be statement errors which need to be queried directly with the bank.

In our example, you may recall, there are two transactions in Sage One which have yet to appear on the bank statement. These two items will be available for reconciliation when the next statement from the bank is received.

You can prove this to yourself by attempting to reconcile the next statement or running the 'Unreconciled Bank Transactions' report:

TotalPhoto Ltd

Unreconciled Bank Transactions Report

Bank: Current (1200) — To Date: 23/02/2015

Account Balance at 'To Date': 8,723.74 — Reconciled Balance at 'To Date': 10,825.29

Date	Name	Reference	Type	Payment	Receipt
01/10/2014	K2 Films Ltd	Chq 246	Supplier Payment	1,726.55	0.00
01/10/2014	The Stationery Cupboard	Chq 245	Supplier Payment	375.00	0.00
				2,101.55	0.00
				Total	-2,101.55

The purpose of a bank reconciliation is to identify:

- transactions which have been posted in the accounting system which have not appeared on the bank statement
- transactions which appear on the bank statement which have not been posted to the accounting system.

The extent of these items will enable you to reconcile the actual bank balance with the balance of the bank account according to the accounting system.

Following a bank reconciliation process in Sage One Accounts, it is possible to run a report to list all total bank account postings which have not appeared on the bank statement. See Unreconciled Bank Transactions report.

The items on this report will continue to show until a bank reconciliation process has been carried out again. When a new (or updated) bank statement is available and a new reconciliation is carried out, the system items for reconciliation/matching will be all transactions in the accounting system which have not yet been reconciled previously – per the report.

Normally, all transactions which appear on the bank statement which have not been recorded in the accounting system will be created and reconciled at the time of processing the reconciliation. Very rarely, there may be some transactions which need to be queried directly with the bank.

In the example you have just seen, there are two transactions in Sage One which have yet to appear on the bank statement. These two items will be available for reconciliation when the next statement from the bank is received.

You can prove this to yourself by clicking on More to reconcile the next statement or by viewing the Unreconciled Bank Transactions report.

Print/Export List

[illegible]

11 Useful reports

LEARNING OBJECTIVES

LO6 Produce reports.

6.1 Produce routine reports for customers and suppliers.

6.2 Produce routine reports from the nominal ledger.

CONTENTS

1 Introduction

There are a number of predefined reports in Sage One, some of which you have already used. Others will be new to you. You should now make yourself familiar with these.

The reports available in Sage One fulfil different functions, statutory (VAT) and operational through to management reports. Have a go at generating these reports using the Reporting tab or using the reports available in the module areas using the 'More' function button.

In order to select the data you wish to view in the report use the 'Refine' button to select dates and transaction types etc.

For more detailed views – use the detailed reports button.

Type to search
Refine
View the detailed report
Export

Ensure you are comfortable with the different output options, i.e. PDF and CSV or on-screen views. Practice saving the file as a PDF. This may be required as part of your assessment so it's an essential part of your studies.

You can practice as much as you like in order to familiarise yourself with the process.

Reporting Menu:

Summary
Sales
Purchases
Contacts
Products & Services
Banking
Journals
Reporting
Reports
Reports

Example of reports available from module areas:

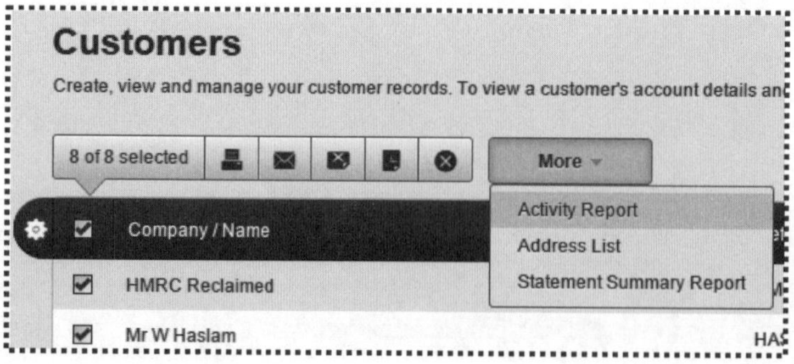
Customers
8 of 8 selected
More
Activity Report
Address List
Statement Summary Report
Company / Name
HMRC Reclaimed
Mr W Haslam

Some reports will display immediately, however certain reports will be generated and accessed from the navigation bar at the top of the screen:

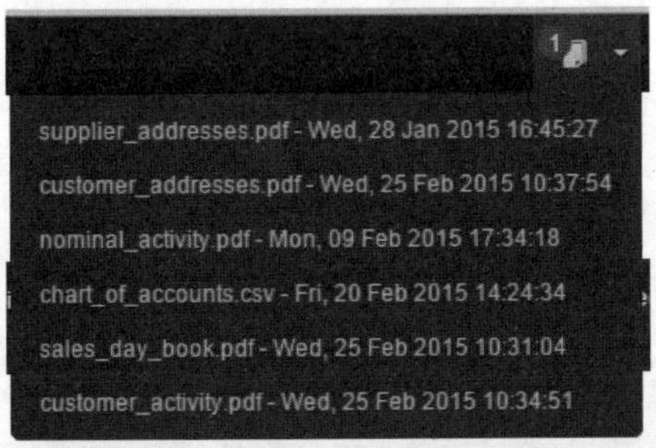
supplier_addresses.pdf - Wed, 28 Jan 2015 16:45:27
customer_addresses.pdf - Wed, 25 Feb 2015 10:37:54
nominal_activity.pdf - Mon, 09 Feb 2015 17:34:18
chart_of_accounts.csv - Fri, 20 Feb 2015 14:24:34
sales_day_book.pdf - Wed, 25 Feb 2015 10:31:04
customer_activity.pdf - Wed, 25 Feb 2015 10:34:51

2 Customer reports

TotalPhoto Ltd

Aged Debtors Report

To Date: 31/10/2014

Customer	O/S Amt	< 30 days	< 60 days	< 90 days	< 120 days	Older
Campbell & Dunn Ltd (CAM004)	£2,110.85	£0.00	£2,110.85	£0.00	£0.00	£0.00
Lullabies Nursery (LUL002)	£120.00	£0.00	£120.00	£0.00	£0.00	£0.00
Miss S Pargenter (PAR006)	£650.00	-£14.40	£664.40	£0.00	£0.00	£0.00
Mr A Smith (SMI009)	£720.00	£0.00	£720.00	£0.00	£0.00	£0.00
Mr W Haslam (HAS004)	£353.65	£0.00	£353.65	£0.00	£0.00	£0.00
Mrs H Poppy (POP002)	£226.00	£0.00	£226.00	£0.00	£0.00	£0.00
Mrs T Pashby (PAS002)	£0.00	£0.00	£0.00	£0.00	£0.00	£0.00
	£4,180.50	**-£14.40**	**£4,194.90**	**£0.00**	**£0.00**	**£0.00**

Shows a list of debtors with analysis of how long the debts have been in existence.

TotalPhoto Ltd

Sales Day Book Report

From Date: 01/10/2014

To Date: 31/10/2014

Trans ID	Type	Date	Name	Invoice Number	Ref	Details	Net	VAT	Total
24	Sales QE Invoice	01/10/2014	Mrs H Poppy	QE-Inv-001	Inv-001		105.00	21.00	126.00
25	Sales QE Invoice	01/10/2014	Mr W Haslam	QE-Inv-002	Inv-002		24.50	4.90	29.40
26	Sales QE Invoice	01/10/2014	Miss S Pargenter	QE-Inv-003	Inv-003		12.00	2.40	14.40
27	Sales QE Invoice	01/10/2014	Lullabies Nursery	QE-Inv-005	Inv-005		100.00	20.00	120.00
28	Sales QE Invoice	01/10/2014	Campbell & Dunn Ltd	QE-Inv-006	Inv-006		45.00	9.00	54.00
29	Sales QE Invoice	01/10/2014	Mr W Haslam	QE-Inv-007	Inv-007		12.00	2.40	14.40
30	Sales QE Invoice	01/10/2014	Mr A Smith	QE-Inv-004	Inv-004		600.00	120.00	720.00
60	Sales QE Credit	01/10/2014	Mrs T Pashby	QE-WO-001	WO-001	Write Off Bad Debt	-74.58	-14.92	-89.50
53	Sales QE Credit	08/10/2014	Miss S Pargenter	QE-CRN-001	CRN-001	Fault - INV-003	-12.00	-2.40	-14.40
							811.92	**162.38**	**974.30**

Shows a list of all invoices & credit notes produced including the Net, VAT and Gross Amounts.

Customer Activity (Accessed from Customer List)

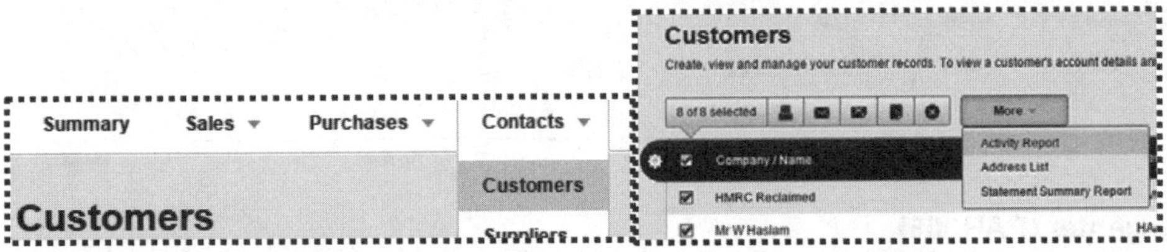
Summary
Sales
Purchases
Contacts
Customers
Customers
Suppliers
Customers
Create, view and manage your customer records. To view a customers account details an
8 of 8 selected
More
Activity Report
Address List
Statement Summary Report
Company / Name
HMRC Reclaimed
Mr W Haslam
HA

TotalPhoto Ltd

Customer Activity Report

From Date: 01/10/2014

To Date: 31/10/2014

HMRC Reclaimed (HMRC Rec)

No activity for the selected date range

Mr W Haslam (HAS004)

Date	Number	Reference	Type	Net	VAT	Total	Discount	Outstanding
01/10/2014	QE-Inv-002	Inv-002	Sales QE Invoice	24.50	4.90	29.40		29.40
01/10/2014	QE-Inv-007	Inv-007	Sales QE Invoice	12.00	2.40	14.40		14.40
						43.80		**43.80**

Mrs H Poppy (POP002)

Date	Number	Reference	Type	Net	VAT	Total	Discount	Outstanding
01/10/2014			Customer Receipt			-120.00	0.00	0.00

Wed 25 Feb 2015, 10:34 Page 1 of 3

01/10/2014	QE-Inv-001	Inv-001	Sales QE Invoice	105.00	21.00	126.00		126.00
						6.00		**126.00**

Mrs T Pashby (PAS002)

Date	Number	Reference	Type	Net	VAT	Total	Discount	Outstanding
01/10/2014	QE-WO-001	WO-001	Sales QE Credit	-74.58	-14.92	-89.50		-89.50
						-89.50		**-89.50**

Campbell & Dunn Ltd (CAM004)

Date	Number	Reference	Type	Net	VAT	Total	Discount	Outstanding
01/10/2014	QE-Inv-006	Inv-006	Sales QE Invoice	45.00	9.00	54.00		54.00
						54.00		**54.00**

Lullabies Nursery (LUL002)

Date	Number	Reference	Type	Net	VAT	Total	Discount	Outstanding
01/10/2014	QE-Inv-005	Inv-005	Sales QE Invoice	100.00	20.00	120.00		120.00
01/10/2014			Customer Receipt			-726.90	0.00	0.00
						-606.90		**120.00**

Miss S Pargenter (PAR006)

Wed 25 Feb 2015, 10:34

Page 2 of 3

Date	Number	Reference	Type	Net	VAT	Total	Discount	Outstanding
01/10/2014	QE-Inv-003	Inv-003	Sales QE Invoice	12.00	2.40	14.40		0.00
08/10/2014	QE-CRN-001	CRN-001	Sales QE Credit	-12.00	-2.40	-14.40		0.00
						0.00		**0.00**

Mr A Smith (SMI009)

Date	Number	Reference	Type	Net	VAT	Total	Discount	Outstanding
01/10/2014	QE-Inv-004	Inv-004	Sales QE Invoice	600.00	120.00	720.00		720.00
						720.00		**720.00**

Shows all transactions for customers (i.e. purchases and receipts)

TotalPhoto Ltd

Customer Address List

Address Types: All

Customer Name	Address	Contact name	Phone	Mobile	Email	Fax
HMRC Reclaimed (HMRC Rec)	United Kingdom	Main Contact				
Mr W Haslam (HAS004)	Mr W Haslam 22 Brown Street Miltonby Lancashire LN87 6FD United Kingdom	Mr W Haslam				
Mrs H Poppy (POP002)	120 Forrest Way Miltonby Lancashire LN87 9YR United Kingdom	Mrs H Poppy				
Mrs T Pashby (PAS002)	30A Andrews Street Killington Lancashire LN85 6TT United Kingdom	Mrs T Pashby				

Shows address details, contact name etc. for customers

3 Supplier reports

TotalPhoto Ltd

Aged Creditors Report

To Date: 31/10/2014

Supplier	O/S Amt	< 30 days	< 60 days	< 90 days	< 120 days	Older
Arthur's Photographic Equipment Ltd (AP004)	£8,743.01	-£2,531.99	£11,275.00	£0.00	£0.00	£0.00
Mackay Films Ltd (MF001)	£595.87	£0.00	£595.87	£0.00	£0.00	£0.00
Mills Paper Products (MP002)	£5,115.32	£0.00	£5,115.32	£0.00	£0.00	£0.00
Octopus Inks Ltd (OI001)	£921.34	£0.00	£921.34	£0.00	£0.00	£0.00
The Stationery Cupboard (SC003)	£112.28	£0.00	£112.28	£0.00	£0.00	£0.00
	£15,487.82	**-£2,531.99**	**£18,019.81**	**£0.00**	**£0.00**	**£0.00**

Shows the outstanding creditor balances and the how long the debts have been in existence. The aging will be dynamic based on the 'To Date' i.e. retrospective aging calculation.

TotalPhoto Ltd

Supplier Activity Report

From Date: 01/10/2014

To Date: 31/10/2014

HMRC Payments (HMRC Pay)

No activity for the selected date range

Mackay Films Ltd (MF001)

Date	Number	Reference	Type	Net	VAT	Total	Discount	Outstanding
01/10/2014	QE-1341	1341	Purchase QE Invoice	208.76	41.75	250.51		250.51
						250.51		**250.51**

K2 Films Ltd (KF001)

Date	Number	Reference	Type	Net	VAT	Total	Discount	Outstanding
01/10/2014		Chq 246	Supplier Payment			-1,726.55	0.00	0.00
						-1,726.55		**0.00**

Wed 25 Feb 2015, 10:47

Page 1 of 3

The Stationery Cupboard (SC003)

Date	Number	Reference	Type	Net	VAT	Total	Discount	Outstanding
01/10/2014	QE-209	209	Purchase QE Invoice	14.65	2.93	17.58		17.58
01/10/2014	QE-216	216	Purchase QE Invoice	78.92	15.78	94.70		94.70
01/10/2014		Chq 245	Supplier Payment			-375.00	0.00	0.00
						-262.72		**112.28**

Mills Paper Products (MP002)

Date	Number	Reference	Type	Net	VAT	Total	Discount	Outstanding
01/10/2014	QE-10092	10092	Purchase QE Invoice	162.52	32.50	195.02		195.02
						195.02		**195.02**

Octopus Inks Ltd (OI001)

Date	Number	Reference	Type	Net	VAT	Total	Discount	Outstanding
01/10/2014	QE-2203	2203	Purchase QE Invoice	309.28	61.86	371.14		371.14
						371.14		**371.14**

Arthur's Photographic Equipment Ltd (AP004)

Date	Number	Reference	Type	Net	VAT	Total	Discount	Outstanding

Wed 25 Feb 2015, 10:47 Page 2 of 3

08/10/2014	QE-134C	134C	Purchase QE Credit	-2,109.99	-422.00	-2,531.99		-2,531.99
						-2,531.99		**-2,531.99**

Shows all transactions for a single, or range of, suppliers, including purchases, returns, payments etc.

TotalPhoto Ltd

Purchase Day Book Report

From Date: 01/10/2014

To Date: 31/10/2014

Trans ID	Type	Date	Name	Invoice Number	Ref	Details	Net	VAT	Total
33	Purchase QE Invoice	01/10/2014	Mackay Films Ltd	QE-1341	1341		208.76	41.75	250.51
34	Purchase QE Invoice	01/10/2014	The Stationery Cupboard	QE-209	209		14.65	2.93	17.58
35	Purchase QE Invoice	01/10/2014	The Stationery Cupboard	QE-216	216		78.92	15.78	94.70
36	Purchase QE Invoice	01/10/2014	Octopus Inks Ltd	QE-2203	2203		309.28	61.86	371.14
37	Purchase QE Invoice	01/10/2014	Mills Paper Products	QE-10092	10092		162.52	32.50	195.02
39	Purchase QE Credit	08/10/2014	Arthur's Photographic Equipment Ltd	QE-134C	134C	Faulty Camera	-2,109.99	-422.00	-2,531.99
							-1,335.86	**-267.18**	**-1,603.04**

Shows the list of all invoices received.

Supplier Address List

TotalPhoto Ltd

SageOne

Address Types: All

Supplier Name	Address	Contact name	Phone	Mobile	Email	Fax
HMRC Payments (HMRC Pay)	United Kingdom	Main Contact				
K2 Films Ltd (KF001)	Tokyo House 72-84 Great Milne Street London WC4 6DD United Kingdom	Kim Nakajima	0207 867 6599			
Mackay Films Ltd (MF001)	33 West Parade Miltonby Lancashire LN87 7HD United Kingdom	Carl Richardson	01828 827493			
Mills Paper Products (MP002)	405 Ream Road Bradford West Yorkshire BD5 6QA United Kingdom	Mr Shaun Squire	01726 378918			

Shows address details, contact name etc. for suppliers

4 Bank reports

Receipts & Payments Day Book Report

This report shows receipt or payment transactions for a selected bank account, for a specified date range.

Bank Account: Current (1200) | Receipt/Payment: Receipts | Type to search | Refine | Export

From Date: 01/10/2014 | To Date: 31/10/2014 | Type: All

Trans ID	Type	Date	Name	Ref	Net	VAT	Total
48	Other Receipt	01/10/2014		Cash Sales	40.00	8.00	48.00
49	Customer Receipt	01/10/2014	Lullabies Nursery				726.90
51	Customer Receipt	01/10/2014	Mrs H Poppy				120.00
71	Bank Receipt	01/10/2014		Interest Earned			11.22

Receipts & Payments Day Book Report

This report shows receipt or payment transactions for a selected bank account, for a specified date range.

Bank Account: Current (1200) | Receipt/Payment: Payments | Type to search | Refine | Export

From Date: 01/10/2014 | To Date: 31/10/2014 | Type: All

Trans ID	Type	Date	Name	Ref	Net	VAT	Total
64	Other Payment	01/10/2014		Chq 242	55.00	0.00	55.00
65	Other Payment	01/10/2014		Chq 243	107.65	21.53	129.18
66	Supplier Payment	01/10/2014	The Stationery Cupboard	Chq 245			375.00
67	Other Payment	01/10/2014		Chq 244	45.00	0.00	45.00
68	Bank Payment	01/10/2014		Bank Charge			31.41
70	Supplier Payment	01/10/2014	K2 Films Ltd	Chq 246			1,726.55
72	Other Payment	06/10/2014		Direct Debit	200.00	40.00	240.00

Shows all payments and/or receipts from the chosen bank account

TotalPhoto Ltd

Unreconciled Bank Transactions Report

Bank: Current (1200)

To Date: 25/02/2015

Account Balance at 'To Date': 8,723.74

Reconciled Balance at 'To Date': 10,825.29

Date	Name	Reference	Type	Payment	Receipt
01/10/2014	K2 Films Ltd	Chq 246	Supplier Payment	1,726.55	0.00
01/10/2014	The Stationery Cupboard	Chq 245	Supplier Payment	375.00	0.00
				2,101.55	**0.00**
				Total	**-2,101.55**

Shows all transactions that have yet to be matched and reconciled to the bank statement.

TotalPhoto Ltd

TotalPhoto Ltd
Unit 63 Bailey Industrial Estate Fornby Road Miltonby Lancashire
LD37 7QZ

Registered in England and Wales number 734928107

Telephone: 01949 969 378 **Website:** www.totalphotoltd.co.uk **VAT Number** 376 096 823

Bank Account Current (1200) **Statement Date** 15/10/2014

Reference Statement 10 **Reconciled By** Pierre Trimm

Date	Reference	Name	Category	Paid	Received
30/09/2014			Bank Opening Balance	0.00	10,293.00
01/10/2014	Cash Sales		Other Receipt	0.00	48.00
01/10/2014		Lullabies Nursery	Customer Receipt	0.00	726.90
01/10/2014		Mrs H Poppy	Customer Receipt	0.00	120.00
10/10/2014	000012345		Deposit: Cash in Hand	0.00	150.00
13/10/2014			Transfer: Cash in Hand	23.24	0.00
01/10/2014	Chq 242		Other Payment	55.00	0.00
01/10/2014	Chq 243		Other Payment	129.18	0.00
01/10/2014	Chq 244		Other Payment	45.00	0.00
01/10/2014	Bank Charge		Bank Payment	31.41	0.00
01/10/2014	Interest Earned		Bank Receipt	0.00	11.22
06/10/2014	Direct Debit		Other Payment	240.00	0.00

Total Received	11,349.12
Total Paid	523.83
Starting Balance	0.00
Statement End Balance	10,825.29
Reconciled Balance	10,825.29
Difference	0.00

Shows all bank transactions that have been successfully matched and reconciled to the bank statement

Recurring entries

12

LEARNING OBJECTIVES

LO4 Record bank and cash transactions and impact on cash flow forecast

4.2 Process recurring receipts and payments.

CONTENTS

1 Introduction

A company often pays and receives money on a regular basis. For example, it may pay bills monthly or quarterly to organisations for payment such as insurance or rates. Also, it may receive money regularly from customers or other parties, for example receipts for rental income. To make life easier, Sage One allows regular payments and receipts to be entered, automatically, as a '*recurring entry*'.

2 Creating a new recurring payment

How to process a recurring entry

Recurring payments and receipts are created from pre-existing transactions.

From the Banking tab, select the Current Account by clicking on it in the list.

From within the 'Activity' area inside the bank account record screen, locate the £240 direct debit payment for marketing from North West Radio.

This can be done simply using the date and/or 'transaction type' filters. In this example a combination of dates and search text 'direct debit' was used.

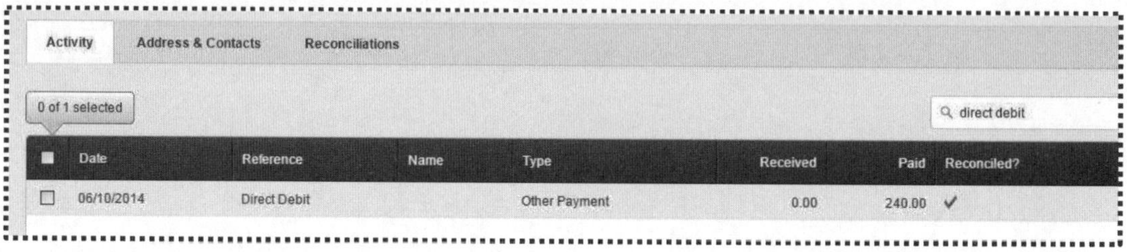

Select the payment transaction by clicking on it.

You will notice this item has been included in a bank reconciliation – it was identified during the bank reconciliation process.

A new button will be displaying on the payment transaction record.

Create Recurring Payment

Using this set up the 'Recurring Payment' as follows:

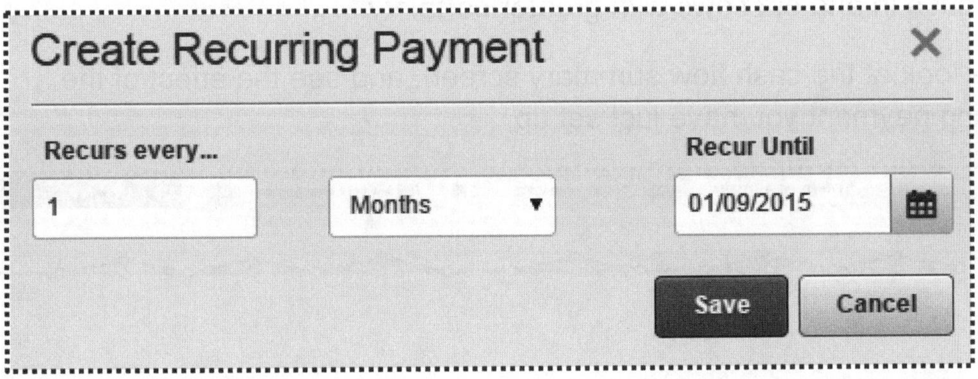
Create Recurring Payment
Recurs every...
1
Months
Recur Until
01/09/2015
Save
Cancel

This set up means the payment will recur once a month until a date set in the future.

The number of recurrences is determined by the numerical value you enter and the frequency you choose, i.e. weekly, monthly etc. ..

Change the refine filter, so that the 'To' date is equal to 'today' and you will notice the recurring transactions have been entered automatically up until either today or to the Recur until date – depending which is the oldest.

☐	06/10/2014	Direct Debit	Other Payment	0.00	240.00	✓
☐	06/11/2014	Direct Debit	Other Payment	0.00	240.00	
☐	06/12/2014	Direct Debit	Other Payment	0.00	240.00	
☐	06/01/2015	Direct Debit	Other Payment	0.00	240.00	
☐	06/02/2015	Direct Debit	Other Payment	0.00	240.00	⟳

The  symbol will appear against the last recurring transaction. If you wish to extend or stop the recurring period, select this item from the activity list and 
Edit Recurring Payment
or 
Stop recurrence
.

Cash flow Management

Sage One supports cash flow management. This topic is not covered in this manual, however it is worth point out that recurring receipts and payments, amongst other transaction types, all contribute to the cash flow forecast. This is particularly useful as Sage One allows you to predict your future cash in and out flows with greater certainty.

Take a look at the cash flow summary screen, and see the effect of the recurring payment you have just set up.

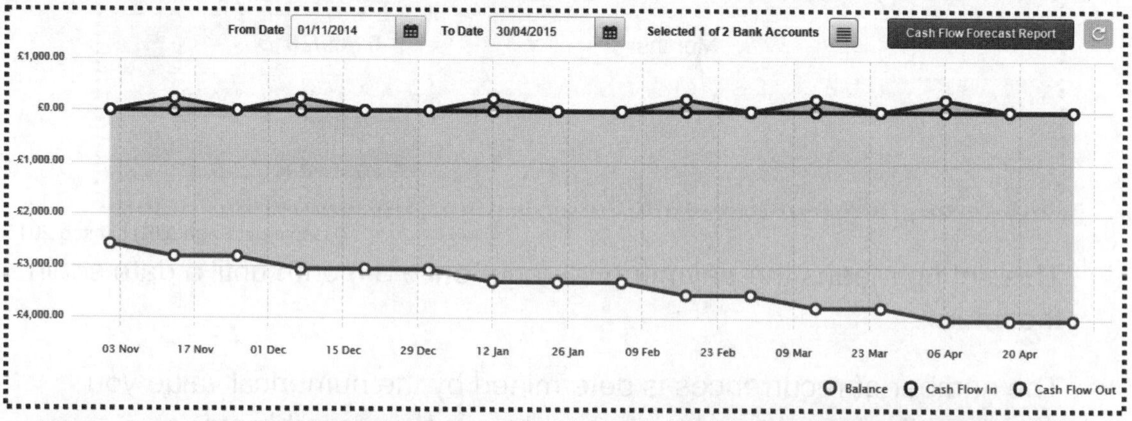

3 Recurring receipts

You are also able to process regular receipts via the recurring entry facility in Sage One. This is particularly useful for regular amounts sent to the business such as 'Rent Received'. These types of transactions would be processed in exactly the same way as a Recurring Payment, except the transaction type will be based on a previously created 'Other Receipt'.

Amending company details and managing data

13

KNOWLEDGE

There are no relevant 'learning outcomes' applicable to this section of the workbook, as the topics covered are not part of the assessment process. However, you are recommend to fully familiarise yourself with all aspects of this chapter.

CONTENTS

1 Amending data

As we have already seen, one way to correct an error is by means of a journal. This is essentially a book-keeping solution, using a double entry to correct or amend an earlier error. In Sage One we need to use a journal when the incorrect transaction is included in a reconciliation, VAT return or allocation. Reconciliations can, however, be reversed to allow amendment – make the amendment directly before reprocessing the allocation or reconciliation.

2 Resetting Data

When you are practising on Sage One, you may need to 'reset' data and start again from scratch. For example, this could be required if you have made significant errors or wish to work through an example again from scratch.

Resetting will remove all of the transactions and accounts set up data that have previously been entered, including any additional nominal codes, suppliers and customers etc. You will need to start right back at the beginning of this text.

Despite the severe implications of a data reset, it is a relatively straightforward process to follow:

From the  icon on the black navigation bar at the top of the screen, select 
Service Settings
and then 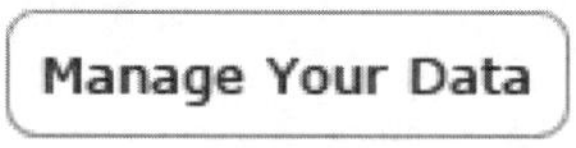
Manage Your Data
.

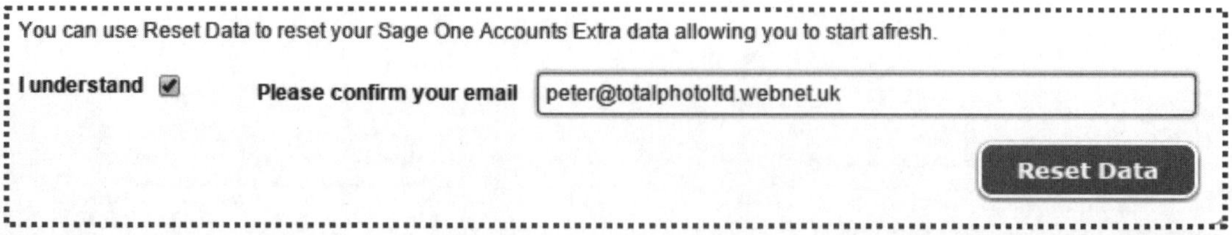
You can use Reset Data to reset your Sage One Accounts Extra data allowing you to start afresh.
I understand
Please confirm your email
peter@totalphotoltd.webnet.uk
Reset Data

This functionality is for use in your studies. You would be unlikely to use it in the workplace.

Creating a password to protect data

14

KNOWLEDGE	
LO7	Maintain the safety and security of data held in the computerised accounting system.
7.2	Use a software password to protect accounting information.

CONTENTS

1 Changing a password to protect data

It is important to protect your accounting data with the sufficient level of security. Sage One is highly secure on-line platform, however it is up to you to make sure your passwords not easily guessed by someone who may know some information about you. Your authentication provider including SageID will however ensure the length and content of the passwords and the types of security questions are of sufficient structure.

Depending how you have signed in to Sage One, will determine how you are authenticated and where you set up and manage your password.

If you have signed up with a SageID you will be able to manage your password and security directly from within Sage One itself.

If you have signed up via a third-party, such as Google or FaceBook, you will need to manage your security settings in those services.

SageID: How to change your password

If you need to change your password, from the icon located on the black navigation bar at the top of the screen, navigate via

User Settings / **Change Password and Security**

You are able to change your password and/or your security settings. Your existing password and questions will be required in order to make changes.

Follow the instructions on the screen.

PRACTICE ASSESSMENT

1 Practice assessment questions

The situation

This assignment is based on an existing business, Justin Timbercrafts, an organisation that makes small wooden toys which it sells to independent toy stores and the public. The owner of the business is Justin Wilson, who operates as a sole trader.

At the start of business, Justin initially operated a manual book-keeping system, but has now decided that from 1st August 2014, the accounting system will become computerised.

Justin's first set of trading accounts will include transactions for a period longer than 12 months, i.e. balances and expenditure from before 1st August 2014.

You are employed as an accounting technician in the business.

You can assume that all documentation within this assessment has been checked for accuracy and duly authorised by Justin.

The company details are:

Justin Timbercrafts
27 West Lane
Dornley
DN22 4RD

Sales are to be analysed in four ways:

- the Jungle Collection
- the Farm Collection
- the Pets Collection
- cash sales – to members of the public at the small factory shop.

The business is registered for VAT (Standard Scheme), and the rate charged on all items is the basic rate of 20%

All expenditure should be analysed as you feel appropriate.

You should set the system accounts start date at 1st August 2014 – the financial year end is 31st July 2015.

Task 1

Refer to the customer details below and set up customer records to open Sales Ledger Accounts for each customer.

Customer details

Customer Name, Address and Contact Details	Customer Account Code	Customer Account Details
Toyways plc 88 Main Street Longstan LG18 5DF Tel: 01872 6281923 Contact: Brian Mason	TW003	Credit Limit = £5,000 Payment Terms = 30 days Opening Balance = £1,235.76 (relates to invoice 00288 dated 15th July 2014)
Perfect Pastimes Ltd Hubley Industrial Estate Hubley HB29 7FD Tel: 07719 3612819 Contact: Stan Hartley	PP002	Credit Limit = £15,000 Payment Terms = 30 days Opening Balance = £13,209.34 (relates to invoice 00291 dated 17th July 2014)
Happykidz Ltd Churchill Shopping Centre Fearnley FN88 3DS Tel: 0727 4792982 Contact: Shane Humphries	HK006	Credit Limit = £8,000 Payment Terms = 30 days Opening Balance = £342.98 (relates to invoice 00299 dated 28th July 2014)
Prettypops Ltd 10 St Bart's Row Ganningly GN33 2WQ Tel: 0845 1982828 Contact: Betty Chamberlain	PP004	Credit Limit = £5,000 Payment Terms = 30 days Opening Balance = £190.87 (relates to invoice 00212 dated 17th July 2014)

Task 2

Refer to the Supplier Details below and create supplier records to open Purchase Ledger Accounts for each supplier.

Supplier name, address and contact details	Supplier Account Code	Supplier Account Details
Matchsticks Ltd Unit 66 Haxton HC99 7TG Tel : 02625 3890101 Contact: Amjid Khan	MCS003	Credit Limit = £5000 Payment Terms = 30 days Opening Balance = £1943.26 (relates to Invoice 2033 dated 18 July 2014)
Willow Works Ltd Ceder House Lanchester LN33 7DK Tel: 07727 3737281 Contact: Hin Lan Hun	WWW002	Credit Limit = £8,500 Payment Terms= 30 days Opening Balance = £288.29 (relates to Invoice 38842 dated 20 July 2014)
Grange Toys Ltd The Lodge Kilminster KG18 6GC Tel : 0845 2831298 Contact: Jake Newlove	GRT005	Credit Limit = £10,000 Payment Terms = 30 days Opening Balance = £4,277.50 (relates to Invoice GT2640 dated 12 July 2014)
FLW Ltd 199 Duncan Avenue Hurtleby HB28 4FS Tel : 07227 2903832 Contact: Emma Rose	FLW002	Credit Limit = £3,000 Payment Terms = 14 days Opening Balance = £923.46 (relates to Invoice 2727 dated 20 July 2014)
Dornley Evening Chronicle 11 Dundee Street Dornley DN22 6FD Tel : 01822 2818811 Contact: Holly Maclay	DEC004	Credit Limit = £1,000 Payment Terms = 30 days Opening Balance = £0.00

Task 3.1

Create new, or amend the following nominal codes

Account number	Account name
4000	Sales – Jungle Collection
4001	Sales – Farm Collection
4002	Sales – Pets Collection
4003	Cash Sales
3260	Drawings
7100	Rent and Rates

Task 3.2

Refer to the list of nominal ledger balances below. Enter the opening balances onto the computerised accounting system, making sure you select the appropriate nominal ledger account codes.

List of nominal ledger closing balances as at the 31st July 2014 i.e. - from the manual system and prior period:

Account Name	£ **DR**	£ **CR**
Motor Vehicles	4,586.00	
IT Equipment	3684.00	
Bank Current Account*	11,203.30	
Petty Cash*	150.00	
*Sales Ledger Control Account**	*14978.95*	
*Purchase Ledger Control Account**		*7432.51*
Sales – Jungle Collection		17,293.50
Sales – Farm Collection		19,224.70
Sales – Pets Collection		10,260.45
Cash Sales		5,431.40
Owner Investment		20,000.00
Rent and Rates	2,400.00	
Insurance	720.00	
Marketing	1,420.00	
Cost of Sales - Materials	28,344.80	
Office costs	2,350.00	
Motor (Expenses)	9805.51	
**You do not need to enter these figures as you have already entered opening balances for customers and suppliers*	**79,642.56**	**79,642.56**

Task 3.3

Transfer £1000.00 from the bank current account to the bank deposit account. Enter this on to the computerised accounting system using reference TRF01 dated 1st August 2014.

You will first need to set up a Bank Deposit Account (Savings).

Task 3.4

Print out the following reports and **identify and correct any errors**.

- Customer Address List
- Supplier Address List
- Trial Balance Report (select dates 1st July 14 until 1st Aug 14)

Task 4

You have received the following e-mail from FLW Ltd (a supplier). Enter the new address and telephone number into the accounting system.

> To: accounts@justintimbercrafts.webnet.uk
>
> From: emmarose@networks.com
>
> Date: 29/07/2014
>
> Hi there
>
> Just to let you know that we are moving! From 31st July our new address will be Emsley House, Radleigh, RD77 3ED.
>
> Our new phone number is 01442 7373218
>
> Please ensure that you update all records with this change in address
>
> Kind regards
>
> Emma

Task 5

Enter the following sales invoices and credit note onto the computerised accounting system – using 'Quick Entries'.

Justin Timbercrafts
27 West Lane
Dornley
DN22 4RD
"Quality Wooden Toys at Affordable Prices"

INVOICE 00300
Tax Point : 2nd August 2014 VAT Registration Number: 4839101298

Happykidz Ltd
Churchill Shopping Centre
Fearnley
FN88 3DS

Farm Collections × 8	£7.00	£56.00
Jungle Collections × 10	£9.00	£90.00
		£146.00
VAT @ 20.0%		£29.20
TOTAL FOR PAYMENT		£175.20

Terms: 30 days

Justin Timbercrafts
27 West Lane
Dornley
DN22 4RD
"Quality Wooden Toys at Affordable Prices"

INVOICE 00301
Tax Point : 2nd August 2014 VAT Registration Number: 4839101298

Toyways plc
88 Main Street
Longstan
LG18 5DF

Farm Collections × 5	£7.00	£35.00
Jungle Collections × 5	£9.00	£45.00
Pets Collections × 5	£9.00	£45.00
		£125.00
VAT @ 20.0%		£25.00
TOTAL FOR PAYMENT		£150.00

Terms: 30 days

Justin Timbercrafts

27 West Lane
Dornley
DN22 4RD

"Quality Wooden Toys at Affordable Prices"

INVOICE 00302
Tax Point : 4th August 2014 VAT Registration Number: 4839101298

Happykidz Ltd
Churchill Shopping Centre
Fearnley
FN88 3DS

Farm Collections × 4	£7.00	£28.00
Pets Collections × 8	£9.00	£72.00
		£100.00
VAT @ 20.0%		£20.00
TOTAL FOR PAYMENT		£120.00

Terms: 30 days

Justin Timbercrafts

27 West Lane
Dornley
DN22 4RD

"Quality Wooden Toys at Affordable Prices"

CREDIT NOTE 55
Tax Point : 2nd August 2014 VAT Registration Number: 4839101298

Happykidz Ltd
Churchill Shopping Centre
Fearnley
FN88 3DS

Farm Collections × 2 (Broken)	£7.00	£14.00
VAT @ 20.0%		£2.80
TOTAL FOR PAYMENT		£16.80

Terms: 30 days

Task 6

Enter the following purchases invoices onto the computer system using 'Quick Entries'.

Date	Supplier	Invoice No	Gross £	VAT £	Net £	Materials	Advertising
2/8/14	Dornley Evening Chronicle	2929/11	156.00	26.00	130.00		130.00
3/8/14	Grange Toys Ltd	GT2882	1,272.00	212.00	1,060.00	1,060.00	
6/8/14	Willow Works Ltd	99128	288.00	48.00	240.00	240.00	
	Totals		**1,716.00**	**286.00**	**1,430.00**	**1,300.00**	**130.00**

Task 7

Refer to the following summary of payments received from customers and made to suppliers. Enter the receipts and payments into the computer, making sure you allocate all amounts as shown in the details column.

Cheque / BACS Receipts Listing

Date	Details	Customer	£	How Received
03 Aug 14	Payment of opening balance	Toyways plc	1235.76	Cheque
05 Aug 14	Payment of opening balance	Happykidz Ltd	342.98	BACS

Cheques Paid Listing

Date	Details	Supplier	£	Cheque Number
04 Aug 14	Payment of opening balance	FLW Ltd	923.46	0012671
04 Aug 14	Payment of opening balance	Matchsticks Ltd	1943.26	0012672

Task 8

Refer to the following email from Justin:

email

From : Justin@justintimbercrafts.co.uk

To : accounts@justintimbercrafts.co.uk

Date: 5 August 2014

Subject: Prettypops Ltd

Hi

I'm afraid that Prettypops Ltd have gone into liquidation – I've just had a letter from their administrators. It looks most unlikely we will get anything for their outstanding account – which stands at £190.87.

Please write this amount off as a bad debt.

Thanks

Justin

Print a new customer 'Activity Report' showing the amount written off and the new balance of nil. Treat using NO VAT.

Note: Before you perform the write-off transaction, you will need to ensure the bad debts nominal account is visible in the sales area – go to chart of accounts set up.

Task 9

Enter the following petty cash payments into the computerised system:-

Petty Cash Voucher
Voucher no 10

Date 5 August 2014

Details	
Window cleaner (*NO VAT*) Receipt attached	£20.00

Petty Cash Voucher
Voucher no 11

Date 5 August 2014

Details	
5 × New calculators	£20.00
VAT	£4.00
Total	£24.00
Receipt attached	

Task 10

Refer to the following cash sales and enter receipts into the computer. Use the bank current account for this transaction and enter 'cash sales' as the optional customer details & reference.

Date	*Receipt type*	*Gross*	*VAT*	*NET*	*Nominal code*
1st Aug	Cash sale	78.24	13.04	65.20	4003
4th Aug	Cash sale	102.30	17.05	85.25	4003

Task 11

Enter the following journal onto the computerised accounting system.

Reference: JNL01			
Date	**Account Name & Code**	**Dr**	**Cr**
25/8/14	Owner Drawings	200.00	
	Bank Current Account		200.00
Being the transfer of cash for Justin Wilson's personal use.			

Task 12

Refer to the following email from Justin:

email

From : Justin@justintimbercrafts.co.uk

To : accounts@justintimbercrafts.co.uk

Date: 6 August 2014

Subject: Opening Balances

Could you please enter the details of a new customer that I have agreed terms with this morning? You will need to set up a new customer record for them with an opening balance of nil.

The details are:

Funnystuff Ltd
31 Yew Tree Way
Hedgefield
HD43 2WA

Contact: James Strong

The settlement terms are 30 days with a credit limit of £1,000.

Please use account code FS001 for this customer

Thanks

Justin

Task 13

Once you have opened up a new customer record for Funnystuff, print the address list report for the new customer showing the name and address details.

Refer to the following sales invoice for the new customer Funnystuff Ltd, and existing customer Toyways Plc. Enter the two invoices (detailed on the following page) onto the computer system.

Justin Timbercrafts
27 West Lane
Dornley
DN22 4RD
"Quality Wooden Toys at Affordable Prices"

INVOICE 00303
Tax Point : 6th August 2014 VAT Registration Number: 4839101298

Funnystuff Ltd
31 Yew Tree Way
Hedgefield
HD43 2WA

Farm Collections × 5	£7.00	£35.00
Pets Collections × 5	£9.00	£45.00
		£80.00
VAT @ 20.0%		£16.00
TOTAL FOR PAYMENT		£96.00

Terms: 30 days

Justin Timbercrafts
27 West Lane
Dornley
DN22 4RD
"Quality Wooden Toys at Affordable Prices"

INVOICE 00304
Tax Point : 6th August 2014 VAT Registration Number: 4839101298

Toyways plc
88 Main Street
Longstan
LG18 5DF

Pets Collections × 30	£9.00	£270.00
VAT @ 20.0%		£54.00
TOTAL FOR PAYMENT		£324.00

Terms: 30 days

Task 14

Enter the following purchase invoices into the computer system.

Date	*Supplier Name*	*Invoice Number*	*Gross £*	*VAT £*	*Net £*	*Materials £*	*Advertising £*
8/8/14	Matchsticks Ltd	3178	1680.00	280.00	1400.00	1400.00	
11/8/14	Grange Toys Ltd	GT2916	672.00	112.00	560.00	560.00	
		Total	**2352.00**	**392.00**	**1960.00**	**1960.00**	

Task 15

Refer to the following summary of payments received from customers and made to suppliers. Enter the receipts and payments into the bank current account, making sure you allocate all amounts as shown in the details column.

Cheque / BACS Receipts Listing

Date	*Details*	*Customer*	*£*	*How Received*
11/8/14	Payment of Invoice 00300 including credit note CN55	Happykidz Ltd	158.40	BACS

Cheques Paid Listing

Date	*Details*	*Supplier*	*£*	*Cheque Number*
11/8/14	Payment of opening balance	Willow Works Ltd	288.29	0012674
14/8/14	Part-payment of opening balance	Grange Toys Ltd	3000.00	0012675
14/8/14	Payment of Invoice 2929/11	Dornley Evening Chronicle	156.00	0012676

Task 16

Refer to the following petty cash vouchers and enter into the computerised system:

Petty Cash Voucher

Voucher 12

Date 12 August 2014

Details	
Train fare – exempt for VAT	
	£14.80
Receipt attached	

Petty Cash Voucher

Voucher 13

Date 14 August 2014

Details	
Photocopy paper	£8.50
VAT	£1.70
Total	£10.20
Receipt attached	

Task 17

Refer to the following e-mail from Justin:

email

From : Justin@justintimbercrafts.co.uk

To : accounts@justintimbercrafts.co.uk

Date: 14 August 2014

Subject: Bank Loan

Hi

I don't know if you remember me telling you but I applied for a business loan of £10,000.00 a few weeks ago. This has been granted and has been received into the bank current account today. Please can you ensure that you enter this into the computer system.

Thanks

Justin

Enter the following bank transfer to record the receipt of the above bank loan. (From loan account to current account.)

You will need to set up a bank account for the loan – account type: loan – ledger code 1230 – no opening balance.

Reference: TFR01			
Date	**Account Name & Code**	**Dr**	**Cr**
14/8/14	Bank Current Account	10000.00	
	Bank Loan Account		10000.00
Being the receipt of loan proceeds.			

Task 18

Refer to the following receipt for the purchase of a new picture, paid for by petty cash. Use voucher code 14 for this transaction. This is a picture for the office wall, so should be coded to 'Office Costs'.

Receipt Number 1289

Art of the Matter

Kitchener Shopping Centre

Miltonby

VAT Reg: 343 4839 47

Date : 14 August 2014

Received from Justin Timbercrafts, by cash, for original print

£25 inc VAT

Task 19

Refer to the following schedule of standing orders. You need to set these up as recurring receipts (using 'Other Payments') on the computer system. Both of the payments should be set up exempt of VAT.

- Post the first payments on the start dates.
- Set up a recurring entry for each transaction as shown in the standing order schedule below.
- Print a screen shot of the screen setting up the recurring entries.

Please note that you do need to set the dates correctly or the recurring entries will continue indefinitely.

Details	**Amount**	**Frequency**	**Total payments**	**Payment start date**	**Payment finish date**
P Smith (Rent)	£400	Monthly	12	18 August 2014	18 July 2015
Details	**Amount**	**Frequency**	**Total payments**	**Payment start date**	**Payment finish date**
Dornley Council (Rates)	£120.00	Monthly	12	28 August 2014	28 July 2015

Task 20

Process the following journal. The sum of £150.00 for insurance costs have been incorrectly posted to the Repairs and renewals account in error. Enter the following journal to correct the error using reference no:

Journal – 20 August 2014		
Ref : JNL02	**Dr £**	**Cr £**
Insurance Repairs and renewals *Being correction of error recording insurance as repair costs*	150.00	 150.00

Task 21

Refer to the email below from Justin:

> **email**
>
> From : Justin@justintimbercrafts.co.uk
>
> To : accounts@justintimbercrafts.co.uk
>
> Date: 31st August 2014
>
> Subject: Petty cash
>
> Hi
>
> Please transfer £94.00 from the bank account to the petty cash account to reimburse the petty cash float – this should reinstate it to £150.00. Use reference TFR02 for this transaction.
>
> Thanks
>
> Justin

Task 22

An office printer has been purchased for £250.00 including VAT. This was paid for via the bank current account (cheque no 0012673 on 9/8/2014). Process this payment on the computer system. (IT equipment cost 0030.)

Task 23

You are given the following bank statement and are asked to produce a bank reconciliation as at 31 August, processing any adjustments that may be necessary. Enter the bank charges (no VAT) which have not yet been accounted for. Reconcile the bank statement.

MIDWEST BANK plc
109 Church Street
Dornley
DN12 5DE

Justin Timbercrafts
27 West Lane
Dornley
DN22 4RD

Account Number : 341723810

31 August 2014

Statement of Account – Sheet 819

Date (2014)	Details	Paid out £	Paid in £	Balance £
1 August	Opening Balance			11203.30 Cr
01/08/2014	Transfer	1000.00		10203.30 Cr
02/08/2014	Counter credit		78.24	10281.54 Cr
04/08/2014	Counter credit		102.30	10383.84 Cr
05/08/2014	BGC		1235.76	11619.60 Cr
05/08/2014	BACS Receipt		342.98	11962.58 Cr
10/08/2014	Chq 0012671	923.46		11039.12 Cr
11/08/2014	BACS receipt		158.40	11197.52 Cr
12/08/2014	Chq 0012672	1943.26		9254.26 Cr
12/08/2014	Chq 0012673	250.00		9004.26 Cr
14/08/2014	Loan proceeds		10000.00	19004.26 Cr
15/08/2014	Chq 0012675	3000.00		16004.26 Cr
15/08/2014	Direct Debit	400.00		15604.26 Cr
16/08/2014	Direct Debit	120.00		15484.26 Cr
25/08/2014	Counter debit	200.00		15284.26 Cr
28/08/2014	Bank Charges	32.00		15252.26 Cr
31/08/2014	Counter credit	94.00		15158.26 Cr
31/08/2014	Closing Balance			15158.26 Cr

CR = Credit
DR = Debit

Task 24

Print the following reports:

- Customer Activity report - for all customers from 31st July until 31st August – print to PDF
- Supplier Activity report - for all customers from 31st July until 31st August - print to PDF
- Trial Balance for the month of August (include opening balance dated 31st July) - print to PDF
- Audit Trail for August (detailed – transactions only) print to CSV
- Aged Creditors Report (summary) as at 31st August 2014 - Screen View
- Aged Debtors Report (summary) as at 31st August 2014 – Screen View
- Nominal Ledger Activity Report for the following accounts from 31st July until 31st August – print to PDF
  - (a) Bank Current Account
  - (b) Petty Cash Account (Cash in Hand)
- Bank Statement Reconciliation Report – Statement 31st Aug 14

PRACTICE ASSESSMENT ANSWERS

2 Practice assessment answers

Task 3.4 Customer Address List

Justin Timbercrafts

Customer Address List

Address Types: All

Customer Name	Address	Contact name	Phone	Mobile	Email	Fax
HMRC Reclaimed (HMRC Rec)	United Kingdom	Main Contact				
Toyways plc (TW003)	88 Main Street Longstan LG18 5DF United Kingdom	Brian Mason	01872 6281923			
Perfect Pastimes Ltd (PP002)	Hubley Industrial Estate Hubley FN88 3DS United Kingdom	Stan Hartley	07719 3612819			
Happykidz Ltd (HK006)	Churchill Shopping Centre Fearnley FN88 3DS United Kingdom	Shane Humphries	07719 3612819			
Prettypops Ltd (PP004)	10 St Bart's Row Ganningly GN33 2WQ United Kingdom	Betty Chamberlain	0845 1982828			

Task 3.4 Supplier Address List

Justin Timbercrafts

Supplier Address List

Address Types: All

Supplier Name	Address	Contact name	Phone	Mobile	Email	Fax
HMRC Payments (HMRC Pay)	United Kingdom	Main Contact				
Matchsticks Ltd (MCS003)	Unit 66 Haxton HC99 7TG United Kingdom	Amjid Khan	02625 3890101			
Willow Works Ltd (WWW002)	Ceder House Lanchester LN33 7DK United Kingdom	Hin Lan Hun	07727 3737281			
Grange Toys Ltd (GRT005)	The Lodge Kilminster KG18 6GC United Kingdom	Jake Newlove	0845 2831298			
FLW Ltd (FLW002)	199 Duncan Avenue Hurtleby HB28 4FS United Kingdom	Emma Rose	07227 2903832			
Domley Evening Chronicle (DEC004)	11 Dundee Street Domley HB28 4FS United Kingdom	Holly Maclay	01822 2818811			

Wed 11 Mar 2015, 16:03

Page 1

Task 3.4 Trial Balance

Justin Timbercrafts

Trial Balance Report

From Date: 01/07/2014 To Date: 01/08/2014

Nominal Code	Name	Debits	Credits
1100	Sales invoices not paid	14,978.95	
1200	Cash at Bank	10,203.30	
1210	Cash in Hand	150.00	
1220	Deposit Account	1,000.00	
2100	Purchase invoices not paid		7,432.51
3200	Owner Investment		20,000.00
4000	Sales - Jungle Collection		17,293.50
4001	Sales - Farm Collection		19,224.70
4002	Sales - Pets Collection		10,260.45
4003	Sales - Cash Sales		5,431.40
5010	Cost of Sales - Materials	28,344.80	
6200	Marketing	1,420.00	
7100	Rent & Rates	2,400.00	
7300	Motor	9,805.51	
7500	Office costs	2,350.00	
7610	Insurance	720.00	
9998	Opening Balances Control Account	8,270.00	
Total		**79,642.56**	**79,642.56**

Task 8 Customer Activity Report

Justin Timbercrafts

Customer Activity Report

From Date: 01/07/2014

To Date: 31/08/2014

Prettypops Ltd (PP004)

Date	Number	Reference	Type	Net	VAT	Total	Discount	Outstanding
17/07/2014		00212	Customer OB Invoice	190.87	0.00	190.87		190.87
05/08/2014		W-OFF	Sales QE Credit	-190.87	0.00	-190.87		-190.87
						0.00		**0.00**

Task 13 New Customer Record

Justin Timbercrafts

Customer Address List

Address Types: All

Customer Name	Address	Contact name	Phone	Mobile	Email	Fax
Funnystuff Ltd (FS001)	31 Yew Tree Way Hedgefield HD43 2WA United Kingdom	James Strong				

Task 19 Recurring entry screen shots

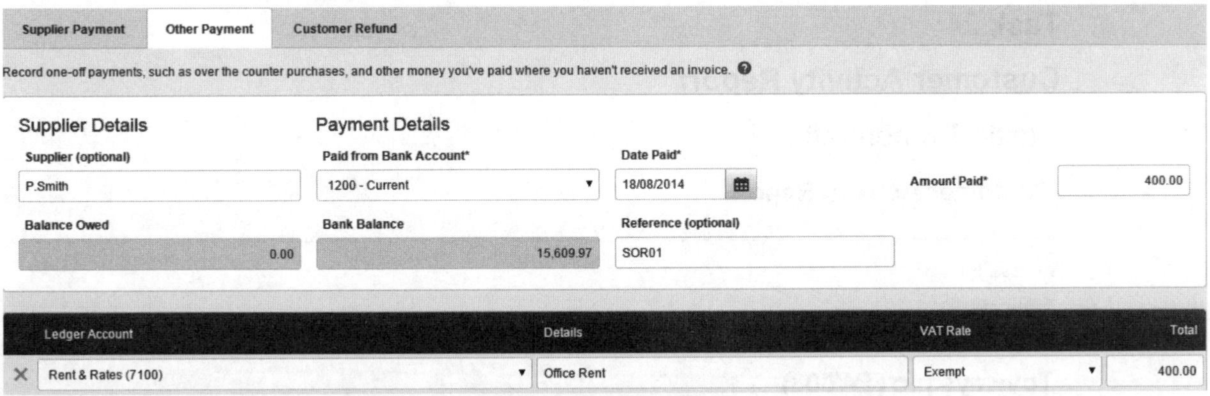
Supplier Payment
Other Payment
Customer Refund
Record one-off payments, such as over the counter purchases, and other money you've paid where you haven't received an invoice.
Supplier Details
Supplier (optional)
P.Smith
Balance Owed
0.00
Payment Details
Paid from Bank Account*
1200 - Current
Bank Balance
15,609.97
Date Paid*
18/08/2014
Reference (optional)
SOR01
Amount Paid*
400.00
Ledger Account
Details
VAT Rate
Total
Rent & Rates (7100)
Office Rent
Exempt
400.00

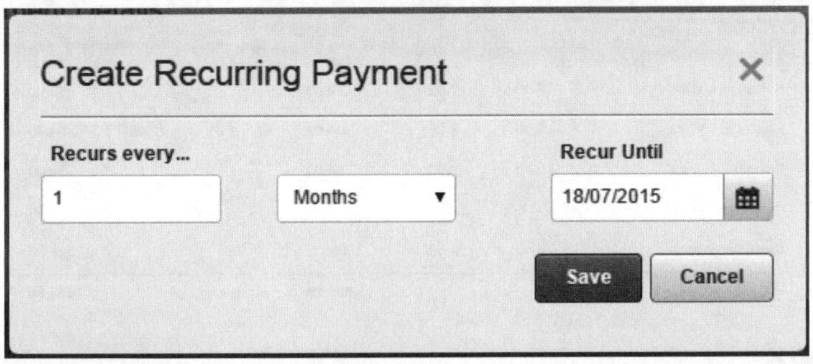
Create Recurring Payment
Recurs every...
1
Months
Recur Until
18/07/2015
Save
Cancel

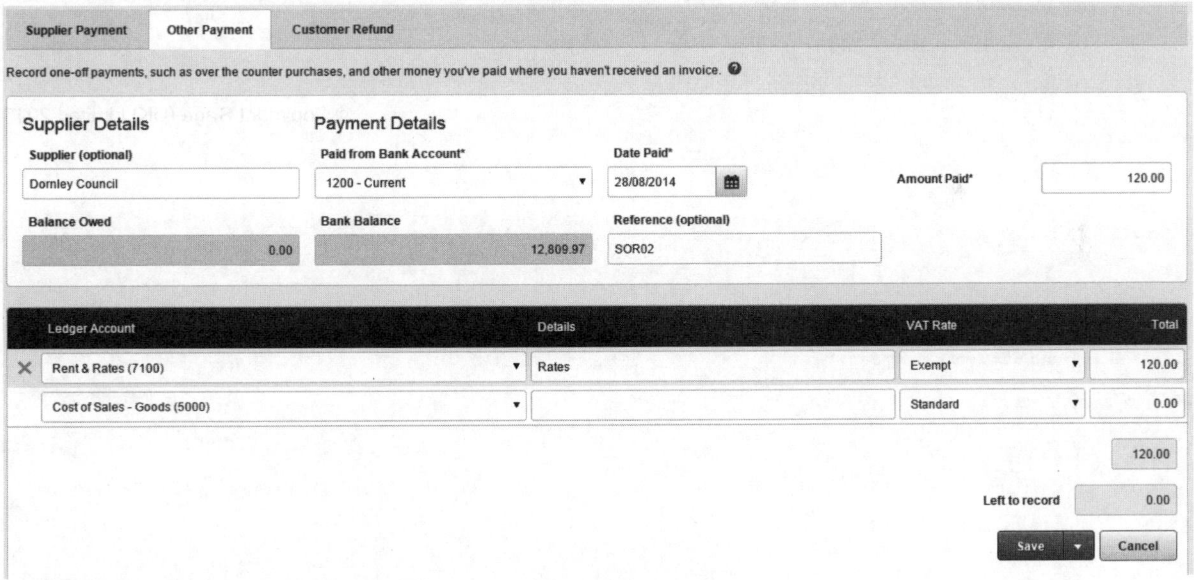
Supplier Payment
Other Payment
Customer Refund
Record one-off payments, such as over the counter purchases, and other money you've paid where you haven't received an invoice.
Supplier Details
Supplier (optional)
Dornley Council
Balance Owed
0.00
Payment Details
Paid from Bank Account*
1200 - Current
Bank Balance
12,809.97
Date Paid*
28/08/2014
Reference (optional)
SOR02
Amount Paid*
120.00
Ledger Account
Details
VAT Rate
Total
Rent & Rates (7100)
Rates
Exempt
120.00
Cost of Sales - Goods (5000)
Standard
0.00
120.00
Left to record
0.00
Save
Cancel

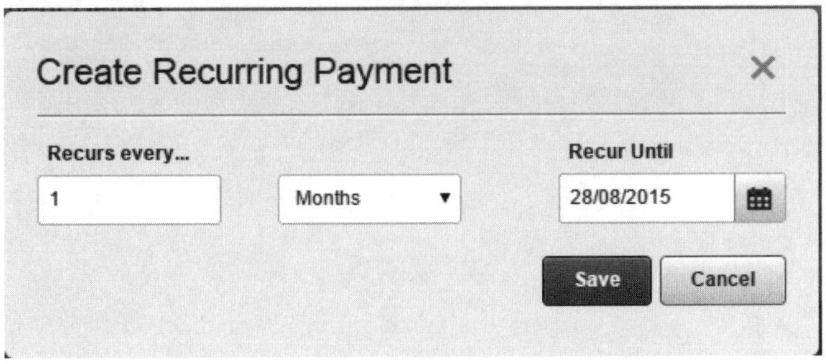
Create Recurring Payment
Recurs every...
1
Months
Recur Until
28/08/2015
Save
Cancel

Task 24

Customer Activity Report

Justin Timbercrafts

Customer Activity Report

From Date: 31/07/2014

To Date: 31/08/2014

Toyways plc (TW003)

Date	Number	Reference	Type	Net	VAT	Total	Discount	Outstanding
02/08/2014		00301	Sales QE Invoice	35.00	7.00	42.00		42.00
02/08/2014		00301	Sales QE Invoice	45.00	9.00	54.00		54.00
02/08/2014		00301	Sales QE Invoice	45.00	9.00	54.00		54.00
03/08/2014		CHEQUE	Customer Receipt			-1,235.76	0.00	0.00
06/08/2014		00304	Sales QE Invoice	270.00	54.00	324.00		324.00
						-761.76		**474.00**

Perfect Pastimes Ltd (PP002)

No activity for the selected date range

Happykidz Ltd (HK006)

Fri 13 Mar 2015, 12:02 Page 1

Date	Number	Reference	Type	Net	VAT	Total	Discount	Outstanding
02/08/2014		00300	Sales QE Invoice	56.00	11.20	67.20		0.00
02/08/2014		00300	Sales QE Invoice	90.00	18.00	108.00		0.00
02/08/2014		55	Sales QE Credit	-14.00	-2.80	-16.80		0.00
04/08/2014		00302	Sales QE Invoice	28.00	5.60	33.60		33.60
04/08/2014		00302	Sales QE Invoice	72.00	14.40	86.40		86.40
05/08/2014		BACS	Customer Receipt			-342.98	0.00	0.00
11/08/2014		BACS	Customer Receipt			-158.40	0.00	0.00
						-222.98		**120.00**

Prettypops Ltd (PP004)

Date	Number	Reference	Type	Net	VAT	Total	Discount	Outstanding
05/08/2014		W-OFF	Sales QE Credit	-190.87	0.00	-190.87		-190.87
						-190.87		**-190.87**

Funnystuff Ltd (FS001)

Date	Number	Reference	Type	Net	VAT	Total	Discount	Outstanding
06/08/2014		00303	Sales QE Invoice	35.00	7.00	42.00		42.00
06/08/2014		00303	Sales QE Invoice	45.00	9.00	54.00		54.00
						96.00		**96.00**

Task 24 Supplier Activity Report

Justin Timbercrafts

Supplier Activity Report

From Date: 31/07/2014

To Date: 31/08/2015

Matchsticks Ltd (MCS003)

Date	Number	Reference	Type	Net	VAT	Total	Discount	Outstanding
04/08/2014		CHEQUE: 0012672	Supplier Payment			-1,943.26	0.00	0.00
08/08/2014		3178	Purchase QE Invoice	1,400.00	280.00	1,680.00		1,680.00
						-263.26		**1,680.00**

Willow Works Ltd (WWW002)

Date	Number	Reference	Type	Net	VAT	Total	Discount	Outstanding
06/08/2014	QE-99128	99128	Purchase QE Invoice	240.00	48.00	288.00		288.00
11/08/2014		Cheque 0012674	Supplier Payment			-288.29	0.00	0.00
						-0.29		**288.00**

Grange Toys Ltd (GRT005)

Fri 13 Mar 2015, 13:05

Page 1

Date	Number	Reference	Type	Net	VAT	Total	Discount	Outstanding
03/08/2014	QE-GT2882	GT2882	Purchase QE Invoice	1,060.00	212.00	1,272.00		1,272.00
11/08/2014		GT2916	Purchase QE Invoice	560.00	112.00	672.00		672.00
14/08/2014		Cheque 0012675	Supplier Payment			-3,000.00	0.00	0.00
						-1,056.00		**1,944.00**

FLW Ltd (FLW002)

Date	Number	Reference	Type	Net	VAT	Total	Discount	Outstanding
04/08/2014		CHEQUE: 0012671	Supplier Payment			-923.46	0.00	0.00
						-923.46		**0.00**

Dornley Evening Chronicle (DEC004)

Date	Number	Reference	Type	Net	VAT	Total	Discount	Outstanding
02/08/2014	QE-2929/11	2929/11	Purchase QE Invoice	130.00	26.00	156.00		0.00
14/08/2014		Cheque 0012676	Supplier Payment			-156.00	0.00	0.00
						0.00		**0.00**

Task 24 Trial Balance as 31st August

Trial Balance Report

From Date: 31/07/2014 To Date: 31/08/2014

Nominal Code	Name	Debits	Credits
0030	IT equipment cost	208.33	
1100	Sales invoices not paid		1,079.61
1200	Cash at Bank	14,713.97	
1210	Cash in Hand	150.00	
1220	Deposit Account	1,000.00	
1230	Business Loan		10,000.00
2100	Purchase invoices not paid	2,243.01	
2200	VAT on Sales		171.49
2201	VAT on Purchases	732.01	
3200	Owner Investment		20,000.00
3260	Owner Drawings	200.00	
4000	Sales - Jungle Collection		17,428.50
4001	Sales - Farm Collection		19,364.70
4002	Sales - Pets Collection		10,692.45
4003	Sales - Cash Sales		5,581.85
5000	Cost of Sales - Goods	560.00	
5010	Cost of Sales - Materials	31,044.80	
6200	Marketing	1,550.00	
7100	Rent & Rates	2,920.00	
7300	Motor	9,805.51	
7400	Travel and Entertainment	12.33	
7500	Office costs	2,419.33	

Fri 13 Mar 2015, 13:18 Page 1 of 2

7610	Insurance	870.00	
7800	Repairs and renewals		150.00
7900	Bank charges & interest	32.00	
8100	Bad debt	190.87	
9998	Opening Balances Control Account	15,816.44	
	Total	84,468.60	84,468.60

Task 24 Audit Trail for August

	A	B	C	D	E	F	G	H	I	J	K
1	From Date	01/08/2014									
2	To Date	31/08/2014									
3	Type	All									
4	Trans ID	Entry Date	Created By	Trans Date	Name	Type	Invoice Number	Ref	Ledger Account	Debit	Credit
5	13	11/03/2015	Justin Wilson	01/08/2014		Bank Transfer		TRF01	Cash at Bank (1200)	0	1,000.00
6	13	11/03/2015	Justin Wilson	01/08/2014		Bank Transfer		TRF01	Deposit Account (1220)	1,000.00	0
7	14	11/03/2015	Justin Wilson	02/08/2014	Happykidz Ltd (HK006)	Sales QE Invoice		300	Sales - Farm Collection (4001)	0	56
8	14	11/03/2015	Justin Wilson	02/08/2014	Happykidz Ltd (HK006)	Sales QE Invoice		300	VAT on Sales (2200)	0	11.2
9	14	11/03/2015	Justin Wilson	02/08/2014	Happykidz Ltd (HK006)	Sales QE Invoice		300	Sales invoices not paid (1100)	67.2	0
10	15	11/03/2015	Justin Wilson	02/08/2014	Happykidz Ltd (HK006)	Sales QE Invoice		300	Sales - Jungle Collection (4000)	0	90
11	15	11/03/2015	Justin Wilson	02/08/2014	Happykidz Ltd (HK006)	Sales QE Invoice		300	VAT on Sales (2200)	0	18
12	15	11/03/2015	Justin Wilson	02/08/2014	Happykidz Ltd (HK006)	Sales QE Invoice		300	Sales invoices not paid (1100)	108	0
13	16	11/03/2015	Justin Wilson	02/08/2014	Toyways plc (TW003)	Sales QE Invoice		301	Sales - Farm Collection (4001)	0	35
14	16	11/03/2015	Justin Wilson	02/08/2014	Toyways plc (TW003)	Sales QE Invoice		301	VAT on Sales (2200)	0	7
15	16	11/03/2015	Justin Wilson	02/08/2014	Toyways plc (TW003)	Sales QE Invoice		301	Sales invoices not paid (1100)	42	0
16	16	11/03/2015	Justin Wilson	02/08/2014	Toyways plc (TW003)	Sales QE Invoice		301	Sales - Farm Collection (4001)	35	0
17	16	11/03/2015	Justin Wilson	02/08/2014	Toyways plc (TW003)	Sales QE Invoice		301	VAT on Sales (2200)	7	0
18	16	11/03/2015	Justin Wilson	02/08/2014	Toyways plc (TW003)	Sales QE Invoice		301	Sales invoices not paid (1100)	0	42
19	17	11/03/2015	Justin Wilson	02/08/2014	Toyways plc (TW003)	Sales QE Invoice		301	Sales - Jungle Collection (4000)	0	45
20	17	11/03/2015	Justin Wilson	02/08/2014	Toyways plc (TW003)	Sales QE Invoice		301	VAT on Sales (2200)	0	9
21	17	11/03/2015	Justin Wilson	02/08/2014	Toyways plc (TW003)	Sales QE Invoice		301	Sales invoices not paid (1100)	54	0
22	17	11/03/2015	Justin Wilson	02/08/2014	Toyways plc (TW003)	Sales QE Invoice		301	Sales - Jungle Collection (4000)	45	0
23	17	11/03/2015	Justin Wilson	02/08/2014	Toyways plc (TW003)	Sales QE Invoice		301	VAT on Sales (2200)	9	0
24	17	11/03/2015	Justin Wilson	02/08/2014	Toyways plc (TW003)	Sales QE Invoice		301	Sales invoices not paid (1100)	0	54
25	18	11/03/2015	Justin Wilson	02/08/2014	Toyways plc (TW003)	Sales QE Invoice		301	Sales - Pets Collection (4002)	0	45
26	18	11/03/2015	Justin Wilson	02/08/2014	Toyways plc (TW003)	Sales QE Invoice		301	VAT on Sales (2200)	0	9
27	18	11/03/2015	Justin Wilson	02/08/2014	Toyways plc (TW003)	Sales QE Invoice		301	Sales invoices not paid (1100)	54	0
28	18	11/03/2015	Justin Wilson	02/08/2014	Toyways plc (TW003)	Sales QE Invoice		301	Sales - Pets Collection (4002)	45	0
29	18	11/03/2015	Justin Wilson	02/08/2014	Toyways plc (TW003)	Sales QE Invoice		301	VAT on Sales (2200)	9	0
30	18	11/03/2015	Justin Wilson	02/08/2014	Toyways plc (TW003)	Sales QE Invoice		301	Sales invoices not paid (1100)	0	54
31	19	11/03/2015	Justin Wilson	02/08/2014	Toyways plc (TW003)	Sales QE Invoice		301	Sales - Farm Collection (4001)	0	35
32	19	11/03/2015	Justin Wilson	02/08/2014	Toyways plc (TW003)	Sales QE Invoice		301	VAT on Sales (2200)	0	7
33	19	11/03/2015	Justin Wilson	02/08/2014	Toyways plc (TW003)	Sales QE Invoice		301	Sales invoices not paid (1100)	42	0
34	20	11/03/2015	Justin Wilson	02/08/2014	Toyways plc (TW003)	Sales QE Invoice		301	Sales - Jungle Collection (4000)	0	45
35	20	11/03/2015	Justin Wilson	02/08/2014	Toyways plc (TW003)	Sales QE Invoice		301	VAT on Sales (2200)	0	9
36	20	11/03/2015	Justin Wilson	02/08/2014	Toyways plc (TW003)	Sales QE Invoice		301	Sales invoices not paid (1100)	54	0
37	21	11/03/2015	Justin Wilson	02/08/2014	Toyways plc (TW003)	Sales QE Invoice		301	Sales - Pets Collection (4002)	0	45
38	21	11/03/2015	Justin Wilson	02/08/2014	Toyways plc (TW003)	Sales QE Invoice		301	VAT on Sales (2200)	0	9
39	21	11/03/2015	Justin Wilson	02/08/2014	Toyways plc (TW003)	Sales QE Invoice		301	Sales invoices not paid (1100)	54	0
40	22	11/03/2015	Justin Wilson	04/08/2014	Happykidz Ltd (HK006)	Sales QE Invoice		302	Sales - Farm Collection (4001)	0	28
41	22	11/03/2015	Justin Wilson	04/08/2014	Happykidz Ltd (HK006)	Sales QE Invoice		302	VAT on Sales (2200)	0	5.6
42	22	11/03/2015	Justin Wilson	04/08/2014	Happykidz Ltd (HK006)	Sales QE Invoice		302	Sales invoices not paid (1100)	33.6	0
43	23	11/03/2015	Justin Wilson	04/08/2014	Happykidz Ltd (HK006)	Sales QE Invoice		302	Sales - Pets Collection (4002)	0	72
44	23	11/03/2015	Justin Wilson	04/08/2014	Happykidz Ltd (HK006)	Sales QE Invoice		302	VAT on Sales (2200)	0	14.4
45	23	11/03/2015	Justin Wilson	04/08/2014	Happykidz Ltd (HK006)	Sales QE Invoice		302	Sales invoices not paid (1100)	86.4	0
46	24	11/03/2015	Justin Wilson	02/08/2014	Happykidz Ltd (HK006)	Sales QE Credit		55	Sales invoices not paid (1100)	0	16.8
47	24	11/03/2015	Justin Wilson	02/08/2014	Happykidz Ltd (HK006)	Sales QE Credit		55	Sales - Farm Collection (4001)	14	0
48	24	11/03/2015	Justin Wilson	02/08/2014	Happykidz Ltd (HK006)	Sales QE Credit		55	VAT on Sales (2200)	2.8	0
49	25	11/03/2015	Justin Wilson	02/08/2014	Dornley Evening Chror	Purchase QE Invc	QE-2929/11	2929/11	Marketing (6200)	130	0
50	25	11/03/2015	Justin Wilson	02/08/2014	Dornley Evening Chror	Purchase QE Invc	QE-2929/11	2929/11	VAT on Purchases (2201)	26	0
51	25	11/03/2015	Justin Wilson	02/08/2014	Dornley Evening Chror	Purchase QE Invc	QE-2929/11	2929/11	Purchase invoices not paid (2100)	0	156
52	26	11/03/2015	Justin Wilson	03/08/2014	Grange Toys Ltd (GRT0(	Purchase QE Invc	QE-GT2882	GT2882	Cost of Sales - Materials (5010)	1,060.00	0
53	26	11/03/2015	Justin Wilson	03/08/2014	Grange Toys Ltd (GRT0(	Purchase QE Invc	QE-GT2882	GT2882	VAT on Purchases (2201)	212	0
54	26	11/03/2015	Justin Wilson	03/08/2014	Grange Toys Ltd (GRT0(	Purchase QE Invc	QE-GT2882	GT2882	Purchase invoices not paid (2100)	0	1,272.00
55	27	11/03/2015	Justin Wilson	06/08/2014	Willow Works Ltd (WW	Purchase QE Invc	QE-99128	99128	Cost of Sales - Materials (5010)	240	0
56	27	11/03/2015	Justin Wilson	06/08/2014	Willow Works Ltd (WW	Purchase QE Invc	QE-99128	99128	VAT on Purchases (2201)	48	0
57	27	11/03/2015	Justin Wilson	06/08/2014	Willow Works Ltd (WW	Purchase QE Invc	QE-99128	99128	Purchase invoices not paid (2100)	0	288
58	28	11/03/2015	Justin Wilson	03/08/2014	Toyways plc (TW003)	Customer Receipt			Cash at Bank (1200)	1,235.76	0
59	28	11/03/2015	Justin Wilson	03/08/2014	Toyways plc (TW003)	Customer Receipt			Sales invoices not paid (1100)	0	1,235.76
60	28	11/03/2015	Justin Wilson	03/08/2014	Toyways plc (TW003)	Customer Receipt			Cash at Bank (1200)	0	1,235.76
61	28	11/03/2015	Justin Wilson	03/08/2014	Toyways plc (TW003)	Customer Receipt			Sales invoices not paid (1100)	1,235.76	0
62	29	11/03/2015	Justin Wilson	05/08/2014	Happykidz Ltd (HK006)	Customer Receipt		BACS	Cash at Bank (1200)	342.98	0
63	29	11/03/2015	Justin Wilson	05/08/2014	Happykidz Ltd (HK006)	Customer Receipt		BACS	Sales invoices not paid (1100)	0	342.98
64	30	11/03/2015	Justin Wilson	03/08/2014	Toyways plc (TW003)	Customer Receipt		CHEQUE	Cash at Bank (1200)	1,235.76	0
65	30	11/03/2015	Justin Wilson	03/08/2014	Toyways plc (TW003)	Customer Receipt		CHEQUE	Sales invoices not paid (1100)	0	1,235.76
66	31	11/03/2015	Justin Wilson	04/08/2014	FLW Ltd (FLW002)	Supplier Payment		CHEQUE: 0012671	Purchase invoices not paid (2100)	923.46	0
67	31	11/03/2015	Justin Wilson	04/08/2014	FLW Ltd (FLW002)	Supplier Payment		CHEQUE: 0012671	Cash at Bank (1200)	0	923.46
68	32	11/03/2015	Justin Wilson	04/08/2014	Matchsticks Ltd (MCS0(	Supplier Payment		CHEQUE 0012672	Purchase invoices not paid (2100)	1,943.26	0
69	32	11/03/2015	Justin Wilson	04/08/2014	Matchsticks Ltd (MCS0(	Supplier Payment		CHEQUE 0012672	Cash at Bank (1200)	0	1,943.26
70	32	11/03/2015	Justin Wilson	04/08/2014	Matchsticks Ltd (MCS0(	Supplier Payment		CHEQUE 0012672	Purchase invoices not paid (2100)	0	1,943.26
71	32	11/03/2015	Justin Wilson	04/08/2014	Matchsticks Ltd (MCS0(	Supplier Payment		CHEQUE 0012672	Cash at Bank (1200)	1,943.26	0
72	33	11/03/2015	Justin Wilson	04/08/2014	Matchsticks Ltd (MCS0(	Supplier Payment		CHEQUE: 0012672	Purchase invoices not paid (2100)	1,943.26	0

73	33	11/03/2015	Justin Wilson	04/08/2014	Matchsticks Ltd (MCS0(	Supplier Payment	CHEQUE: 0012672	Cash at Bank (1200)	0	1,943.26
74	34	12/03/2015	Justin Wilson	05/08/2014	Prettypops Ltd (PP004)	Sales QE Credit	W-OFF	Sales invoices not paid (1100)	0	190.87
75	34	12/03/2015	Justin Wilson	05/08/2014	Prettypops Ltd (PP004)	Sales QE Credit	W-OFF	Bad debt (8100)	190.87	0
76	35	12/03/2015	Justin Wilson	05/08/2014		Other Payment	Voucher 10	Cash at Bank (1200)	0	20
77	35	12/03/2015	Justin Wilson	05/08/2014		Other Payment	Voucher 10	Office costs (7500)	16.67	0
78	35	12/03/2015	Justin Wilson	05/08/2014		Other Payment	Voucher 10	VAT on Purchases (2201)	3.33	0
79	35	12/03/2015	Justin Wilson	05/08/2014		Other Payment	Voucher 10	Cash at Bank (1200)	20	0
80	35	12/03/2015	Justin Wilson	05/08/2014		Other Payment	Voucher 10	Office costs (7500)	0	16.67
81	35	12/03/2015	Justin Wilson	05/08/2014		Other Payment	Voucher 10	VAT on Purchases (2201)	0	3.33
82	36	12/03/2015	Justin Wilson	05/08/2014		Other Payment	Voucher 11	Cash in Hand (1210)	0	24
83	36	12/03/2015	Justin Wilson	05/08/2014		Other Payment	Voucher 11	Office costs (7500)	20	0
84	36	12/03/2015	Justin Wilson	05/08/2014		Other Payment	Voucher 11	VAT on Purchases (2201)	4	0
85	37	12/03/2015	Justin Wilson	05/08/2014		Other Payment	Voucher 10	Cash in Hand (1210)	0	20
86	37	12/03/2015	Justin Wilson	05/08/2014		Other Payment	Voucher 10	Office costs (7500)	20	0
87	37	12/03/2015	Justin Wilson	05/08/2014		Other Payment	Voucher 10	Cash in Hand (1210)	20	0
88	37	12/03/2015	Justin Wilson	05/08/2014		Other Payment	Voucher 10	Office costs (7500)	0	20
89	38	12/03/2015	Justin Wilson	05/08/2014		Other Payment	Voucher 10	Cash in Hand (1210)	0	20
90	38	12/03/2015	Justin Wilson	05/08/2014		Other Payment	Voucher 10	Office costs (7500)	20	0
91	38	12/03/2015	Justin Wilson	05/08/2014		Other Payment	Voucher 10	Cash in Hand (1210)	20	0
92	38	12/03/2015	Justin Wilson	05/08/2014		Other Payment	Voucher 10	Office costs (7500)	0	20
93	39	12/03/2015	Justin Wilson	05/08/2014		Other Payment	Voucher 10	Cash in Hand (1210)	0	20
94	39	12/03/2015	Justin Wilson	05/08/2014		Other Payment	Voucher 10	Office costs (7500)	20	0
95	40	12/03/2015	Justin Wilson	01/08/2014		Other Receipt	Cash Sales	Sales - Cash Sales (4003)	0	65.2
96	40	12/03/2015	Justin Wilson	01/08/2014		Other Receipt	Cash Sales	VAT on Sales (2200)	0	13.04
97	40	12/03/2015	Justin Wilson	01/08/2014		Other Receipt	Cash Sales	Cash at Bank (1200)	78.24	0
98	41	12/03/2015	Justin Wilson	04/08/2014		Other Receipt	Cash Sales	Sales - Cash Sales (4003)	0	85.25
99	41	12/03/2015	Justin Wilson	04/08/2014		Other Receipt	Cash Sales	VAT on Sales (2200)	0	17.05
100	41	12/03/2015	Justin Wilson	04/08/2014		Other Receipt	Cash Sales	Cash at Bank (1200)	102.3	0
101	42	12/03/2015	Justin Wilson	25/08/2014		Journal	JNL01	Owner Drawings (3260)	200	0
102	42	12/03/2015	Justin Wilson	25/08/2014		Journal	JNL01	Cash at Bank (1200)	0	200
103	43	12/03/2015	Justin Wilson	06/08/2014	Funnystuff Ltd (FS001)	Sales QE Invoice	303	Sales - Farm Collection (4001)	0	35
104	43	12/03/2015	Justin Wilson	06/08/2014	Funnystuff Ltd (FS001)	Sales QE Invoice	303	VAT on Sales (2200)	0	7
105	43	12/03/2015	Justin Wilson	06/08/2014	Funnystuff Ltd (FS001)	Sales QE Invoice	303	Sales invoices not paid (1100)	42	0
106	44	12/03/2015	Justin Wilson	06/08/2014	Funnystuff Ltd (FS001)	Sales QE Invoice	303	Sales - Pets Collection (4002)	0	45
107	44	12/03/2015	Justin Wilson	06/08/2014	Funnystuff Ltd (FS001)	Sales QE Invoice	303	VAT on Sales (2200)	0	9
108	44	12/03/2015	Justin Wilson	06/08/2014	Funnystuff Ltd (FS001)	Sales QE Invoice	303	Sales invoices not paid (1100)	54	0
109	45	12/03/2015	Justin Wilson	06/08/2014	Toyways plc (TW003)	Sales QE Invoice	304	Sales - Pets Collection (4002)	0	270
110	45	12/03/2015	Justin Wilson	06/08/2014	Toyways plc (TW003)	Sales QE Invoice	304	VAT on Sales (2200)	0	54
111	45	12/03/2015	Justin Wilson	06/08/2014	Toyways plc (TW003)	Sales QE Invoice	304	Sales invoices not paid (1100)	324	0
112	46	12/03/2015	Justin Wilson	08/08/2014	Matchsticks Ltd (MCS0(	Purchase QE Invoice	3178	Cost of Sales - Materials (5010)	1,400.00	0
113	46	12/03/2015	Justin Wilson	08/08/2014	Matchsticks Ltd (MCS0(	Purchase QE Invoice	3178	VAT on Purchases (2201)	280	0
114	46	12/03/2015	Justin Wilson	08/08/2014	Matchsticks Ltd (MCS0(	Purchase QE Invoice	3178	Purchase invoices not paid (2100)	0	1,680.00
115	47	12/03/2015	Justin Wilson	11/08/2014	Grange Toys Ltd (GRT0(	Purchase QE Invoice	GT2916	Cost of Sales - Goods (5000)	560	0
116	47	12/03/2015	Justin Wilson	11/08/2014	Grange Toys Ltd (GRT0(	Purchase QE Invoice	GT2916	VAT on Purchases (2201)	112	0
117	47	12/03/2015	Justin Wilson	11/08/2014	Grange Toys Ltd (GRT0(	Purchase QE Invoice	GT2916	Purchase invoices not paid (2100)	0	672
118	48	12/03/2015	Justin Wilson	11/08/2014	Happykidz Ltd (HK006)	Customer Receipt	BACS	Sales invoices not paid (1100)	16.8	0
119	48	12/03/2015	Justin Wilson	11/08/2014	Happykidz Ltd (HK006)	Customer Receipt	BACS	Cash at Bank (1200)	158.4	0
120	48	12/03/2015	Justin Wilson	11/08/2014	Happykidz Ltd (HK006)	Customer Receipt	BACS	Sales invoices not paid (1100)	0	67.2
121	48	12/03/2015	Justin Wilson	11/08/2014	Happykidz Ltd (HK006)	Customer Receipt	BACS	Sales invoices not paid (1100)	0	108
122	49	12/03/2015	Justin Wilson	11/08/2014	Willow Works Ltd (WW	Supplier Payment	Cheque 0012674	Purchase invoices not paid (2100)	288.29	0
123	49	12/03/2015	Justin Wilson	11/08/2014	Willow Works Ltd (WW	Supplier Payment	Cheque 0012674	Cash at Bank (1200)	0	288.29
124	50	12/03/2015	Justin Wilson	14/08/2014	Grange Toys Ltd (GRT0(	Supplier Payment	Cheque 0012675	Purchase invoices not paid (2100)	3,000.00	0
125	50	12/03/2015	Justin Wilson	14/08/2014	Grange Toys Ltd (GRT0(	Supplier Payment	Cheque 0012675	Cash at Bank (1200)	0	3,000.00
126	51	12/03/2015	Justin Wilson	14/08/2014	Dornley Evening Chror	Supplier Payment	Cheque 0012676	Purchase invoices not paid (2100)	156	0
127	51	12/03/2015	Justin Wilson	14/08/2014	Dornley Evening Chror	Supplier Payment	Cheque 0012676	Cash at Bank (1200)	0	156
128	52	12/03/2015	Justin Wilson	12/08/2014		Other Payment	Voucher 12	Cash in Hand (1210)	0	14.8
129	52	12/03/2015	Justin Wilson	12/08/2014		Other Payment	Voucher 12	Travel and Entertainment (7400)	12.33	0
130	52	12/03/2015	Justin Wilson	12/08/2014		Other Payment	Voucher 12	VAT on Purchases (2201)	2.47	0
131	53	12/03/2015	Justin Wilson	14/08/2014		Other Payment	Voucher 13	Cash in Hand (1210)	0	10.2
132	53	12/03/2015	Justin Wilson	14/08/2014		Other Payment	Voucher 13	Office costs (7500)	8.5	0
133	53	12/03/2015	Justin Wilson	14/08/2014		Other Payment	Voucher 13	VAT on Purchases (2201)	1.7	0
134	54	13/03/2015	Justin Wilson	14/08/2014		Bank Transfer	TFR01	Cash at Bank (1200)	0	10,000.00
135	54	13/03/2015	Justin Wilson	14/08/2014		Bank Transfer	TFR01	Business Loan (1230)	10,000.00	0
136	54	13/03/2015	Justin Wilson	14/08/2014		Bank Transfer	TFR01	Cash at Bank (1200)	10,000.00	0
137	54	13/03/2015	Justin Wilson	14/08/2014		Bank Transfer	TFR01	Business Loan (1230)	0	10,000.00
138	55	13/03/2015	Justin Wilson	14/08/2014		Bank Transfer	TFR01	Business Loan (1230)	0	10,000.00
139	55	13/03/2015	Justin Wilson	14/08/2014		Bank Transfer	TFR01	Cash at Bank (1200)	10,000.00	0
140	56	13/03/2015	Justin Wilson	14/08/2014		Other Payment	Voucher 14	Cash in Hand (1210)	0	25
141	56	13/03/2015	Justin Wilson	14/08/2014		Other Payment	Voucher 14	Office costs (7500)	20.83	0
142	56	13/03/2015	Justin Wilson	14/08/2014		Other Payment	Voucher 14	VAT on Purchases (2201)	4.17	0
143	57	13/03/2015	Justin Wilson	18/08/2014		Other Payment	SOR01	Cash at Bank (1200)	0	400
144	57	13/03/2015	Justin Wilson	18/08/2014		Other Payment	SOR01	Rent & Rates (7100)	400	0

145	57	13/03/2015	Justin Wilson	18/08/2014		Other Payment		SOR01	VAT on Purchases (2201)	0	0
146	57	13/03/2015	Justin Wilson	18/08/2014		Other Payment		SOR01	Cash at Bank (1200)	400	0
147	57	13/03/2015	Justin Wilson	18/08/2014		Other Payment		SOR01	Rent & Rates (7100)	0	400
148	57	13/03/2015	Justin Wilson	18/08/2014		Other Payment		SOR01	VAT on Purchases (2201)	0	0
149	58	13/03/2015	Justin Wilson	18/08/2014		Other Payment		SOR01	Cash at Bank (1200)	0	400
150	58	13/03/2015	Justin Wilson	18/08/2014		Other Payment		SOR01	Rent & Rates (7100)	400	0
151	58	13/03/2015	Justin Wilson	18/08/2014		Other Payment		SOR01	VAT on Purchases (2201)	0	0
152	65	13/03/2015	Justin Wilson	28/08/2014		Other Payment		SOR02	Cash at Bank (1200)	0	120
153	65	13/03/2015	Justin Wilson	28/08/2014		Other Payment		SOR02	Rent & Rates (7100)	120	0
154	65	13/03/2015	Justin Wilson	28/08/2014		Other Payment		SOR02	VAT on Purchases (2201)	0	0
155	65	13/03/2015	Justin Wilson	28/08/2014		Other Payment		SOR02	Cash at Bank (1200)	120	0
156	65	13/03/2015	Justin Wilson	28/08/2014		Other Payment		SOR02	Rent & Rates (7100)	0	120
157	65	13/03/2015	Justin Wilson	28/08/2014		Other Payment		SOR02	VAT on Purchases (2201)	0	0
158	66	13/03/2015	Justin Wilson	28/08/2014		Other Payment		SOR02	Cash at Bank (1200)	0	120
159	66	13/03/2015	Justin Wilson	28/08/2014		Other Payment		SOR02	Rent & Rates (7100)	120	0
160	66	13/03/2015	Justin Wilson	28/08/2014		Other Payment		SOR02	VAT on Purchases (2201)	0	0
161	73	13/03/2015	Justin Wilson	20/08/2014		Journal		JNL02	Insurance (7610)	150	0
162	73	13/03/2015	Justin Wilson	20/08/2014		Journal		JNL02	Repairs and renewals (7800)	0	150
163	74	13/03/2015	Justin Wilson	31/08/2014		Bank Transfer		TFR02	Cash at Bank (1200)	0	94
164	74	13/03/2015	Justin Wilson	31/08/2014		Bank Transfer		TFR02	Cash in Hand (1210)	94	0
165	75	13/03/2015	Justin Wilson	09/08/2014		Other Payment		Cheque 0012673	Cash at Bank (1200)	0	250
166	75	13/03/2015	Justin Wilson	09/08/2014		Other Payment		Cheque 0012673	IT equipment cost (0030)	208.33	0
167	75	13/03/2015	Justin Wilson	09/08/2014		Other Payment		Cheque 0012673	VAT on Purchases (2201)	41.67	0
168	76	13/03/2015	Justin Wilson	28/08/2014		Bank Payment		Bank Charge	Cash at Bank (1200)	0	32
169	76	13/03/2015	Justin Wilson	28/08/2014		Bank Payment		Bank Charge	Bank charges & interest (7900)	32	0

Task 24 Aged Creditors Report

Aged Creditors Report

This report shows all outstanding or unallocated supplier transactions, broken down by the ageing periods specified in Default Settings.

Type to search | Refine | View the detailed report | Export ▾

To Date 31/08/2014 | Sort by Name

Supplier	Credit limit	O/S Amt	< 30 days	< 60 days	< 90 days	< 120 days	Older
Grange Toys Ltd (GRT005)	£10,000.00	£3,221.50	£1,944.00	£1,277.50	£0.00	£0.00	£0.00
Matchsticks Ltd (MCS003)	£5,000.00	£1,680.00	£1,680.00	£0.00	£0.00	£0.00	£0.00
Willow Works Ltd (WWW002)	£8,500.00	£288.00	£288.00	£0.00	£0.00	£0.00	£0.00
TOTAL		£5,189.50	£3,912.00	£1,277.50	£0.00	£0.00	£0.00

Task 24 Aged Debtors Report

Aged Debtors Report

This report shows all outstanding or unallocated customer transactions, broken down by the ageing periods specified in Default Settings.

Type to search | Refine | View the detailed report | Export ▾

To Date 31/08/2014 | Sort by Name

Customer	Credit limit	O/S Amt	< 30 days	< 60 days	< 90 days	< 120 days	Older
Funnystuff Ltd (FS001)	£1,000.00	£96.00	£96.00	£0.00	£0.00	£0.00	£0.00
Happykidz Ltd (HK006)	£8,000.00	£120.00	£120.00	£0.00	£0.00	£0.00	£0.00
Perfect Pastimes Ltd (PP002)	£15,000.00	£13,209.34	£0.00	£13,209.34	£0.00	£0.00	£0.00
Prettypops Ltd (PP004)	£5,000.00	£0.00	-£190.87	£190.87	£0.00	£0.00	£0.00
Toyways plc (TW003)	£5,000.00	£474.00	£474.00	£0.00	£0.00	£0.00	£0.00
TOTAL		£13,899.34	£499.13	£13,400.21	£0.00	£0.00	£0.00

Task 24 Nominal activity – Bank Current Account and Petty Cash (Cash in Hand)

Justin Timbercrafts

Nominal Activity Report

From Date: 31/07/2014 To Date: 31/08/2014

Category: All Ledger Account: Cash at Bank (1200)

Category	Ledger Account	Date	Reference	Type	Debit	Credit
Bank	Cash at Bank (1200)	31/07/2014		Bank Opening Balance	11,203.30	0.00
Bank	Cash at Bank (1200)	01/08/2014	Cash Sales	Other Receipt	78.24	0.00
Bank	Cash at Bank (1200)	01/08/2014	TRF01	Bank Transfer	0.00	1,000.00
Bank	Cash at Bank (1200)	03/08/2014	CHEQUE	Customer Receipt	1,235.76	0.00
Bank	Cash at Bank (1200)	04/08/2014	CHEQUE: 0012672	Supplier Payment	0.00	1,943.26
Bank	Cash at Bank (1200)	04/08/2014	CHEQUE: 0012671	Supplier Payment	0.00	923.46
Bank	Cash at Bank (1200)	04/08/2014	Cash Sales	Other Receipt	102.30	0.00
Bank	Cash at Bank (1200)	05/08/2014	BACS	Customer Receipt	342.98	0.00
Bank	Cash at Bank (1200)	09/08/2014	Cheque 0012673	Other Payment	0.00	250.00
Bank	Cash at Bank (1200)	11/08/2014	Cheque 0012674	Supplier Payment	0.00	288.29
Bank	Cash at Bank (1200)	11/08/2014	BACS	Customer Receipt	158.40	0.00
Bank	Cash at Bank (1200)	14/08/2014	TFR01	Bank Transfer	10,000.00	0.00
Bank	Cash at Bank (1200)	14/08/2014	Cheque 0012676	Supplier Payment	0.00	156.00
Bank	Cash at Bank (1200)	14/08/2014	Cheque 0012675	Supplier Payment	0.00	3,000.00
Bank	Cash at Bank (1200)	18/08/2014	SOR01	Other Payment	0.00	400.00
Bank	Cash at Bank (1200)	25/08/2014	JNL01	Journal	0.00	200.00
Bank	Cash at Bank (1200)	28/08/2014	Bank Charge	Bank Payment	0.00	32.00
Bank	Cash at Bank (1200)	28/08/2014	SOR02	Other Payment	0.00	120.00
Bank	Cash at Bank (1200)	31/08/2014	TFR02	Bank Transfer	0.00	94.00

Justin Timbercrafts

Nominal Activity Report

From Date: 31/07/2014 To Date: 31/08/2014

Category: All Ledger Account: Cash in Hand (1210)

Category	Ledger Account	Date	Reference	Type	Debit	Credit
Bank	Cash in Hand (1210)	31/07/2014		Bank Opening Balance	150.00	0.00
Bank	Cash in Hand (1210)	05/08/2014	Voucher 11	Other Payment	0.00	24.00
Bank	Cash in Hand (1210)	05/08/2014	Voucher 10	Other Payment	0.00	20.00
Bank	Cash in Hand (1210)	12/08/2014	Voucher 12	Other Payment	0.00	14.80
Bank	Cash in Hand (1210)	14/08/2014	Voucher 13	Other Payment	0.00	10.20
Bank	Cash in Hand (1210)	14/08/2014	Voucher 14	Other Payment	0.00	25.00
Bank	Cash in Hand (1210)	31/08/2014	TFR02	Bank Transfer	94.00	0.00
				Total	244.00	94.00

Task 24 Current Account - Bank Reconciliation

Justin Timbercrafts

Justin Timbercrafts
27 West Lane Dornley DN22 4RD

Telephone: +44 (0)1912944080
VAT Number 12345678

Bank Account	Current (1200)	**Statement Date**	31/08/2014
Reference	Sheet 819	**Reconciled By**	Justin Wilson

Date	Reference	Name	Category	Paid	Received
31/07/2014			Bank Opening Balance	0.00	11,203.30
01/08/2014	TRF01		Transfer: Deposit Account	1,000.00	0.00
05/08/2014	BACS	Happykidz Ltd	Customer Receipt	0.00	342.98
03/08/2014	CHEQUE	Toyways plc	Customer Receipt	0.00	1,235.76
04/08/2014	CHEQUE: 0012671	FLW Ltd	Supplier Payment	923.46	0.00
04/08/2014	CHEQUE: 0012672	Matchsticks Ltd	Supplier Payment	1,943.26	0.00
01/08/2014	Cash Sales		Other Receipt	0.00	78.24
04/08/2014	Cash Sales		Other Receipt	0.00	102.30
25/08/2014	JNL01		Journal	200.00	0.00
11/08/2014	BACS	Happykidz Ltd	Customer Receipt	0.00	158.40
14/08/2014	Cheque 0012675	Grange Toys Ltd	Supplier Payment	3,000.00	0.00
14/08/2014	TFR01		Transfer: Business Loan	0.00	10,000.00
18/08/2014	SOR01		Other Payment	400.00	0.00
28/08/2014	SOR02		Other Payment	120.00	0.00
31/08/2014	TFR02		Transfer: Cash in Hand	94.00	0.00
09/08/2014	Cheque 0012673		Other Payment	250.00	0.00
28/08/2014	Bank Charge		Bank Payment	32.00	0.00

Total Received	23,120.98
Total Paid	7,962.72
Starting Balance	0.00
Statement End Balance	15,158.26
Reconciled Balance	15,158.26
Difference	0.00

INDEX